T

The Emergence of the Muse

MAJOR CANADIAN POETS FROM CRAWFORD TO PRATT

Bryan N.S. Gooch and Maureen Niwa

Toronto OXFORD UNIVERSITY PRESS 1993

Oxford University Press, 70 Wynford Drive, Don Mills, Ontario M3C 1J9

Toronto Oxford New York
Delhi Bombay Calcutta Madras Karachi Kuala Lumpur
Singapore Hong Kong Tokyo Nairobi Dar es Salaam
Cape Town Melbourne Auckland Madrid

and associated companies in
Berlin Ibadan

This book is printed on permanent (acid-free) paper ∞.

Canadian Cataloguing in Publication Data

Main entry under title:

The Emergence of the muse : major Canadian poets from
Crawford to Pratt

ISBN 0-19-540911-6

1. Canadian poetry (English) – 20th century.*
2. Canadian poetry (English) – 19th century.*
I. Gooch, Bryan N. S., 1937– . II. Niwa, Maureen.

PS8291.E54 1993 C811′.508 C93-093178-5
PR9195.7.E54 1993

1 2 3 4 - 96 95 94 93

Design by Heather Delfino

Printed in Canada

TABLE OF CONTENTS

PREFACE

To explore in detail the Canadian poetry of the late nineteenth and early twentieth centuries is to come to know our country in a way that is simply not possible by studying it only, say, in terms of politics and economics—important as those contexts are, even in relation to Canadian cultural development. A consideration of the cultural record is essential for an understanding of any nation's character and, for obvious reasons, it is often easier to focus exclusively on recent artistic activities; however, earlier work forms a crucial historical background for the study of modern and postmodernist Canadian poetry, despite what might be seen as modernism's dismissive reaction to its precursors. Certainly, dismissal characterized the general critical reaction to the work of poets such as William Wilfred Campbell, Archibald Lampman, and Marjorie Pickthall. After all, each age usually seeks to find its own measure of artistic merit and nearly always attempts to avoid reproducing an older stylistic manner. For this reason, the reaction to Canadian poetry published between 1850 and 1950 has perhaps been based on the notion that the work of the "Confederation poets"—a general description which suggests historical context and not artistic nature—is basically post-Romantic/Victorian naturalism transported to a land of maple leaves, clear lakes, and innumerable crimson sunsets.

Some generalizations concerning Canadian poets' use of existing poetic conventions may be close to the mark, but the assumption that their poetry is simply post-Romantic naturalism is not. Certainly, Isabella Valancy Crawford, William Wilfred Campbell, Charles G.D. Roberts, and other nineteenth-century Canadian poets had read—studied avidly, even—their Classics, Wordsworth, Keats, and Tennyson, for example, but they also found their own voices in the new land, not simply producing derivative poetic descriptions of serene landscapes. Although descriptions of idyllic beauty abound in later nineteenth- and early twentieth-century Canadian poetry, equally predominant is the realistic portrayal of the sublimity of nature. The notion that the land can defeat the strongest of physical onslaughts and negate humankind's ingenuity is repeatedly found in poems such as Campbell's "The Dread Voyage", Scott's "At the Cedars", and Pratt's "The Titanic".

Mid- and latter nineteenth-century Canadian poets say a great deal about the unappealing features of the new country's society and climate, the human conflict, urban mechanization, current politics, greed, and materialism, yet they also emphasize the human spirit necessary to counter these negative aspects as they reveal thematic preoccupations with physical courage, selflessness, and religious transcendence.

Thus, to underrate the originality of nineteenth-century Canadian poets—if only because their voices are not modern—is to lose sight of a great portion of our literary heritage, for they often comprise the most eloquent portrayals of it. Also, it is not only valuable but engaging to set this poetry within the cultural context of the music and painting of the same period, such as the compositions of W.O. Forsyth, Clarence Lucas, Edward Manning, and Ernest White, and the painting of Lucius O'Brien, Frances Anne Hopkins, John Fraser, and Allan Edson.

In order to provide a fairly extensive selection of authors' pieces and to reflect a range of thematic and stylistic elements across the chronology of each one's canon, this volume contains works of only eight major poets: Isabella Valancy Crawford, William Wilfred Campbell, Charles G.D. Roberts, Bliss Carman, Archibald Lampman, Duncan Campbell Scott, Marjorie Pickthall, and E.J. Pratt. Inevitably, given the limitations of space, the difficulty in the editorial task has been to decide not what to include, but what to leave out. However, it is fair to say that many of the familiar works will be found in these pages along with a large number which are lesser known. Rejection of poems simply on the basis of general currency is unwise, because it tends to fly in the face of oft-admitted merit. Equally, omission of lesser-known works because of unfamiliarity fails to broaden the available reading spectrum; nor does it substantiate the claim that other compositions by these poets are interesting and deserving of careful attention and study.

The overall arrangement within the volume is essentially chronological and moves forward from Crawford, whose vibrant imagery, extraordinary strength of line, and concern for the ills of society deserve more critical attention. Familiar poets such as William Wilfred Campbell, Charles G.D. Roberts, and Archibald Lampman are too often dismissed as being bathed in romantic syrup and, with the exception of Roberts, emblazoned with the national leaf. Though D.C. Scott was not a declared modernist, his freedom with forms and line lengths is undeniable. A selection of Majorie Pickthall's work follows. Of all writers included here, she is probably the least known and the most undervalued. As the selection shows, her poetic strengths are far greater than her present reputation generally allows. Poems by E.J. Pratt, many of which reflect an increasing concern with technology in both theme and image, conclude the text. This selection comprises the greatest number of pages simply because he often tended to work within the genre of the long poem. Short fragments of the major poems do not offer sufficient opportunity to become attuned to his symphonic sweeps.

Within each author's selection, works are arranged chronologically according to year—or probable year—of composition. That date is provided at the end of each piece, along with details of first publication in a newspaper, magazine, or periodical (if known), and the first publication in a collection. Prefacing each section of the anthology are brief biographical notes, which are not in any way intended to be exhaustive, but rather, to suggest certain thematic, structural, and stylistic issues of particular interest. Each one of these carries a short, selected bibliography that points to primary sources as well as to current critical statements that will aid further study. Here again, though, the lists of secondary material are not designed to be complete, and the reader is cautioned that, such is the growing body of criticism in Canadian letters, details of many other important monographs and articles should be sought elsewhere. Title line and first line indices conclude the volume.

Bryan N.S. Gooch
Maureen Niwa

August 1992

ACKNOWLEDGEMENTS

The editors would like to express their appreciation to the following individuals for their assistance in the preparation of this volume: Dr. Laura Groening and Ellen Quigley for help with the dating of certain poems by D.C. Scott; Dr. Leonard Early for help dating the poems by Archibald Lampman; Dr. Laurel Boone for help with the dating of some of Campbell's poems; Dr. John R. Sorfleet for help in dating some of the poems of Carman; Dr. Misao Dean and Douglas Beardsley for offering suggestions about the inclusion of particular poems by Archibald Lampman and D.C. Scott; Kathleen Niwa for advice regarding the cover plate and for help with the proofreading; and Diana Rutherford for her careful attention and diligence in typing the text.

The editors would also like to express their gratitude to the following individuals and firms for permission to reprint particular works:

E.J. Pratt. All poems reprinted from *E.J. Pratt Complete Poems,* edited by Sandra Djwa and R.G. Moyles. Reprinted by permission of University of Toronto Press.

Duncan Campbell Scott. All poems reprinted by permission of John G. Aylen.

Isabella Valancy Crawford

1850–1887

Born in Dublin, Ireland, Crawford emigrated in 1858 with her parents and surviving siblings to Paisley in Bruce County, Canada West (Ontario), where her father practised medicine. Her early pioneering life has provided some of the background for her narrative poems, but the nobility of the venture, that is, the challenge of coming to terms with our often harsh environment and finding an unspoiled ethos in which culture could flourish, was not to prevail against a financial scandal involving Dr. Crawford. Perhaps as early as 1862 or 1863, the Crawfords retreated to the Kingston area and subsequently to Lakefield in 1864. By 1872 they were in Peterborough; soon after Dr. Crawford's death in the mid-70s the family moved to Toronto. Many of Crawford's poems found outlets in *The Favorite*, *The Mail*, *The National*, *The Evening Telegram*, and *The Globe*, as well as in *Old Spookses' Pass, Malcolm's Katie, and Other Poems* (1884), but many more—including most of the remarkably strong extended fragment "Hugh and Ion"—remained in manuscript. Although John W. Garvin's edition of 1905 gave much of her work continued currency, it was not until the middle and latter decades of this century that a critical assessment was developed, stimulated in part by James Reaney's thoughtful introduction to his reprint of Garvin's edition, and also by the work of A.J.M. Smith, E.K. Brown, and Northrop Frye.

While critical views have not offered unqualified praise of her work—Desmond Pacey and Louis Dudek, for example, have certainly not bestowed unstinting accolades—there can be no doubt that Crawford's poetry is marked by a strength of creativity and uniqueness of voice which, in the view of many, allow her—rather than Charles Sangster—the place of the first truly Canadian poet of major importance. Certainly, thematic conventions are there—the commonplace rivalries of good and evil, of rural and urban, for instance—but the way in which she creates figures for these dichotomies in well-known pieces like "The City Tree" and "The Roman Rose-Seller" bear witness to her success. Not even the greatest of writers will produce a masterpiece on every occasion; hence, the criticism of unevenness loses its force and one can only wonder what poetry might have resulted had she lived longer—or later—and had the benefits of a burgeoning literary circle.

What also marks Crawford's work is her strong social sense; she was neither an easy conformist nor a comfortable conservative and was prepared to put forward her views—often with more than a touch of irony—as bluntly as Blake, Kingsley, or Dickens. Ultimately hopeful, she nevertheless had a realist's eye for humankind's potential for destruction in the new, unspoiled land. Neither was Crawford naive about the difficulties of survival, for her family's removal to the relative comforts of more urban locations (echoing, in some respects, that of Susanna Moodie and her family a few decades earlier) was evidently much on her mind. She was by no means a traditional painter of poetic dappling streams and crimson maple trees, for she equally represented the perils of nature. With Crawford's work, the unqualified notion that prior to 1920 our poets sang unceasingly about sunsets and idyllic prospects falls flat, and it is often that superb amalgam of realism and romance which marks the best of her work: her image of the rose with its canker is one of which even Keats would probably have approved.

The most definitive edition of Isabella Valancy Crawford's poetry to date is *The Collected Poems: Isabella Valancy Crawford* (1905), ed. John Garvin. Her major long poem, which is not included in this anthology, *Malcolm's Katie: A Love Story* has been edited and introduced by D.M.R. Bentley (1987). Her manuscripts are located in the Lorne Pierce Collection at the Douglas Library, Queen's University, Kingston.

Works on Crawford include: Katherine Hale, *Isabella Valancy Crawford* (1923); James Reaney, "Isabella Valancy

Crawford", *Our Living Tradition* (1959), 268-86; Ann Yeoman, "Towards a Native Mythology: The Poetry of Isabella Valancy Crawford," *Canadian Literature* 52 (1972), 39-47; Dorothy Livesay, "The Hunters Twain", *Canadian Literature* 55 (Winter 1973), 75-98; *The Isabella Valancy Crawford Symposium*, ed. and intro. Frank Tierney (1979); Dorothy Farmiloe, *Isabella Valancy Crawford: The Life and the Legends* (1983); Robert Alan Burns, "Isabella Valancy Crawford's Poetic Technique", *Studies in Canadian Literature* 10 (1985), 1-2, 53-80; Mary Joy Macdonald, "Inglorious Battles: People and Power in Crawford's 'Malcolm's Katie' ", *Canadian Poetry* 23 (Fall-Winter 1988), 31-46; Robert Alan Burns, "The Poet in Her Time: Isabella Valancy Crawford's Social, Economic and Political Views", *Studies in Canadian Literature* 14:1 (1989), 30-53; and Wanda Campbell's "Isabella Valancy Crawford and Elizabeth Barrett Browning", *Canadian Poetry* 29 (Fall-Winter 1991), 25-37.

THE ROMAN ROSE-SELLER

Not from Pæstum come my roses; Patrons, see
My flowers are Roman-blown; their nectaries
Drop honey amber, and their petals throw
Rich crimsons on the lucent marble of the shrine
Where snowy Dian lifts her pallid brow,
As crimson lips of Love may seek to warm
A sister glow in hearts as pulseless hewn.
Cæsar from Afric wars returns to-day;
Patricians, buy my royal roses; strew
His way knee-deep, as though old Tiber roll'd
A tide of musky roses from his bed to do
A wonder, wond'rous homage. Marcus Lucius, thou
To-day dost wed; buy roses, roses, roses,
To mingle with the nuptial myrtle; look,
I strip the polish'd thorns from the stems,
The nuptial rose should be a stingless flower;
Lucania, pass not by my roses. Virginia,
Here is a rose that has a canker in't, and yet
It is most glorious-dyed and sweeter smells
Than those death hath not touched. To-day they bear
The shield of Claudius with his spear upon it,
Close upon Cæsar's chariot—heap, heap it up
With roses such as these; 'tis true he's dead
And there's the canker! but, Romans, he
Died glorious, there's the perfume! and his virtues
Are these bright petals; so buy my roses, Widow.
No Greek-born roses mine. Priestess, priestess!
Thy ivory chariot stay; here's a rose and not
A white one, though thy chaste hands attend
On Vesta's flame. Love's of a colour—be it that
Which ladders Heaven and lives amongst the Gods;
Or like the Daffodil blows all about the earth;
Or, Hesperus like, is one sole star upon
The solemn sky which bridges some sad life,
So here's a crimson rose: Be thou as pure
As Dian's tears iced on her silver cheek,
And know no quality of love, thou art
A sorrow to the Gods! Oh mighty Love!
I would my roses could but chorus Thee.
No roses of Persepolis are mine. Helot, here—
I give thee this last blossom: A bee as red

As Hybla's golden toilers sucked its sweets;
A butterfly, wing'd like to Eros, nipp'd
Its new-pinked leaves; the sun, bright despot, stole
The dew night gives to all. Poor slave, methinks
A bough of cypress were as a gay a gift, and yet
It hath some beauty left! a little scarlet—for
The Gods love all; a little perfume, for there is no life,
Poor slave, but hath its sweetness. Thus I make
My roses Oracles. O hark! the cymbals beat
In god-like silver bursts of sound; I go
To see great Cæsar leading Glory home,
From Campus Martius to the Capitol!

c. 1874
The Mail, 7 March 1874
"Old Spookses' Pass," "Malcolm's Katie," and Other Poems, 1884

ESTHER

Unheard of others, voices called all night:—
The babble of young voices, the strong cries
Of men and women mourned amid the palms,
And gathered in mine ear, as winds that blow
About the earth and, gathering in some cave,
Give ghostly utterance of ghostly things—
"Esther, the Queen, arise and move the King
To sheathe the sword that lies upon the throats
Of thine own people!"

When the sun sprang up
His tresses were as blood that stained the courts
And beat upon the walls, and sent its tide
To bathe my naked feet when I thrust back
The golden tissue of the door to catch
Some sweetness of the morn upon my brow;
And lo! my God, a sweetness filled my soul
That came not from the morning but from Thee!

The winds that stirred the foldings of my robe
Were children's fingers—ghostly, clinging clasps

That said, "O Esther, plead before the King!"
Ah me! how often when a little maid,
Playing amid the fountains and the flowers
Of mine own people, have such dimpled hands
Caught at my flying robe in mimic fright,
And great round eyes buried themselves therein;
But then the voices laughed, "O Esther, stay
That wicked brother, for he chases us,
And pelts with blushing roses." Now I hear,
"O Esther, stay the King, he slaughters us!"

Alas! my courage is so weak a blade
It trembles at a breath. God, temper it to strength!
I perish if I go uncalled before the King.
Yea! let him smite me down a sacrifice
For Israel! Perchance that, dying thus, my blood
May creep about his heart and soften it
To those for whom I die. O God, when Thou
Didst veil Thy handmaid's soul in this fair flesh
'Twas for some strait sore as the present need!

What is it that glimmers ready by my couch?
The symbol of my state, the crown the King
Hath set upon my brows. On, crown, and deck
My triumph or my death! O robes of state,
Ye jewelled splendours, how ye mock this flesh
That quivers with monitions of that hour
When this night's moon shall peer above the palms
And find no life in Esther but that cold, cold life,
Blazing from diamond crown and golden robe,
Mocks of her life's brief sun and briefer state.

But still will Esther go. Jehovah calls!
And if I die—Hark! as I go by court
And golden pillar, sweet, shrill voices cry,
Unheard of others, "Esther, stay the King!"
O yea, my lambs of Israel! how your hands
Cling to my robes and pluck me to the King!
God, lift his sceptre up before my face!
But if I die—I die!

c. 1874
The Mail, 28 July 1874
The Collected Poems of Isabella Valancy Crawford, 1905

CANADA TO ENGLAND

Gone are the days, old Warrior of the Seas,
When thine armed head, bent low to catch my voice,
Caught but the plaintive sighings of my woods,
And the wild roar of rock-dividing streams,
And the loud bellow of my cataracts,
Bridged with the seven splendours of the bow.
When Nature was a Samson yet unshorn,
Filling the land with solitary might,
Or as the Angel of the Apocalypse,
One foot upon the primeval bowered land,
One foot upon the white mane of the sea,
My voice but faintly swelled the ebb and flow
Of the wild tides and storms that beat upon
Thy rocky girdle,—loud shrieking from the Ind
Ambrosial-breathing furies; from the north
Thundering with Arctic bellows, groans of seas
Rising from tombs of ice disrupted by
The magic kisses of the wide-eyed sun.

The times have won a change. Nature no more
Lords it alone and binds the lonely land
A serf to tongueless solitudes; but Nature's self
Is led, glad captive, in light fetters rich
As music-sounding silver can adorn;
And man has forged them, and our silent God
Behind His flaming worlds smiles on the deed.
"Man hath dominion"—words of primal might;
"Man hath dominion"—thus the words of God.

If destiny is writ on night's dusk scroll,
Then youngest stars are dropping from the hand
Of the Creator, sowing on the sky
My name in seeds of light. Ages will watch
Those seeds expand to suns, such as the tree
Bears on its boughs, which grows in Paradise.

How sounds my voice, my warrior kinsman, now?
Sounds it not like to thine in lusty youth—
A world-possessing shout of busy men,
Veined with the clang of trumpets and the noise
Of those who make them ready for the strife,

And in the making ready bruise its head?
Sounds it not like to thine—the whispering vine,
The robe of summer rustling thro' the fields,
The lowing of the cattle in the meads,
The sound of Commerce, and the music-set,
Flame-brightened step of Art in stately halls,—
All the infinity of notes which chord
The diapason of a Nation's voice?

My infants' tongues lisp word for word with thine;
We worship, wed, and die, and God is named
That way ye name Him,—strong bond between
Two mighty lands when as one mingled cry,
As of one voice, Jehovah turns to hear.
The bonds between us are no subtle links
Of subtle minds binding in close embrace,
Half-struggling for release, two alien lands,
But God's own seal of kindred, which to burst
Were but to dash His benediction from
Our brows. "Who loveth not his kin,
Whose face and voice are his, how shall he love
God whom he hath not seen?"

c. 1874
The Mail, 28 July 1874
The Collected Poems of Isabella Valancy Crawford, 1905

WAR

Shake, shake the earth with giant tread,
  Thou red-maned Titan bold;
For every step a man lies dead,
  A cottage hearth is cold.
Take up the babes with mailèd hands,
  Transfix them with thy spears,
Spare not the chaste young virgin-bands,
  Tho' blood may be their tears.

Beat down the corn, tear up the vine,
  The waters turn to blood;
And if the wretch for bread doth whine,

Give him his kin for food.
Ay, strew the dead to saddle-girth,
They make so rich a mold,
Thou wilt enrich the wasted earth—
They'll turn to yellow gold.

On with thy thunders! Shot and shell
Send screaming, featly hurled—
Science has made them in her cell
To *civilize* the world.
Not, not alone where Christian men
Pant in the well-armed strife,
But seek the jungle-throttled glen—
The savage has a life!

He has a soul—so priests will say—
Go, save it with thy sword!
Thro' his rank forests force thy way,
Thy war cry, "For the Lord!"
Rip up his mines, and from his strands
Wash out the gold with blood—
Religion raises blessing hands,
"War's evil worketh good!"

When striding o'er the conquered land
Silence thy rolling drum,
And, led by white-robed choiring band,
With loud *"Te Deum"* come.
Seek the grim chancel, on its wall
Thy blood-stiff banner hang;
They lie who say thy blood is gall,
Thy tooth the serpent's fang.

See, the white Christ is lifted high,
Thy conquering sword to bless!
Smiles the pure Monarch of the sky—
Thy king can do no less.
Drink deep with him the festal wine,
Drink with him drop for drop;
If like the sun his throne doth shine,
Of it *thou* art the prop.

If spectres wait upon the bowl,
Thou needst not be afraid;
Grin hell-hounds for thy bold, black soul,
His purple be thy shade.
Go, feast with Commerce, be her spouse!
She loves thee, thou art hers;

For thee she decks her board and house,
Then how may others curse

If she, mild-seeming matron, leans
Upon thine iron neck,
And leaves with thee her household scenes
To follow at thy beck?
Bastard in brotherhood of kings,
Their blood runs in thy veins;
For them the crowns; the sword that swings
For thee, to hew their chains.

For thee the rending of the prey;
They, jackals to the lion,
Tread after in the gory way
Trod by the mightier scion.
O slave, that slayest other slaves,
O'er vassals crowned a king,
O War, build high thy throne with graves,
High as the vulture's wing!

c. 1879
The Evening Telegram, 4 August 1879
The Collected Poems of Isabella Valancy Crawford, 1905

THE CAMP OF SOULS

My white canoe, like the silvery air
O'er the River of Death that darkly rolls
When the moons of the world are round and fair,
I paddle back from the "Camp of Souls."
When the wishton-wish in the low swamp grieves
Come the dark plumes of red "Singing Leaves."

Two hundred times have the moons of spring
Rolled over the bright bay's azure breath
Since they decked me with plumes of an eagle's wing,
And painted my face with the "paint of death,"
And from their pipes o'er my corpse there broke
The solemn rings of the blue "last smoke."

Two hundred times have the wintry moons
  Wrapped the dead earth in a blanket white;
Two hundred times have the wild sky loons
  Shrieked in the flush of the golden light
Of the first sweet dawn, when the summer weaves
Her dusky wigwam of perfect leaves.

Two hundred moons of the falling leaf
  Since they laid my bow in my dead right hand
And chanted above me the "song of grief"
  As I took my way to the spirit land;
Yet when the swallow the blue air cleaves
Come the dark plumes of red "Singing Leaves."

White are the wigwams in that far camp,
  And the star-eyed deer on the plains are found;
No bitter marshes or tangled swamp
  In the Manitou's happy hunting-ground!
And the moon of summer forever rolls
Above the red men in their "Camp of Souls."

Blue are its lakes as the wild dove's breast,
  And their murmurs soft as her gentle note;
As the calm, large stars in the deep sky rest,
  The yellow lilies upon them float;
And canoes, like flakes of the silvery snow,
Thro' the tall, rustling rice-beds come and go.

Green are its forests; no warrior wind
  Rushes on war trail the dusk grove through,
With leaf-scalps of tall trees mourning behind;
  But South Wind, heart friend of Great Manitou,
When ferns and leaves with cool dews are wet,
Blows flowery breaths from his red calumet.

Never upon them the white frosts lie,
  Nor glow their green boughs with the "paint of death";
Manitou smiles in the crystal sky,
  Close breathing above them His life-strong breath;
And He speaks no more in fierce thunder sound,
So near is His happy hunting-ground.

Yet often I love, in my white canoe,
  To come to the forests and camps of earth:
'Twas there death's black arrow pierced me through;
  'Twas there my red-browed mother gave me birth;
There I, in the light of a young man's dawn,
Won the lily heart of dusk "Springing Fawn."

And love is a cord woven out of life,
  And dyed in the red of the living heart;
And time is the hunter's rusty knife,
  That cannot cut the red strands apart:
And I sail from the spirit shore to scan
Where the weaving of that strong cord began.

But I may not come with a giftless hand,
  So richly I pile, in my white canoe,
Flowers that bloom in the spirit land,
  Immortal smiles of Great Manitou.
When I paddle back to the shores of earth
I scatter them over the white man's hearth.

For love is the breath of the soul set free;
  So I cross the river that darkly rolls,
That my spirit may whisper soft to thee
  Of *thine* who wait in the "Camp of Souls."
When the bright day laughs, or the wan night grieves,
Come the dusky plumes of red "Singing Leaves."

c. 1880
The Evening Telegram, 4 September 1880
The Collected Poems of Isabella Valancy Crawford, 1905

THE CITY TREE

I stand within the stony, arid town,
  I gaze forever on the narrow street,
I hear forever passing up and down
  The ceaseless tramp of feet.

I know no brotherhood with far-locked woods,
  Where branches bourgeon from a kindred sap,
Where o'er mossed roots, in cool, green solitudes,
  Small silver brooklets lap.

No emerald vines creep wistfully to me
  And lay their tender fingers on my bark;
High may I toss my boughs, yet never see
  Dawn's first most glorious spark.

When to and fro my branches wave and sway,
   Answ'ring the feeble wind that faintly calls,
They kiss no kindred boughs, but touch alway
   The stones of climbing walls.

My heart is never pierced with song of bird;
   My leaves know nothing of that glad unrest
Which makes a flutter in the still woods heard
   When wild birds build a nest.

There never glance the eyes of violets up,
   Blue, into the deep splendour of my green;
Nor falls the sunlight to the primrose cup
   My quivering leaves between.

Not mine, not mine to turn from soft delight
   Of woodbine breathings, honey sweet and warm;
With kin embattled rear my glorious height
   To greet the coming storm!

Not mine to watch across the free, broad plains
   The whirl of stormy cohorts sweeping fast,
The level silver lances of great rains
   Blown onward by the blast!

Not mine the clamouring tempest to defy,
   Tossing the proud crest of my dusky leaves—
Defender of small flowers that trembling lie
   Against my barky greaves!

Not mine to watch the wild swan drift above,
   Balanced on wings that could not choose between
The wooing sky, blue as the eye of love,
   And my own tender green!

And yet my branches spread, a kingly sight,
   In the close prison of the drooping air:
When sun-vexed noons are at their fiery height
   My shade is broad, and there

Come city toilers, who their hour of ease
   Weave out to precious seconds as they lie
Pillowed on horny hands, to hear the breeze
   Through my great branches die.

I see no flowers, but as the children race
   With noise and clamour through the dusty street,
I see the bud of many an angel face,
   I hear their merry feet.

No violets look up, but, shy and grave,
The children pause and lift their crystal eyes
To where my emerald branches call and wave
As to the mystic skies.

c. 1880
The Evening Telegram, 4 September 1880
"Old Spookses' Pass," "Malcolm's Katie," and Other Poems, 1884

[SOME OF] FARMER STEBBINS' OPINIONS[1]

No, Parson, 'tain't bin in my style
(Nor none uv my relations)
Tew dig about the gnarly roots
Uv prophetic spekkleations,
Tew see what Malachai meant
Or Solomon wus hintin',
Or round what jog o' futur's road
Isaiah wus a-squintin'.

I've lost my rest a-keepin' out
The hogs frum our cowcumbers,
But never lost a wink, ye bet,
By 'rastlin' over Numbers.
I never took no comfort, when
The year wus bald with losses,
A-spekkleatin' on them chaps
Thet rode them varus hosses.

It never gev my soul a boost,
When grief an' it wus matin',
Tew figger out thet thet thar Pope
Wus reely twins with Satan.
I took no stock in countin' up
How menny head uv cattle

[1]Published as "Farmer Stebbins' Opinions" in John Garvin's 1905 collected edition.

Frum Egypt's ranches Moses drove;
I never fit a battle
On p'ints thet frequently giv rise
Tew pious spat an' grumble,
An' make the brethren clinch an' yell
In spiritooal rough-an'-tumble.

I never bet on Paul agin
The argyments uv Peter;
I never made the good old Book
A kind uv moral teeter
Tew pass a choreless hour away,
An' get the evenin' over;
I swallered it jest as it stood,
Frum cover clar tew cover.

Hain't hed no time tew disputate,
Except with axe an' arm,
With stump an' rampike an' with stuns,
Upon my half-clared farm;
An' when sech argyments as them
Fill six days out uv seven,
A man on Sabbath wants tew crawl
By quiet ways tew Heaven.

Agin he gets the waggon out,
An' hitches up the sorrels
An' rides ten miles tew meetin', he
Ain't braced fur pious quarrels;
No, sir, he ain't! thet waggon rolls
Frum corduroy to puddle,
An' thet thar farmer gets his brains
Inter an easy muddle.

His back is stiff frum six days' toil—
So God takes hold an' preaches
In boughs uv rustlin' maple an'
In whisperin' leaves uv beeches.
Sez He tew thet thar farmin' chap
(Likewise tew the old woman),
"I guess I'm built tew comprehend
Thet you an' her be's human.

"So jest take hold on this here day,
Recowperate yer muscle;
Let up a mite this day on toil,
'Tain't made fur holy bustle.
Let them old sorrels jog along

With mighty slack-like traces,
Half dreamin', es My sunbeams fleck
Their venerable faces.

"I guess they did their share uv work
Since Monday's dew wus hoary;
Don't try tew lick 'em tew a trot
Upon the road tew Glory;
Jest let 'em laze a spell whar thick
My lily-buds air blowin',
An' whar My trees cast shadders on
My silver cricklet flowin'.

"An' while their red, rough tongues push back
The stems uv reed an' lily,
Jest let 'em dream uv them thar days
When they wus colt an' filly,
An' spekkleate, es fetlock deep
They eye My cool crick flowin',
On whar I loosed it frum My hand,
Whar be its crisp waves goin';
An' how in snow-white lily cup
I built them yaller fires,
An' bronzed them reeds thet rustle up
Agin the waggon tires;

"An' throw a forrard eye along
Whar thet bush roadway passes,
A-spekkleating on the chance
Uv nibbling roadside grasses.
Jest let them lines rest on their necks—
Restrain yer moral twitters—
An' paste this note inside yer hat:
I talk tew all My critters,

"Be they on four legs or on two,
In broadcloth, scales or feathers,
No matter what may be the length
Uv all their mental tethers,
In ways mayn't suit the minds uv them
Thet thinks themselves their betters,—
I talk tew them in simple style
In words uv jest three letters,
Spelled out in lily-blow an' reed,
In soft winds on them blowin',
In juicy grass by wayside streams,
In coolin' waters flowin'.

"An' so jest let them sorrels laze
  My ripplin' silver creek in;
They're listenin' in their own dumb way,
  An' I, Myself, am speakin'."

c. 1882
The Evening Telegram, 2 June 1882
"Old Spookses' Pass," "Malcolm's Katie," and Other Poems,
  1884

[SAID] THE CANOE[1]

My masters twain made me a bed
Of pine-boughs resinous, and cedar;
Of moss, a soft and gentle breeder
Of dreams of rest; and me they spread
With furry skins and, laughing, said:
"Now she shall lay her polished sides
As queens do rest, or dainty brides,
Our slender lady of the tides!"

My masters twain their camp-soul lit;
Streamed incense from the hissing cones;
Large crimson flashes grew and whirled;
Thin golden nerves of sly light curled
Round the dun camp; and rose faint zones,
Half way about each grim bole knit,
Like a shy child that would bedeck
With its soft clasp a Brave's red neck,
Yet sees the rough shield on his breast,
The awful plumes shake on his crest,
And, fearful, drops his timid face,
Nor dares complete the sweet embrace.

Into the hollow hearts of brakes—
Yet warm from sides of does and stags
Passed to the crisp, dark river-flags—

[1]Published as "Said the Canoe" in John Garvin's 1905 collected edition.

Sinuous, red as copper-snakes,
Sharp-headed serpents, made of light,
Glided and hid themselves in night.

My masters twain the slaughtered deer
Hung on forked boughs with thongs of leather:
Bound were his stiff, slim feet together,
His eyes like dead stars cold and drear.
The wandering firelight drew near
And laid its wide palm, red and anxious,
On the sharp splendour of his branches,
On the white foam grown hard and sere
   On flank and shoulder.
Death—hard as breast of granite boulder—
   Under his lashes
Peered thro' his eyes at his life's grey ashes.

My masters twain sang songs that wove—
As they burnished hunting-blade and rifle—
A golden thread with a cobweb trifle,
Loud of the chase and low of love:

"O Love! art thou a silver fish,
Shy of the line and shy of gaffing,
Which we do follow, fierce, yet laughing,
Casting at thee the light-winged wish?
And at the last shall we bring thee up
From the crystal darkness, under the cup
   Of lily folden
   On broad leaves golden?

"O Love! art thou a silver deer
With feet as swift as wing of swallow,
While we with rushing arrows follow?
And at the last shall we draw near
And o'er thy velvet neck cast thongs
Woven of roses, stars and songs—
   New chains all moulden
   Of rare gems olden?"

They hung the slaughtered fish like swords
   On saplings slender; like scimitars,
   Bright, and ruddied from new-dead wars,
Blazed in the light the scaly hordes.

They piled up boughs beneath the trees,
   Of cedar web and green fir tassel.
   Low did the pointed pine tops rustle,
The camp-fire blushed to the tender breeze.

The hounds laid dewlaps on the ground
  With needles of pine, sweet, soft and rusty,
  Dreamed of the dead stag stout and lusty;
A bat by the red flames wove its round.

The darkness built its wigwam walls
  Close round the camp, and at its curtain
  Pressed shapes, thin, woven and uncertain
As white locks of tall waterfalls.

8 December 1883
The Evening Telegram, 26 February 1884
The Collected Poems of Isabella Valancy Crawford, 1905

TORONTO

She moves to meet the centuries, her feet
All shod with emerald, and her light robe
Fringed with leaves singing in the jazel air.
Her tire is rich, not with stout battlements,
Prophets of strife, but wealthy with tall spires
All shining Godward, rare with learning's domes,
And burning with young stars that promise suns
To clasp her older brows. On her young breast
Lie linked the fair, clear pearls of many homes,—
Mighty and lovely chain, from its white strength
Hangs on her heart the awful jewel, Hope.

She moves to meet the centuries, nor lies
All languid waiting, with the murmuring kiss
Of the large waters on white, nerveless feet,
And dim, tranced gaze upon the harbour bar,
And dusk, still boughs knit over her prone head,
And rose-soft hands that idly pluck the turf,
And rose lips singing idly thro' her dream.

She hears the marching centuries which Time
Leads up the dark peaks of Eternity:
The pulses of past warriors bound in her;
The pulses of dead sages beat in her;
The pulses of dead merchants stir in her;

The roses of her young feet turn to flame,
Yet ankle-deep in tender buds of spring;
Till, with the perfumes of close forests thick
Upon her tender flesh, she to her lips
Lifts the bold answering trump, and, winding shrill
With voices of her people and her waves
Notes of quick joy, half queen, half child, she bounds
To meet the coming Time, and climbs the steps
Of the tall throne he builds upon her strand.

Toronto, joy and peace! When comes the day
Close domes of marble rich with gold leap up
From porphyry pillars to the eye-clear sky,
And when the wealthy fringes of thy robe
Sweep outward league on league, and to thee come
The years all bowed with treasures for thy house,
On lusty shoulders, still remember thee
Of thy first cradle on the lilies' lap
In the dim woods; and tho' thy diadem
Make a new sunrise, still, amid its flame,
Twine for the nursing lilies' sake the glow
Of God-like lilies round about thy brows—
Honour and Peace and sweet-breathed Charity!

c. 1884
The Evening Telegram, 25 June 1884
The Collected Poems of Isabella Valancy Crawford, 1905

THE HIDDEN ROOM

I marvel if my heart
Hath any room apart,
Built secretly its mystic walls within,
With subtly warded key
Ne'er yielded unto me,
Where even I have surely never been.

Ah, surely I know all
The bright and cheerful hall,
With the fire ever red upon its hearth;
My friends dwell with me there,

Nor comes the step of Care
To sadden down its music and its mirth.

Full well I know as mine
The little cloistered shrine
No foot but mine alone hath ever trod;
There come the shining wings,
The face of One who brings
The prayers of men before the throne of God.

And many know full well
The busy, busy cell
Where I toil at the work I have to do;
Nor is the portal fast
Where stand phantoms of the past,
Or grow the bitter plants of darksome rue.

I know the dainty spot
(Ah, who doth know it not?)
Where pure young Love his lily-cradle made,
And nestled some sweet springs
With lily-spangled wings—
Forget-me-nots upon his bier I laid.

Yet marvel I, my soul,
Know I thy very whole,
Or dost thou hide a chamber still from me?
Is it built upon the wall?
Is it spacious? Is it small?
Is it God, or man, or I who hold the key?

c. 1884
"Old Spookses' Pass," "Malcolm's Katie," and Other Poems, 1884

HUGH AND ION[1]

I

She had the full, fell frankness of her kind
Nor made a rose-ball of the saucy "No"
She flung across her tea-cup at his heart.
She had within the strong stone of her soul
A little feeble seed of womanhood,
That stirr'd, and pitied when the blow went home.
"Now, now," she said, "for comfort here's a tale.
For some fell tyrant's freak, once was a man
Condemned to crucifixion. In deep dark
They laid his long, strong limbs upon a cross
And bound his great thews to it with thin cords
Then said, 'lie there, thou valiant fool, and die.'
And so he lay, and wither'd inch by inch,
In the dense dark—nor mov'd a finger-tip
To test the ropes that bound him. Came a day,
The Sultan miss'd his beauty and his sword,
And said 'If still he live, why, bring him forth.'
Then the grim gaoler flash'd a torch on him
And seeing he still liv'd, cried 'Up, and come—
The Sultan needs thee.' As the light stream'd wide
He saw his cross—a shadow built of wings
Of moth and butterfly, and wither'd limbs
Of feeble rose-vines—and about him blaz'd
The long, free halls that once had own'd him lord
And nought had held him to his deadly cross,
And Liberty had waited for one leap
Of his into wide arms—a Sultan's jest,
With death its grim wit-sparkle. Come, my friend
Leap from thy phantom little cross of love,
Burst on the world unshackl'd by thy dreams—
My 'no' the torch to light thy freedom up.
Love is the deep dense darkness of the soul
Beaten by arms that passionately grope
And catch the void. Away with Love, away!"

[1]At the time of Crawford's death, this incomplete manuscript was untitled. Glenn Clever titled it "Hugh and Ion" in his 1977 edition of the poem—a title which has been accepted for the purposes of scholarship and criticism.

"And give us up Barabbas," said the man
Looking to where the other lover lean'd
A portly shoulder by a distant door
And cup in hand, laid all the little light
Of dull and dreamy eyes—not on his love
But on the phantom of the dead day's "deal"
On stocks and margins, "long" and "short," and all
The licens'd weapons of the world's wild war
Against large Plenty, where, all pitiful,
She holds to Want the wealth of weighty sheaves.

She laugh'd—the light, shrill laughter of her kind,
The fell frank music of a hard, high soul,
That knows not Love, lie, tenderness, nor shame.
"Barabbas was a robber. Lack-a-day!
We of the golden tissues floating far
And sandals jewel-lac'd—we need our thieves
Our Benedict Barabbas who can steal
With such bland gestures, and wise brows bent down
In plans financial, that the feeble folk
Stand all at gaze in envy and delight
Yes—even while he plucks the crusts from lips
Blue with their torture for it. Away with Love
Dark God of voids. And if his frame be knit
Of any tissue tougher than a dream
Crucify him—pierce him to death with doubt,
Loose us Barabbas—we of the Jewell'd coifs!"
She sleek'd the pansy darkness of her robe
With the pale pearl of a rose-lin'd palm
And drove the rubied arrow through the dusk
And stormy purple of the raven braid
That built its blackness over falcon eyes
Hooded by lashes like the fall of night
Over sharp, shining waters. Then she smote
Him in the heart with that keen, kindly smile
(Sharp *coup de grace* for many a sturdy stag)
Of wider wisdom—and she knew he knew
Her soul was blind, and could not look on Love.
"Blind, blind so safe," she answer'd to the scorn
That slowly rose against her in his gaze.
"If there be pits, I pass them on a hair
If there be heights, they breed no whirling brain;
If Love bask like a serpent by my feet
If Love lie like a lion in my way
If Love lure like a lily to dark deeps
I see him not—so blind and blessèd pass!"

"So creeps the slow-worm, blind and blessed thing
Not knowing heights nor depths, nor if it cling
To the peak'd mountain lording all the land;
Or to the leaf that rolls along the mire
In Autumn's blast. But you, fierce falcon soul
You pluck the jewell'd hood across keen eyes
And dash bold wings against the face of God
Who loos'd you to the air—and cry 'Blind, blind!
Blame not the blind!' And when you plunge your beak
In some strong quarry breasting up the sky
You cry for pardon with that lying plaint
'Blind, blind, blame not the blind!' O wing'd keen curse
Blind by strong willing that you will not see!"

She drew the golden glamour of a rose
Across her eyes. "Hooded with joys and blind
To dreams and ghosts and phantoms of delight,
Where is this Love? God! if he have his birth
As love—but watch him as he walks the world
And see him at the end, stretch'd stark, and chang'd
To Hate, and dead, with cold veins virus fill'd.
These wedded lovers—like twin seraphs clasp'd
Within the arms of a meek, bright moon
Whose light is honey dripping from clear cusps
Eternity is theirs—until Time rounds
Some twenty fiery pathways round the world
Lo, then the man—why, watch him stand at gaze
At ev'ry budding girl that matches May,
His wife the pale, wan priestess at a shrine
Whose star has faded to a ball of dust,
Dead in dark space! O if Love be born
Strangle the imp while yet the dimples stray
Across full baby cheeks—before he change
To virile Hate—or to languid Loathing
Or merge his modern monogamic mind
For patriarchal mood plus many wives."
She laugh'd, and he that lov'd her sigh'd and went.

II

Without the West drew flaming gates across
The grey, gaunt distance of the wintry street
Low down were welded fast against the sky
Dull, purple bars that held the first, fine snow.
Lower, the old unutterable pray'r
That glows in golden script behind the day
Stretch'd its still strength about the dark'ning world

And as a cobweb delicately spun
Bare black thin boughs hung orb'd against the sky
And in their subtle lacings seem'd to cling
Arachne-like, the round, full Evening Star.
Dark on near hills the primal forest heav'd
Its haughty heart against the City's claws
That lengthen'd towards its ramparts day by day;
Dark on near sands the tideless waters stood
Meek with dun mist—moaning against wan wharves
Dying to dumbness as the fierce young frost
Gaz'd on the shudd'ring world, ere serpent-wise
He coil'd chill crystal folds about its breast.
On such an eve despair seems no strange growth,
But a chief vein that feeds the chilling heart,
With pausing billows stiff'ning as they burst
And Hope an alien flame fall'n from the wick
Of a cold lamp that chills the failing hand.
Dust, sharp as spear points in the rising frost
Whirl'd in keen simoons, and, sullen orbs
The base stars of the city lamps, leap'd up.

III

Where's speech in anguish? O she never throve
On the high swell of Sorrow's bursting heart.
Two groans are hers that give themselves to speech
"God, God!" with this she wails Him up before
Her Bar of Desolation—then, "Why? Why?"
Spurts through her hollowed graves and empty shrines
For who will fling the iron doors apart
Where naked Sorrow sits, and free her shriek
To beat in strength against the granite world?
One caught the mutter of his cag'd despair
And passing, struck a light, lascivious palm
Upon his arm, and serpent-like her glance
Curv'd at him over plump and ruddy cheeks
For she no draggled weed, but tense and hale
Strong Flower of Vice, and foliag'd soberly
In rich demureness of all sombre hues
A fine aesthetic motion of the mind
To suit her colours to the tow'ring walls
Of churches churches pressing on her path
And the grave grey-beards tott'ring in her wake.
Behind the springing of her sudden look
She solv'd swift problems on the problem, man;
So laugh'd and pass'd, and, looking at the gates

He stood by, mutter'd, "Aye—he freezes now
Before some sudden frost in woman's shape,
Or in some blast that burst some shard apart
And let the half-blown, half-seen bud he lov'd
Swing all its stinging poison on the air.
Lord, what an interchange of wonderment
There is when man finds ev'ry woman foul
And woman weeds her dreams away, and through
Clear spaces sees the strong, smooth tiger, Man.
Tush! let him be—he's in the wonder-throe"—
And the sharp dust caught, and veil'd her, and she pass'd.

IV

The bitter eve grew vocal as he went.
The infant city nursing on the breast
Of unhewn woods found virile voice to shout
The cry of eighteen hundred years ago.
The church tow'rs roar'd it on their ev'ning chime
"Loose us Barabbas!—he will rear us high;
Will lay his gold upon our organ pipes;
Will beat his stolen silver in our bells;
And stain our windows with the blood he robs
From the free Helot's heart. O Christ, O Christ!
Thy robe is sordid and Thy palms are hard
Hang on Thy cross! Loose us Barabbas, yes!
And while Christ hangs, the thief shall build to Him."
"Loose us Barabbas!" all the busy marts
Buzzed with the cry, "for none but robber thews
Can wrestle with fierce Fortune, now-a-days."
Vice rear'd its supple, serpent-head and hiss'd
"Loose us Barabbas—let our fellow free."

Want, lean, lank giant, honest hunger-blind
Stood groaning 'tween the cries, and questioning
Might not Barabbas be a newer Christ?
With newer gospel fitter for the time?

V

With the illimitable wilderness around
From the close city hives rang up the groan
"So little space!—we starve—we faint, we die!"
Lord! Lord! to see the gaping city sewer
Beaded with haggard heads—and hungry eyes
Peering above the heaving of the drains
And hear the harsh, unreasonable cry
"We starve, we starve!" While half a world lay fresh

And teeming, out beyond the city gates!
Alas, for him who feels a Samson soul
Within the sinews of a medium mind
And lays weak willing hands on lion jaws
And clasps strong columns in a flaccid arm,
One such there was—the Samson in him grew
At sight of pillars bearing wrongs aloft
On firm, flint shoulders, and of lions crouch'd
To guard grim evils tott'ring on their staves,
By the fierce, tender wonder of his mind
That what man calls "a man," should choose to pave
The city kennels with his juiceless bones,
To lick the city dust with siccous tongue,
To raven at its flesh marts with fierce eyes,
And feel the iron soles of rushing feet
Crush his lean breast, trample his puny babes
And bring the dark divorce of hunger pangs
Between all life and him—while prairie breasts
Mounded, all teeming with the milk of life,
And forests shouted to his leaden ears
Of food and shelter. He who pities man
Has keener sword pricks on his tender breast
Than the gaunt bosom of the victim bears
Aye, though the sword is hilt deep in his heart
And he who sees the mountain reel and fall
Had more of death than him that falls with it.
For Hugh, the giant in him hurl'd the clay
He groan'd in, blindly up against the rocks,
And flung it on the levell'd spears, and thrust
It close against the furnaces, and play'd
A thousand antics with the shade of earth
It scorn'd, and lov'd and loath'd; and the poor ghost
Of flesh and blood lay at the strong soul's feet
Trembling to dust, and smitten with despair.
Then, almost free, the soul had clearer light
And lifting high the pale clay on its breast
Mourn'd the young fury of its holy rage
And on its necessary brother blew
The strong breath of its mouth, and sought to slip
The vital fetter in its place again.

"Up, up, thou weakling! Wouldst thou lay thy palms
Against a stubborn world, to hurl it fair
Into a truer orbit—up, up and forge
Strong sinews for the deed: I, fed of God,
Grow lusty—feed thy fainting flesh beside
His lowlier fountains running for thy lips—

Weld strength with strength, so let us face the world.
I err'd in hate of thee—arise—forgive!"
So spake his Soul, and pluck'd him from the town
With its young walls and venerable sins,
The smell of primal woods upon its air
The groans of Ancient Famine in its slums.

VI

There came an April day all tremulous
And shaking like a shining reed between
Two soft winds blowing at it with purs'd lips
That drove its polish'd stem now into shade
Now into sunshine. Then there came a night
That bore between its dark still palms a cloud
An alabaster box that held the balm
Bright, in the sunset, as a yellow gourd—
She bore it to the peak of midnight—there
With thunder claps she burst its darken'd sides
And through warm blackness fell the bless'd spring balm
Of rain upon the world. All through the night
Life loos'd the awful fountain of his heart,
And earth grew tremulous with pulsing seeds
And leaping stems, and juices rushing up
From her wide veins along the barren woods.
And all the budding boughs in that short night,
Did dimple with small leaves a dew drop large.

VII

Hugh caught the dove of Spring between his palms,
And unasham'd before his large thew'd soul
Drew her soft plumes against his worn breast
And held her to his ear to coo her rime
Of deep green woods, and creeks and purple hills.
"I'll plunge to drowning depth in leaf-built waves,
And let them wash me from this clanging world
That shrieks with steam—where mostly men are merely
ghosts
That tend on iron tyrants—solid kings
That turn and rend the dream-like flesh and blood
That forms and serves them—I saw one monster take
A serf that serv'd it, in its mighty maw
And comb his sweating flesh sheer from his bones
With glitt'ring fangs. The leafy waves shall wash
The roaring of the city from my ears
And drive before their sibilant strong rush

The weak despair that sickens all my soul,
Bores through my brittle bones, and nips apart
The very sinews of my straining mind.
Then will I come again when I am heal'd
And shout such gospel of the woods and plains
As, like the music of the lean Hindoo,
Shall drag from sewers and drains, and noisesome holes
The worm-like men who bore their abject way
In pain and darkness through the city mire,
Who crack their stiff'ning sinews for a crust
And need an alms to screw their coffin-lids.
I'll have them out!—a saviour of their flesh—
Yes—even while they howl about the streets
'Loose us Barabbas—we will cheapen toil
For him, and throne the robber on our necks.'
I'll have them out! God, knit my sinews up."

VIII

The primal savage in him shook his gyves
And stirr'd great shoulders in his narrow cell
And star'd with lusty looks about the earth
And like a hawk peer'd up the very sky
For quarry, and asham'd he felt great throbs
Wing his dull heels behind the scudding deer
Beat at his wrists above the bending rod
And leap from out his very breast along
The keen, clear sky behind some dappl'd wing.
What honey made the marrow of the food
He chas'd and slew? And like a hunter God
The fumes of little lives rose round his heart
And strengthen'd it. And from the very leaves
Joy wrung strong wine into his weary soul.

"Now see," he said to one that shared his tent,
"How buxom Hope becomes with Diane's bow
Laid on her shoulder, and her rosy foot
Inlaid with dew from fern and from flag.
Come, grasp her hand, and stumble to your feet."

"Nay," answer'd his plagu'd friend, "Hope built to brawn
From venison and trout and oxygen
Has so much clay knit in her throbbing flesh
That clay will pluck her back to clay again—
Could I clasp Hope, she should be all a God
The Builder not the built—and move strong wings
Wide as a world cleft into semi-spheres
And have great arms to thrust malignant stars

Back from her course along the universe
And a broad foot to crush the serpent's head
That lifts, and spits his poison in her face.
Hopeless the Godhood—bury her for me!"

"There cries a loon," said Hugh. "And all our tent
Glows shiftingly; and on its canvas roof
Dance the dark shadows of deep leaves above.
Come, burst our linen lintels, and behold
Hope swimming up the dawn upon the world!"

"Strong with deer's flesh," laugh'd Ion, "and the curd
Of tricky trout—stand you, my friend, at gaze.
I'll build the fire, and brew the natant maid
A draught to cheer the kernel of her heart.
Hope, without breakfast, has a swooning trick."

Dawn swam the east; against her breast the night
Broke purple, and her curving arms beat back
The starry surf—she reach'd the shining shoals
And slipp'd the crimson of her lusty foot
On the firm ground and from her breast and knee
Her opal shoulder, and the ruddy palms
That smote the misty tresses from her eyes
Light fell, in half heard music, on the earth.
Naked, a second, on the shore she stood
With all the innocent, small feather'd things
Flying to touch the scarlet, lucid bars
Of her stretch'd fingers, and against her knees
Rubb'd the soft sides of shadowy deer, and high
The squirrels chatter'd at her from rich boughs
Then warmer wound the blood wide in her veins.
She mov'd an ardent palm, and drew the mists
From lakes, and swamps and valleys; and their folds
Spic'd with the cedar and the balsam—bright
On their curl'd edges with a saffron dye
She upward drew along her rosy knees
Her ivory thighs, the silver of her breast.
So veil'd and drap'd she waited for the sun.

"These mists are prophets of a torrid day,"
Said Ion, wearily, "a fierce, red day
Of zenith summer, snorting in sharp peals
Of dry, short thunder, as a stallion snorts
At gaze at midday on an arid plain
The herd afar—wher'ere the fever'd palm
Falls on him, leaps an artery of fire.
What see you in the dawn—come, prophet, speak!"

"I see dead night," said Hugh, "and tears that dry
In aching eyes turned on the growing light."

"But that dead night!" said Ion, "many slaves
Died at his burial; where may be their dawn?
Stark at his feet they lie—their leaping hearts
Dust on his sere cloths! Lo, for some the dawn
Is named despair!—and you—you call her Hope!"

"Aye, Hope," said Hugh, "and by her sturdy side
And ruddy kertle clings my flutt'ring soul.
No Goddess she—but God's own very breath
Shap'd into one grave splendour of the East.
Come, Ion, love her! clasp strong palms with her."

"Your Dawn," laugh'd Ion. "Often times she smites
The last nail in the gallows—and the wretch
Wakes to the rope beneath her rosy palms.
O God, you Hope! A smoke wreath of the soul.
Despair a firm flint rock beneath the feet!
Give me despair's strong certainty—I'll stand
On that grim cliff, and dominate the world
Aye—use it tripod-wise, and sybil-like
Look from it through the universe, and see
The birth of ruins, and the horrid flames
Of bursting worlds—the man who hopes and laughs
Is Nature's fool and wears her motley well."

"Then am I grateful for my cap and bells,"
Said Hugh, "and Nature's zany is her king!
Shame, Ion, shame! You of the feeble folk
Who bend their own weak knees and wav'ring spines
To God, and chitter-chatter of despair
Of ruins and of chaos—nor have sheer strength
To clamber up God's breast, and look abroad
From thence across the universe, and see
All His broad purpose."

"An ultimate of calm,"
Said Ion, "and a plain of stolid peace
The world dew-pure—stormy souls of men
Tether'd with rose-boughs—the tiger's tawny paw
Laid round the lamb for love—the lion's cub
Cradl'd with babes. O mild millennial days
Your round ey'd Hope may see their dulcet dawn
Strong with prime ven'son she, and tip-toe with
Warm wealth of blood, and wine of kindliness.
Despair is cold and lean, and logic-full,

Seasons her rue with reason—from the past
Builds up the dreadful future—O God, your Hope
Full-fed and prating peace from dimpling lips."

"Aye so," said Hugh, "and mild millennial days
Where brawny Peace shall lie, fair and full stretch
Upon charg'd Gatlings, smiling in the sun
And ev'ry man shall sit beneath his vine
A snug torpedo buried by its roots
To greet a foe with! So my round ey'd Hope
Sees Peace in her best prime upon this world.
Not on this shaping-place of souls broods Peace
Unarmed—As in the horrible long crash
Of falling mountains and conflicting seas
God shapes His earth—so are the souls of men
Caught from the secret spaces—in the war
Of circumstances moulded, and sped on
Along eternity from sphere to sphere
Polish'd in speeding—O this clanging world
Is no snug nest for doves! My Hope, you see
Faces eternities—Archangels hold
Her torches high against the mysteries
Their soaring wings still seek—and yet she smiles
Into the violet on the drying grave,
And leaves the dewy jewel of her dawn
Starr'd in its with'ring breast. Despair, Despair!
Have I not seen that hooded spectre steal
Among my many graves? have I not fought
His misty arms? Where be your rounded graves
That hold the seeds of sorrow? O patience yields
To see you standing in the very sun
And chanting lamentations! While neck deep
The many from black waters reach at Hope."

"I hope," said Ion, "faith, so keenly hope
I see some half hour hence the flashing trout
Yet snug in yonder pool—yield mellowly
His rose-leaf flakes, and opal curds to us.
In the meanwhile I'll sing the Dawn, I love.

A startl'd stag the blue grey night
Leaps down beyond dark pines
Behind, a length of yellow light,
  The Hunter's arrow shines
His moccasins are stain'd with red
  He bends upon his knee
From cov'ring peaks his shafts are sped

The blue mists plume his mighty head!
  Well may the dark stag flee!

The pale moon like a snow-white doe
  Bounds by his dappl'd flank;
They beat the stars down as they go
  As wood-bells growing rank.
The winds lift dew-laps from the ground
  Leap from dry shaking reeds
Their hoarse bays shake the cedars round—
With keen cries on the trail they bound—
  Swift, swift the dark stag speeds!

Roar the rent lakes, as through the waves
  Their silver warriors plunge
As vaults from core of crystal caves
  The vast, fierce Maskelonge.
Red torches of the sumach glow
  Fall's council fires are lit
The bittern, squaw-like scolds the air
The wild duck splashes loudly, where
  The waving rice-spears knit.

Shaft after shaft the red sun speeds—
  Rent the stag's dappl'd side,
His breast to fangs of hoarse winds bleeds
  He staggers on the tide.
He feels the hungry waves of space
  Rush at him high and blue
The white spray smites his dusky face
Swifter the sun's swift arrows race
  And pierce his strong heart through.

Away! his white doe far behind
  Lies wounded on the plain
Yells at his flank the nimblest wind—
  His large tears fall like rain
Like lily-pads shall clouds grow white
  About his darkling way
From her bald nest upon the height
The red-ey'd eagle sees his flight
He falters—turns—the antler'd night
  The black stag stands at bay!

His feet are in the waves of space
  His antlers broad and dun,
He low'rs, and turns his velvet face
  To front the hunter sun,
He stamps the lilied clouds and high,
  His branches fill the west—
The lean stork sails across the sky—

The shy loon shrieks to see him die
  The winds leap at his breast.

His antlers fall—once more he spurns
  The hoarse hounds of the day
His blood upon the crisp blue burns
  Reddens the mounting spray.
His branches smite the wave—with cries
  The shrill winds pausing, flag
He sinks in space—red glow the skies;
The brown earth crimsons as he dies,
  The stout and lusty stag!

Later they laid the silver birch canoe
On the fresh tide—and paddl'd from the shore.

"Hush, hush," said Hugh, "O paddle, noiseless slip
Through velvet waters dusky, deep and still,
As hearts of unblown flow'rs; and thou, canoe,
Make smooth thy birchen sides, and like a beam
That pushes night all noiselessly aside
Part the still lake—Lo, all the little isles
Seem at a mid air, mystic anchorage
Sky lav'd at granite plinth, and cedar crest
As though a God stood doubting—holding them
Between the wave and sky."

"And shall I pluck
Them up to gem my calm immortal lakes?
Or shall I spare them yet a space to man?"

"Eastward the large, long shadows lie and gaze
Into brown waters—westward on gold feet
The sultry light stands on the polish'd lakes
And eyes the raven thunder cloud that flies
With plumes all rent far down the curving wave.
Ion, behold!—here lies the old, moss'd crib,
Knit to yon isle by weft of reaching vines,
Fring'd with round lilies; and a bubble floats
On the sleek wave—a little rainbow world
With isles and pines and lilies set in it!
Cool, cool the smooth brown shadows! lo, how quakes
Yon lily in the deep core of the shade!
"There drop the line—there lurks the spangl'd fin!"

Said Ion, "we will bait the hook with Hope
And with keen hope the trout will nibble it!
And then to one—despair—to trout or man!"

"The trout is welcome to the hope a trout
Can nibble from the hook," Hugh laugh'd. "Now draw
The paddle in—like a swan's foot it shines
And frights the fish—Against this lily bed
We'll lie—and silence gild our dangling bait."

IX

Hugh's eyes held all the heritage of light,
From Council fires that fac'd a thousand moons,
And warm'd the tribal wisdom into life,
From age to age—so loved he prairie crests
And awful forests, and the might of hills,
The surfs of quaking lakes—and like a net
His heart cast out at men to draw them up
From swarming city shallows—light the locks
Of Saxon yellow fell on Saxon brows
And the stern humour of the Saxon stood
Built of firm flint within his steadfast soul
With flames to leap against a trial touch
Of cynic steel, and all his creeds and faiths
Had flinty feet, and iron in their veins.
For Ion, ere the ague of despair
Shook his young soul, the hale and healthy pang
Fame-famine, nipp'd him, through the very mists of Death
He saw, with eager vision, and beheld
The white, strong swan-wings over Lethe's wave,
And heard the mighty music of their sweep
As down the dark they hurl'd—beheld the bird
Seize from the dreamless terrors of the stream
His name, his name! And upward from the mists
Bear it, star-burning, to immortal fanes
To blaze across all ages to all men—
Nor knew the longest fame the longest death.
Yet fame's keen pang is pulse of God that stirs
In the strong soul that fain would help to mould
A Universe, or, like the Titan, leave
An awful foot-print sunken in the rock
God-eloquent of giants in the earth.
He lov'd the wilds, Athenian-wise, so lov'd
His little Athens more—his canvas best
His patient and impatient eyes beheld
The leprosies of Nature, and her soul
Of beauty hidden under twisted limbs
And so his spirit at his canvas stood

And painted spirit—never burst a vine
Of Spring beneath his brush, but men beheld
The grapes of Autumn on it, and foresaw
The vintages, and felt the soft winds move
Behind its leaves, and all its juices steal
Luminous from the pulses of the God.
Then Love came troublous with his languid lutes
And danc'd before Despair, whose canker'd feet[2]
Bled on Love's arm'd roses—and Ion flung
His canvas to the dust—and being young
Built a large pompous guest-room on his heart
For bleak Despair; and Love, well mask'd in weeds
And prettily demure, with dimples dark
With ashes, and his arrows hidden in
A cypress wreathèd urn, play'd the page part
To the grim guest, and waiting for his day
Laugh'd in the darkness of the tyrant's shade.
And Ion wing'd his heels, and hurri'd far
Into the wilds from his false falcon love.

His cedar paddle, scented red,
He thrust down through the lily-bed.

Cloak'd in a golden pause he lay
Lock'd in the arms of the bay.

Trembl'd alone his bark canoe
As shocks of bursting lilies flew—

Through the still pulses of the tide,
And smote the frail boat's silv'ry side.

Or when, beside the sedges thin
Flash'd the sharp jewel of a fin.

Or when, a wizard swift and bold
A dragon fly dash'd out in gold

And fire and flame, the wid'ning rings
Of waters whisp'ring to his wings.

Or when, like wing'd and burning soul
Dropp'd from the gloom an oriole—

On the cool wave, as to the balm
Of the Great Spirit's open palm—

The freed soul flies. Soft silence clung
To the still hours as tendrils hung,

[2]Glenn Clever notes that this line is crossed out in the manuscript (*Hugh and Ion*, 1977; p. 31).

In darkness carven, from the trees
Sedge-buried to their burly knees.

Stillness sat in her lodge of leaves,
Clung golden shadows to its eaves:

And on its spicy floor like maize
Red-ripe fell sheaves of knotted rays.

The wood, a proud and crested brave;
Bead-bright, a maiden, stood the wave.

And he had told his tale of love
With voice of eagle and of dove

Of loud, peak'd pines his tongue had made
His lips soft blossoms of the shade

That kiss'd her silver lips—hers cool
As lilies on his inmost pool.

Till now he stood in triumph's rest
His image in her crystal breast.

One isle, 'tween blue and blue did melt
A bead of wampum from the belt,

Of Manitou—a purple rise
On the far shore slipp'd up the skies.

His cedar paddle scented red
He drew up from the lily-bed.

All lily-lock'd, all lily-lock'd
The light bark on the blossoms rock'd—

Their cool lips round the sharp prow sang,
Their soft palms to the pale sides sprang.

With breasts and lips they wove a bar—
Stole from her lodge the Ev'ning Star

With golden hand she grasp'd the mane
Of a red cloud on the azure plain—

It by the con'd red sunset flew
Cool winds from its bright nostrils blew.

They sway'd the high dark trees and low
Swept the lock'd lilies to and fro.

With cedar paddle, scented red
He push'd out from the lily-bed!

Thus Ion sang, and rustl'ing through the rice
They met the shining fingers of the moon
Thrust through the woods to touch the shining lake;
She lifted mellow lips to dying day

And all her kisses quiver'd into stars.
Then from the large rose of the lake leap'd up
A million little lillied mists that play'd
And curl'd before the prow like naiad hands
Bore the birch bark in snowy palms, and hid
The rice, the lilies, and the flashing wave.
A camp-fire flared far on an ebon spear
Of pine-black land that split the lake, and pale
Their tent gleam'd in the light—And Hugh beheld
And sang a paean to its canvas eaves.

There stands my tent secure between
Two pointed pines—twin guards of green.

My palace of mid-June delight!
The canvas walls no longer white:

By smoke from camp-fires keenly kist
Into a dim, dun coil of mist.

By past long summers, bronz'd as brown
As cones from pine peaks shaken down.

Would I thy mellow walls exchange
For snowy canvas fresh and strange?

Perish the thought there's not a rent
Or stain, I'd spare from thee, my tent!

Lo, that long wound heal'd with a seam
Thou hadst it in Walpurgian dream,

Of branches bellowing through the night
As when strong, leafy giants fight.

A smitten pine, his dying grip
Laid on thee with faint finger tip—

And jagg'd thee sore—that russet stain
The fire-kiss of a flaming plain!

That patch—tis victory's squalid flag
Against thee hurl'd the hounded stag—

Fangs at his throat. He reels! he falls!
His antlers in thy yielding walls.

Thy linen lintel bears a blot
I would not move a single jot.

Oh misty, mellow, murm'rous eves,
Oh crooked sticks displum'd of leaves

I hung beneath thy trembling thatch,
The scaly treasures of my "catch"

The speck'ld sweetmeat of the stream—
The darling of the angler's dream.

The silver spirit of the creek
That leaps, a pale nymph, from the peak

Of woody hill, and on her way,
Snares such sun flashes, as she may;

And from the glitt'ring rays, small doubt
Evolves her jewell'd sprite, the trout!

Then later, simple ecstasy
That grew between my pipe and me,

Impletion of serene content—
Joy to thy smoky walls, my tent!

So sped the eve, and lying on piled spruce
Beside the red camp-fire, Hugh mused and planned
And Ion smok'd, or sang his sorrow songs
That sounded merrily, to say the least.

Thus Hugh, with eyes large on the ebon woods
"A fine, full soil—free grants for every soul—
Pure water—timber—hills for little towns—
Shelter for cattle in the valley dips
I'll search no further—hither my colony
Shall tramp; here tent, and touch red Plenty's robe."

Thus Ion: "Yes—and yonder frowning isle
That burst the lake so furiously at birth,
The wave still hisses round it—there your jails
Can cage their birds—Oh, all fits well!
Heights for your towns and temples—rugged rocks
To hold your ready rogues, meek murderers,
Your multi-marri'd, and the hoary heads
That whiten'd churches, while their hungry hands
Pluck'd at the public placket—or betray'd
The orphan's trust—Oh! all fits very well.
Prepare the wilderness for crime—and Man!"

"Nay—man and crime," said Hugh, "Name man the first,
He is the stronger—yield him all his rights."

"O optimist! O owl that through the pitch
Of midnight gazes clearest! And small doubt
Sees the grim ruins gay to his round orbs!"

Then Hugh: "Behold this bay, how firm the sweep
Of the high headlands heav'd from its deep heart.

Here wharves shall grow, and docks, and sails shall set
To this large shelter—from the furious leaps
Of yon unsalted sea."

"True, true," said Ion, "true
And to their slimy lips shall steal at night
Lost mothers with their bastards at their breasts—
And stare a moment at the town behind,
A moment at the stars—then make the choice
Of filthy water. Spurn'd merrily by Fate
The madmen of Despair shall leap from them
And rotting ships, brave in fresh paint, shall swing
Loose from them to the wrecking. Thus it holds
In my young, leafy Athens—thus it holds
In Babylon."

"And thus," said Hugh, "it holds
Round our rude star—from hurricanes slip up
Sleek calms, and healthier airs—and hideous slimes
Labour with lilies—O, God's moulding place
Is full of riot, roar of furnaces
Glaring of metal, running in fierce tides
Smoke, violence, and strife—but ever tends
The storm to music, and the strife to peace
Mayhap the music sounds dim aeons hence
Perchance the Peace shapes on immortal shores."

"Hope is your creed," said Ion, "and you cling
To rainbows, like the elves in picture books!
You ride the moth, and clasp the trembling reed!"

"Ion I worship—sets my soul that way,
And Hope is Pythia to the God I know
Utters His will, and looks along His Hand
Stretch'd through the coming ages shaping them.
Shall I pass sentence and condemn myself
To present Hell, and consort with damn'd souls?
Kiss future fiends? and touch the tender hand
That yet shall glow in torment? bow before
The sage, and see him, kernel-wise, set in
Ripe flames? Nay, pledge my constant friend
And see, by faith, the wine kiss on his lips
Already hot with Hell? Shall I behold
The earth round out with dust by devils shed
And dwarf tremendous Hope to that slight thing
That from man's billions culls her, here and there,
A Soul she fancies? God is God and Hope
His chiefest Prophet!"

"Prove that!" said Ion,
"I'll be your pupil then—yes, faith, I will."

"Proof, proof!" said Hugh. "Nay, work the problem out
Alone; nor waste your toil on it unless
You feel at times the passionate, plain pang
Of adoration paining all your soul
And hear ''Tis well to worship!' from her lips.
Then seek my God, and you shall find His Hope.
In the mean-time, roll up that lusty log
Astride the flames—the night grows pale and chill."

X

Hugh lay and dream'd, with movements of the feet
And starting fingers, and with pricking ears
Full of the crash of stags, through brush and fern
And ripping of deep waves by dappl'd breasts
And so his spirit struggl'd with the earth
Then upward burst to the clear airs of sleep.

XI

He clung against the blackness of a cliff
With bat-sharp nails, and felt against his lips
The awful granite that he could not see.
Against his naked soles he felt a cloud,
Rub its dark down as if an eagle pass'd.
Thunder fill'd space: the thunder spirits roll'd
Their balls in such hot sport, the roaring orbs
Smote side to side—then to the south some sped
A riot of red arrows rushing down
On the swift bird that ever flies before
Their ruddy shafts yet never drops to them.
Below him leaped the thunders of the lake;
Against his breast, reverberant, the cliff
Belch'd brittle echoes; burst from ev'ry pass
Responsive floods of sound, as to the joy
Of the wild thunders they lent their rocky throats.
Night! was this night, or some space set apart
For lasting dark scorch'd with the lightning's blast?
His soul stood tip-toe for the groan of woods
For forests grow by sun—but stone and wave
Made all this world—and thunders all its voice.
Deep dawns of newer darkness fill'd the east
Till, like a swamp-bred monster's hide, the sky
Grew wrinkl'd with them—and the lightning's shafts

Broke on their thicker blackness—wave on wave
Sprang as a brawny buck leaps on his foe
That fights him for his mate, and rearing high
Grew lank against his stretching foe, and roar'd
And with white branches lock'd they strove and reel'd
And crashed to death together—Then there fell

[manuscript ends here]

Undated
Hugh and Ion, 1977

THE GHOSTS OF THE TREES

The silver fangs of the mighty axe
  Bit to the blood of our giant boles;
It smote our breasts and smote our backs.
  Thundered the front-cleared leaves.
    As sped in fire
  The whirl and flame of scarlet leaves,
    With strong desire
  Leaped to the air our captive souls.
While down our corpses thundered,
The Air at our strong souls gazed and wondered,
  And cried to us, "Ye
Are full of all mystery to me.
  I saw but your plumes of leaves,
  Your strong, brown greaves,
Your sinewy roots and lusty branches;
And, fond and anxious,
  I laid my ear and my restless breast
  By each pride-high crest;
    And softly stole
And listened by limb and listened by bole,
Nor ever the stir of a soul
    Heard I in ye.
  Great is the mystery!"

The strong brown Eagle plunged from his peak;
From the hollow iron of his beak

The wood pigeon fell, its breast of blue
Cold with sharp death all thro' and thro'.
        To our ghosts he cried,
        "With talons of steel
        I hold the storm;
    Where the high peaks reel
        My young lie warm;
In the wind-rocked spaces of air I bide,
    My wings too wide,
Too angry-strong, for the emerald gyves
Of woodland cell where the meek dove thrives.
    And when at the bar
Of morn I smote with my breast its star,
        And under
My wings grew purple the jealous thunder,
    With the flame of the skies
Hot in my breast and red in my eyes,
    From peak to peak of sunrise piled,
That set space glowing
With flames from air-based craters blowing,
    I downward swept, beguiled
By the close-set forest, gilded and spread,
A sea for the lordly tread
    Of a god's war-ship.
I broke its leafy surf with my breast;
        My iron lip
I dipped in the cool of each whispering crest.
    From your leafy steeps
    I saw in the deeps
Red coral, the flame-necked oriole;
But never the stir of a soul
        Heard I in ye.
    Great is the mystery!"

        From its ferny coasts
The River gazed at our strong, free ghosts,
    And with rocky fingers shed
    Apart the silver curls of its head;
Laid its murmuring hands
On the reedy bands;
        And at gaze
Stood in the half-moon of brown, still bays.
Like glossed eyes of stags
Its round pools gazed from the rusty flags
    At our ghostly crests,
At the bark-shields strong on our phantom breasts;

And its tide
Took lip and tongue and cried:

"I have pushed apart
The mountain's heart,
I have trod the valley down;
With strong hands curled,
Have caught and hurled
To the earth the high hill's crown.

"My brow I thrust
Through sultry dust
That the lean wolf howled upon;
I drove my tides
Between the sides
Of the bellowing canyon.

"From crystal shoulders
I hurled my boulders
On the bridge's iron span;
When I reared my head
From its old-time bed,
Shook the pale cities of man.

"I have run a course
With the swift, wild horse;
I have thundered pace for pace
With the rushing herds;
I have caught the beards
Of the swift stars in the race.

"Neither moon nor sun
Could me outrun;
Deep caged in my silver bars,
I hurried with me
To the shouting sea
Their light and the light of the stars.

"The reeling earth,
In furious mirth,
With sledges of ice I smote;
I whirled my sword
Where the pale berg roared,
I took the ship by the throat.

"With stagnant breath
I called chill Death,
My guest, to the hot bayou;

I built men's graves
With strong-thewed waves.
That thing that my strength might do

"I did right well.
Men cried, 'From Hell
The might of thy hand is given!'
By loose rocks stoned,
The stout quays groaned;
Sleek sands by my spear were riven.

"O'er shining slides
On my glossèd tides
The brown cribs, close woven, rolled;
The stout logs sprung
Their height among
My loud whirls of white and gold.

"The great raft prest
My calm, broad breast—
A dream thro' my shady trance;
The light canoe
A spirit flew—
The pulse of my blue expanse.

"Winged swift, the ships
My foaming lips
Made rich with dewy kisses,
All night and morn,
Thro' fields of corn;
And where the mill-wheel hisses,

"And shivers and sobs
With labouring throbs,
With its whirls my strong palms played.
I parted my flags
For thirsty stags;
On the necks of arches laid,

"To the dry-vined town
My tide rolled down:
Dry lips and throats a-quiver
Rent sky and sod
With shouts, 'From God
The strength of the mighty river!'

"I, listening, heard
The soft-songed bird,
The beetle about your boles,
The calling breeze

   In your crests, O trees,—
Never the voices of souls!"

We, freed souls of the trees, looked down
On the River's shining eyes of brown;
   And upward smiled
At the tender Air and its warrior child,
   The iron Eagle strong and wild.

   No will of ours,
The captive souls of our barky towers;
   His the deed
Who laid in the secret earth the seed,
And with strong hand
Knitted each woody fetter and band.

c. 1884
"Old Spookses' Pass," "Malcolm's Katie," and Other Poems, 1884

THE ROSE OF A NATION'S THANKS

A welcome? Oh, yes, 'tis a kindly word, but why will they plan and prate
Of feasting and speeches and such small things, while the wives and mothers wait?
Plan as ye will, and do as ye will, but think of the hunger and thirst
In the hearts that wait; and do as ye will, but lend us our laddies first!
Why, what would ye have? There is not a lad that treads in the gallant ranks
Who does not already bear on his breast the Rose of a Nation's Thanks!

A welcome? Why, what do you mean by that, when the very stones must sing
As our men march over them home again; the walls of the city ring

With the thunder of throats and the tramp and tread of feet
  that rush and run?—
I think in my heart that the very trees must shout for the bold
  work done!
Why, what would ye have? There is not a lad that treads in the
  gallant ranks
Who does not already bear on his breast the Rose of a
  Nation's Thanks!

A welcome? There is not a babe at the breast won't spring at
  the roll of the drum
That heralds them home—the keen, long cry in the air of
  "They come! They come!"
And what of it all if ye bade them wade knee-deep in a wave
  of wine,
And tossed tall torches, and arched the town in garlands of
  maple and pine?
All dust in the wind of a woman's cry as she snatches from the
  ranks
Her boy who bears on his bold young breast the Rose of a
  Nation's Thanks!

A welcome? There's a doubt if the lads would stand like stone
  in their steady line
When a babe held high on a dear wife's hand or the stars that
  swim and shine
In a sweetheart's eyes, or a mother's smile, flashed far in the
  welded crowd,
Or a father's proud voice, half-sob and half-cheer, cried on a
  son aloud.
O the billows of waiting hearts that swelled would sweep
  from the martial ranks
The gallant boys who bear on their breasts the Rose of a
  Nation's Thanks!

A welcome? O Joy, can they stay your feet, or measure the
  wine of your bliss?
O Joy, let them have you alone to-day—a day with a pulse
  like this!
A welcome? Yes, 'tis a tender thought, a green laurel that laps
  the sword—
But Joy has the wing of a wild white swan, and the song of a
  free wild bird!
She must beat the air with her wing at will, at will must her
  song be driven
From her heaving heart and tremulous throat through the
  awful arch of heaven.

And what would ye have? There isn't a lad will burst from the
  shouting ranks
But bears like a star on his faded coat the Rose of a Nation's
  Thanks!

c. 1885
The Evening Telegram, 11 June 1885
The Collected Poems of Isabella Valancy Crawford, 1905

William Wilfred Campbell

***c.* 1860–1918**

Campbell was born in Berlin, Canada West (now Kitchener, Ontario), the son of a Church of England priest. He came to know eastern Ontario and some of the area around Georgian Bay, a land which was to figure in a number of his poems. He attended the University of Toronto, Wycliffe College, and the Episcopal Theological School (Cambridge, Massachusetts). While in the United States, he was somewhat influenced by the work of Emerson and became interested in mythology. After a short time in the clergy, he joined the Canadian civil service in 1892 in Ottawa, where he came in contact with both Archibald Lampman and Duncan Campbell Scott. He was first a clerk in the Department of the Secretary of State and in 1908 moved to the Public Archives. His poetry reveals some of the difficulty he had in coming to terms with his world: "Lazarus" is one example, and others are "How One Winter Came in the Lake Region" and "The Dread Voyage", which were written just before his turn to a secular career. Some of his later works demonstrate his passionate attachment to the idea of the British empire and imperial imperatives. Although it recently has been unfashionable to admire the writings of such a monarchist spirit—much of Kipling's work suffered latter-day rejection for the same reason—such is the context in which some of Campbell's poems need to be read. By the time he died, Campbell's reputation as a poet, prose writer, editor, journalist, and speaker was certainly significant—and with cause; and after all, the twentieth century is not unique in finding one generation's ideals to be another's embarrassments. Furthermore, Campbell's imperial views were sustained by his desire for the betterment of the world; he was a man of principle offering strong criticism of his own times—"The Politician", for example, offers more than faint echoes of Lampman's much earlier "The Modern Politician". In an age that was feeling the effects of Darwinian theory, conflicts in Africa (including the Boer War), and the rising tension that was to explode in the Great War, it is hardly surprising that Campbell, like many, should grasp whatever strands of ethical hope he could recognise.

Certainly, Campbell was more of a traditionalist than Crawford—particularly in his political stance—but his views of his age and environment were tempered by a realism which again belies the idea that our early poets were content simply to admire their surroundings in an aura of unquestioning innocence. The early poems offer the painterly small canvases "Indian Summer" and "Vapour and Blue", for example, but recognition of the harsh side is evident, even if somewhat veiled, as in "How One Winter Came in the Lake Region". His canon displays a growing maturity and craft, a willingness to accept more difficult challenges of both artistic and intellectual nature. The apparent experimentation in some of his texts is a measure of his skill, rather than a failure to come to grips with a modernist spirit. "Out of Pompeii" and "Bereavement of the Fields" contain their own individual appeal and the latter has a special poignancy because of Campbell's regard for Lampman. "The Grim Builders" reflects his refusal to accept blindly the benefits of the "money-god hour". Even the apparent romance of "The Avenging Angel" is influenced by a confessed hatred of war and contains the implication that victory over the foe was neither easily won nor, indeed, certain. While it is easy for a modern reader to label such a piece militarist propaganda, the reality of the struggle remains. No doubt the ghastliness of the conflict in 1917 had to promote the kind of hope to which Campbell could give eloquent voice. Ultimately, in Campbell's works there is a sense of beauty and strength; his work demands a sensitive ear and often, as well, a visual response. The rewards are well worth the effort of careful and repeated readings.

Major primary texts for Campbell's poetry are *The Poetical Works of Wilfred Campbell*, ed. W.J. Sykes (1923) and "The Complete Poems of William Wilfred Campbell", ed. Laurel

Boone (Ph.D. Diss., University of New Brunswick, 1981). A useful edition is *William Wilfred Campbell: Selected Poetry & Essays*, ed. and intro. by Laurel Boone (1987). Manuscripts are located in the following repositories: Special Collections, Douglas Library, Queen's University, Kingston; Lorne Pierce Collection, Queen's University Archives, Kingston; Logan Collection, Acadia University, Wolfville; Rare Books Division, McGill University Library, Montreal; Public Archives of Canada, National Library, Ottawa; and Ottawa Public Library, Ottawa.

Secondary sources for Campbell include: Carl Klinck's *Wilfred Campbell: A Study in Late Provincial Victorianism* (1942); W.J. Sykes, "Wilfred Campbell", *Leading Canadian Poets*, ed. W.P. Percival (1948); Judith Miller, "Towards a Canadian Aesthetic: Descriptive Colour in the Landscape Poetry of Duncan Campbell Scott, Archibald Lampman, and William Wilfred Campbell" (M.A. Thesis, University of Waterloo, 1970); John Ower, "Portraits of the Landscapes as a Poet: Canadian Nature as Aesthetic Symbol in Three Confederation Writers", *Journal of Canadian Studies* 6 (February 1971), 27-32; Terry Whalen, "Wilfred Campbell: The Poetry of Celebration and Harmony", *Journal of Canadian Poetry* 1 (Autumn 1978) 2, 27-42; Terry Whalen, "Wilfred Campbell: The Poetry of Mysticism", *Journal of Canadian Poetry* 3 (Winter 1980) 1, 39-61; Laurel Boone, "Evolution and Idealism: Wilfred Campbell's 'The Tragedy of Man' and Its Place in Canadian Intellectual History", *Studies in Canadian Literature* 8 (1983) 1, 93-116, and George Wicken, *William Wilfred Campbell and His Works* (1983).

INDIAN SUMMER

Along the line of smoky hills
The crimson forest stands,
And all the day the blue jay calls
Throughout the autumn lands.

Now by the brook the maple leans
With all his glory spread,
And all the sumachs on the hills
Have turned their green to red.

Now by great marshes wrapt in mist,
Or past some river's mouth,
Throughout the long, still autumn day
Wild birds are flying south.

c. 1881
As "Autumn" with two additional stanzas, *Varsity*, 21 October 1881
Poems!, 1881

THE WINTER LAKES

Out in a world of death far to the northward lying,
Under the sun and the moon, under the dusk and the day;
Under the glimmer of stars and the purple of sunsets dying,
Wan and waste and white, stretch the great lakes away.

Never a bud of spring, never a laugh of summer,
Never a dream of love, never a song of bird;
But only the silence and white, the shores that grow chiller and dumber,
Wherever the ice winds sob, and the griefs of winter are heard.

Crags that are black and wet out of the grey lake looming,
Under the sunset's flush and the pallid, faint glimmer of dawn;
Shadowy, ghost-like shores, where midnight surfs are booming
Thunders of wintry woe over the spaces wan.

Lands that loom like spectres, whited regions of winter,
Wastes of desolate woods, deserts of water and shore;
A world of winter and death, within these regions who enter,
Lost to summer and life, go to return no more.

Moons that glimmer above, waters that lie white under,
Miles and miles of lake far out under the night;
Foaming crests of waves, surfs that shoreward thunder,
Shadowy shapes that flee, haunting the spaces white.

Lonely hidden bays, moon-lit, ice-rimmed, winding,
Fringed by forests and crags, haunted by shadowy shores;
Hushed from the outward strife, where the mighty surf is grinding
Death and hate on the rocks, as sandward and landward it roars.

c. 1885-7 (Lorne Pierce Collection MS)
Century, 28 January 1889
Lake Lyrics and Other Poems, 1889

AUGUST EVENING ON THE BEACH, LAKE HURON

A lurid flush of sunset sky,
An angry sketch of gleaming lake,—
I will remember till I die
The sound, of pines that sob and sigh,
Of waves upon the beach that break.

'Twas years ago, and yet it seems,
O love, but only yesterday

We stood in holy sunset dreams,
While all the day's diaphanous gleams
  Sobbed into silence bleak and grey.

We scarely knew, but our two souls
  Like night and day rushed into one;
The stars came out in gleaming shoals:
While, like a far-off bell that tolls,
  Came voices from the wave-dipped sun.

We scarcely knew, but hand in hand,
  With subtle sense, was closer pressed;
As we two walked in that old land
Forever new, whose shining strand
  Goes gleaming round the world's great breast.

What was it, sweet, our spirits spoke?
  No outward sound of voice was heard.
But was it bird or angel broke
The silence, till a dream voice woke
  And all the night was music-stirred?

1888
Lake Lyrics and Other Poems, 1889

VAPOUR AND BLUE

Domed with the azure of heaven,
  Floored with a pavement of pearl,
Clothed all about with a brightness
  Soft as the eyes of a girl,

Girt with a magical girdle,
  Rimmed with a vapour of rest—
These are the inland waters,
  These are the lakes of the west.

Voices of slumberous music,
  Spirits of mist and of flame,
Moonlit memories left here
  By gods who long ago came,

And vanishing left but an echo
   In silence of moon-dim caves,
Where haze-wrapt the August night slumbers,
   Or the wild heart of October raves,

Here where the jewels of nature
   Are set in the light of God's smile,
Far from the world's wild throbbing,
   I will stay me and rest me awhile.

And store in my heart old music,
   Melodies gathered and sung
By the genies of love and of beauty
   When the heart of the world was young.

c. 1889
Century, July 1889; *The Week*, July 1889
Lake Lyrics and Other Poems, 1889

LAZARUS

O Father Abram, I can never rest
   Here in thy bosom in the whitest heaven,
   Where love blooms on through days without an even;
   For up through all the paradises seven,
There comes a cry from some fierce, anguished breast.

A cry that comes from out of hell's dark night,
   A piercing cry of one in agony,
   That reaches me here in heaven white and high;
   A call of anguish that doth never die,
Like dream-waked infant wailing for the light.

O Father Abram, heaven is love and peace,
   And God is good; eternity is rest.
   Sweet would it be to lie upon thy breast
   And know no thought but loving to be blest,
Save for that cry that nevermore will cease.

It comes to me above the angel-lyres,
   The chanting praises of the cherubim;
   It comes between my upward gaze and Him,

All-blessed Christ. A voice from the vague dim,
"*O Lazarus, come and ease me of these fires!*

"*O Lazarus, I have called thee all these years,*
It is so long for me to reach to thee,
Across the ages of this mighty sea,
That loometh dark, dense, like eternity,
Which I have bridged by anguished prayers and tears.

"*Which I have bridged by knowledge of God's love,*
That even penetrates this anguished glare;
A gleaming ray, a tremulous star-built stair,
A road by which love-hungered souls may fare
Past hate and doubt, to heaven and God above."

So calleth it ever upward unto me.
It creepeth in through heaven's golden doors,
It echoes all along the sapphire floors,
Like smoke of sacrifice, it soars and soars,
It fills the vastness of eternity.

Until my sense of love is waned and dimmed,
The music-rounded spheres do clash and jar,
No more those spirit-calls from star to star,
The harmonies that float and melt afar,
The belts of light by which all heaven is rimmed.

No more I hear the beat of heavenly wings,
The seraph chanting in my rest-tuned ear;
I only know a cry, a prayer, a tear,
That rises from the depths up to me here;
A soul that to me suppliant leans and clings.

O Father Abram, thou must bid me go
Into the spaces of the deep abyss;
Where far from us and our God-given bliss,
Do dwell those souls that have done Christ amiss;
For through my rest I hear that upward woe.

I hear it crying through the heavenly night,
When curvèd, hung in space, the million moons
Lean planet-ward, and infinite space attunes
Itself to silence, as from drear grey dunes
A cry is heard along the shuddering light,

Of wild dusk-bird, a sad, heart-curdling cry,
So comes to me that call from out hell's coasts;
I see an infinite shore with gaping ghosts;
This is no heaven, with all its shining hosts;
This is no heaven until that hell doth die.

So spake the soul of Lazarus, and from thence,
Like new-fledged bird from its sun-jeweled nest,
Drunk with the music of the young year's quest,
He sank out into heaven's gloried breast,
Spaceward turned, toward darkness dim, immense.

Hellward he moved like a radiant star shot out
From heaven's blue with rain of gold at even,
When Orion's train and that mysterious seven
Move on in mystic range from heaven to heaven.
Hellward he sank, followed by radiant rout.

The liquid floor of heaven bore him up
With unseen arms, as in his feathery flight
He floated down toward the infinite night;
But each way downward, on the left and right,
He saw each moon of heaven like a cup

Of liquid, misty fire that shone afar
From sentinel towers of heaven's battlements;
But onward, winged by love's desire intense,
And sank, space-swallowed, into the immense,
While with him ever widened heaven's bar.

'Tis ages now long-gone since he went out,
Christ-urged, love-driven, across the jasper walls.
But hellward still he ever floats and falls,
And ever nearer come those anguished calls;
And far behind he hears a glorious shout.

c. 1889
Toronto Globe, 18 June 1892
Lake Lyrics and Other Poems, 1889

HOW ONE WINTER CAME IN THE LAKE REGION

For weeks and weeks the autumn world stood still,
Clothed in the shadow of a smoky haze;
The fields were dead, the wind had lost its will,
And all the lands were hushed by wood and hill,
In those grey, withered days.

Behind a mist the blear sun rose and set,
At night the moon would nestle in a cloud;
The fisherman, a ghost, did cast his net;
The lake its shores forgot to chafe and fret,
And hushed its caverns loud.

Far in the smoky woods the birds were mute,
Save that from blackened tree a jay would scream,
Or far in swamps the lizard's lonesome lute
Would pipe in thirst, or by some gnarlèd root
The tree-toad trilled his dream.

From day to day still hushed the season's mood,
The streams stayed in their runnels shrunk and dry;
Suns rose aghast by wave and shore and wood,
And all the world, with ominous silence, stood
In weird expectancy:

When one strange night the sun like blood went down,
Flooding the heavens in a ruddy hue;
Red grew the lake, the sere fields parched and brown,
Red grew the marshes where the creeks stole down,
But never a wind-breath blew.

That night I felt the winter in my veins,
A joyous tremor of the icy glow;
And woke to hear the north's wild vibrant strains,
While far and wide, by withered woods and plains,
Fast fell the driving snow.

c. 1890
Century, March 1890
The Dread Voyage, 1893

PAN THE FALLEN

He wandered into the market
With pipes and goatish hoof;
He wandered in a grotesque shape,
And no one stood aloof.
For the children crowded round him,

The wives and greybeards, too,
To crack their jokes and have their mirth,
And see what Pan would do.

The Pan he was they knew him,
Part man, but mostly beast,
Who drank, and lied, and snatched what bones
Men threw him from their feast;
Who seemed in sin so merry,
So careless in his woe,
That men despised, scarce pitied him,
And still would have it so.

He swelled his pipes and thrilled them,
And drew the silent tear;
He made the gravest clack with mirth
By his sardonic leer.
He blew his pipes full sweetly
At their amused demands,
And caught the scornful earth-flung pence
That fell from careless hands.

He saw the mob's derision,
And took it kindly, too,
And when an epithet was flung,
A coarser back he threw;
But under all the masking
Of a brute, unseemly part,
I looked, and saw a wounded soul,
And a god-like, breaking heart.

And back of the elfin music,
The burlesque, clownish play,
I knew a wail that the weird pipes made,
A look that was far away,—
A gaze into some far heaven
Whence a soul had fallen down;
But the mob only saw the grotesque beast
And the antics of the clown.

For scant-flung pence he paid them
With mirth and elfin play,
Till, tired for a time of his antics queer,
They passed and went their way;
Then there in the empty market
He ate his scanty crust,
And, tired face turned to heaven, down
He laid him in the dust.

And over the wild, strange features
  A softer light there fell,
And on his worn, earth-driven heart
  A peace ineffable.
And the moon rose over the market,
  But Pan the beast was dead;
While Pan the god lay silent there,
  With his strange, distorted head.

And the people, when they found him,
  Stood still with awesome fear.
No more they saw the beast's rude hoof,
  The furtive, clownish leer;
But the lightest spirit in that throng
  Went silent from the place,
For they knew the look of a god released
  That shone from his dead face.

c. 1890
The Atlantic Monthly, December 1890
The Dread Voyage, 1893

THE MOTHER

(This poem was suggested by the following passage in Tyler's Animism: *The pathetic German superstition that the dead mother's coming back in the night to suckle the baby she has left on earth may be known by the hollow pressed down in the bed where she lay.*)

It was April, blossoming Spring,
They buried me when the birds did sing;

Earth in clammy wedging earth,
They banked my bed with a black, damp girth.

Under the damp and under the mould,
I kenned my breasts were clammy and cold.

Out from the red beams, slanting and bright,
I kenned my cheeks were sunken and white.

I was a dream, and the world was a dream,
And yet I kenned all things that seem.

I was a dream, and the world was a dream,
But you cannot bury a red sunbeam.

For though in the under-grave's doom-night
I lay all silent and stark and white,

Yet over my head I seemed to know
The murmurous moods of wind and snow,

The snows that wasted, the winds that blew,
The rays that slanted, the clouds that drew

The water-ghosts up from lakes below,
And the little flower-souls in earth that grow.

Under earth, in the grave's stark night,
I felt the stars and the moon's pale light.

I felt the winds of ocean and land
That whispered the blossoms soft and bland.

Though they had buried me dark and low,
My soul with the season's seemed to grow.

II

From throes of pain they buried me low,
For death had finished a mother's woe.

But under the sod, in the grave's dread doom,
I dreamed of my baby in glimmer and gloom.

I dreamed of my babe, and I kenned that his rest
Was broken in wailings on my dead breast.

I dreamed that a rose-leaf hand did cling:
Oh, you cannot bury a mother in spring.

When the winds are soft and the blossoms are red
She could not sleep in her cold earth-bed.

I dreamed of my babe for a day and a night,
And then I rose in my grave-clothes white.

I rose like a flower from my damp earth-bed
To the world of sorrowing overhead.

Men would have called me a thing of harm,
But dreams of my babe made me rosy and warm.

I felt my breasts swell under my shroud;
No stars shone white, no winds were loud;

But I stole me past the graveyard wall,
For the voice of my baby seemed to call;

And I kenned me a voice, though my lips were dumb:
Hush, baby, hush! for mother is come.

I passed the streets to my husband's home;
The chamber stairs in a dream I clomb;

I heard the sound of each sleeper's breath,
Light waves that break on the shores of death.

I listened a space at my chamber door,
Then stole like a moon-ray over its floor.

My babe was asleep on a stranger arm,
'O baby, my baby, the grave is so warm,

'Though dark and so deep, for mother is there!
O come with me from the pain and care!

'O come with me from the anguish of earth,
Where the bed is banked with a blossoming girth,

'Where the pillow is soft and the rest is long,
And mother will croon you a slumber-song,—

'A slumber-song that will charm your eyes
To a sleep that never in earth-song lies!

'The loves of earth your being can spare,
But never the grave, for mother is there.'

I nestled him soft to my throbbing breast,
And stole me back to my long, long rest.

And here I lie with him under the stars,
Dead to earth, its peace and its wars;

Dead to its hates, its hopes, and its harms,
So long as he cradles up soft in my arms.

And heaven may open its shimmering doors,
And saints make music on pearly floors.

And hell may yawn to its infinite sea,
But they never can take my baby from me.

For so much a part of my soul he hath grown
That God doth know of it high on His throne.

And here I lie with him under the flowers
That sun-winds rock through the billowy hours,

With the night-airs that steal from the murmuring sea,
Bringing sweet peace to my baby and me.

c. 1890
Harper's Monthly, April 1891; *The Week*, April 1891; *Toronto Globe*, April 1891
The Dread Voyage, 1893

THE DREAD VOYAGE

Trim the sails the weird stars under—
Past the iron hail and thunder,
Past the mystery and the wonder,
  Sails our fated bark;
Past the myriad voices hailing,
Past the moaning and the wailing,
The far voices failing, failing,
  Drive we to the dark.

Past the headlands grim and sombre,
Past the shores of mist and slumber,
Leagues on leagues no man may number,
  Soundings none can mark;
While the olden voices calling,
One by one behind are falling;
Into silence dread, appalling,
  Drift we to the dark.

Far behind, the sad eyes yearning,
Hands that wring for our returning,
Lamps of love yet vainly burning:
  Past the headlands stark!
Through the wintry snows and sleeting,
On our pallid faces beating,
Through the phantom twilight fleeting,
  Drive we to the dark.

Without knowledge, without warning,
Drive we to no lands of morning;

Far ahead no signals horning
   Hail our nightward bark.
Hopeless, helpless, weird, outdriven,
Fateless, friendless, dread, unshriven,
For some race-doom unforgiven,
   Drive we to the dark.

Not one craven or unseemly;
In the flare-light gleaming dimly,
Each ghost-face is watching grimly:
   Past the headlands stark!
Hearts wherein no hope may waken,
Like the clouds of night wind-shaken,
Chartless, anchorless, forsaken,
   Drift we to the dark.

1890-1 (Lorne Pierce Collection MS)
The Dread Voyage, 1893

THE NIGHT WATCHER

Black rolls the phantom chimney-smoke
Beneath the wintry moon.
For miles on miles, by sound unbroke,
The world lies wrapt in ermine cloak
And the night's icy swoon
Sways earthward in great brimming wells
Of luminous frosty particles.

Far up the roadway drifted deep,
Where frost-etched fences gleam
Beneath the sky's wan shimmering sleep,
My solitary way I keep
Across the world's white dream,
The only living moving thing
In all this mighty slumbering.

Up in the western range of hill,
The thin wood spectrally
Stirs in its sleep and then is still,
Like querulous age, at the wind's will.

My shadow doggedly
Follows my footsteps where I go,
A grotesque giant on the snow.

Out where the river's arms are wound,
And icy sedges cling,
There comes to me as in a swound
A far-off, clear, thin, vibrant sound,
The distant hammering
Of frost-elves as they come and go,
Forging, in silver chains, his woe.

I stand upon the hill's bleak crest
And note the far-night-world:
The mighty lake, whose passionate breast,
Manacled into arctic rest,
In shrouded sleep is furled;
The steely heavens whose mighty host
Wheel white from flaming coast to coast.

Then down the night's dim luminous ways
Meseems they come once more,
Those great star-watchers of old days,
The mighty calm ones whose still gaze
On old time orient shore
Dreamed in the wheeling sons of Light
The awful secrets of earth's night.

They come, those lofty ones of old,
And take me by the hand,
And call me brother. Ages rolled
Are but a smoke-mist; kindred-souled,
They lift me to their band;
Like lights that from pale star-beams shine
Their clear eyes look with peace on mine,

And lend me all the rest the night
To east and west hath given:
This tremulous sphere of misty light
One giant bubble poised in sight
The shimmering arch of heaven,
Until the fiery breath of day
Burst and dissolve its dreams away.

In language of no common kind
These watchers speak to me;
Their thoughts the depths of heaven find
Like plummets true. It were a kind

Of immortality
To spend with them one holy hour,
And know their love and grasp their power.

Till, wrapt around with glad content,
I learn with soul serene,
Caught from the beauty that is blent
In earth, the heaven's luminous tent,
The frost-lit dreams between,
And something holier out of sight,
Glad visions of the infinite.

Then backward past the sere hill's breast,
The spectral moaning wood,
With great peace brooding in my breast,
I turn me toward the common rest
Of life's worn brotherhood;
But as I pass, a sacred sign,
Each lays his holy lips on mine,

Gives me the golden chrism of song,
Tips my hushed heart with fire;
Till, far in heaven, I hear that throng
Who march in mystic paths along;
Great Pleiades, the Lyre,
The te deum of the ages swell,
To earth-tuned ear inaudible.

1890-1 (Lorne Pierce Collection MS)
The Poetical Works of Wilfred Campbell, 1923

OUT OF POMPEII

She lay, face downward, on her bended arm,
  In this her new, sweet dream of human bliss,
Her heart within her fearful, fluttering, warm,
  Her lips yet pained with love's first timorous kiss.
She did not note the darkening afternoon,
  She did not mark the lowering of the sky
O'er that great city. Earth had given its boon
  Unto her lips, love touched her and passed by.

In one dread moment all the sky grew dark,
  The hideous rain, the panic, the red rout,
Where love lost love, and all the world might mark
  The city overwhelmed, blotted out
Without one cry, so quick oblivion came,
  And life passed to the black where all forget;
But she—we know not of her house or name—
  In love's sweet musings doth lie dreaming yet.

The dread hell passed, the ruined world grew still,
  And the great city passed to nothingness:
The ages went and mankind worked its will.
  Then men stood still amid the centuries' press,
And in the ash-hid ruins opened bare,
  As she lay down in her shamed loveliness,
Sculptured and frozen, late they found her there,
  Image of love 'mid all that hideousness.

Her head, face downward, on her bended arm
  Her single robe that showed her shapely form,
Her wondrous fate love keeps divinely warm
  Over the centuries, past the slaying storm;
The heart can read in writings time hath left,
  That linger still through death's oblivion;
And in this waste of life and light bereft,
  She brings again a beauty that had gone.

And if there be a day when all shall wake,
  As dreams the hoping, doubting human heart,
The dim forgetfulness of death will break
  For her as one who sleeps with lips apart;
And did God call her suddenly, I know
  She'd wake as morning wakened by the thrush,
Feel that red kiss across the centuries glow,
  And make all heaven rosier by her blush.

1892
Century, September 1892
The Dread Voyage, 1893

BEREAVEMENT OF THE FIELDS

(In Memory of Archibald Lampman, who died February 10th, 1899)

Soft fall the February snows, and soft
Falls on my heart the snow of wintry pain;
For never more, by wood or field or croft,
Will he we knew walk with his loved again;
No more, with eyes adream and soul aloft,
In those high moods where love and beauty reign,
Greet his familiar fields, his skies without a stain.

Soft fall the February snows, and deep,
Like downy pinions from the moulting breast
Of all the mothering sky, round his hushed sleep,
Flutter a million loves upon his rest,
Where once his well-loved flowers were fain to peep,
With adder-tongue and waxen petals prest,
In young spring evenings reddening down the west.

Soft fall the February snows, and hushed
Seems life's loud action, all its strife removed,
Afar, remote, where grief itself seems crushed,
And even hope and sorrow are reproved;
For he whose cheek erstwhile with hope was flushed,
And by the gentle haunts of being moved,
Hath gone the way of all he dreamed and loved.

Soft fall the February snows, and lost,
This tender spirit gone with scarce a tear,
Ere, loosened from the dungeons of the frost,
Wakens with yearnings new the enfranchised year,
Late winter-wizened, gloomed, and tempest-tost;
And Hesper's gentle, delicate veils appear,
When dream anew the days of hope and fear.

And Mother Nature, she whose heart is fain,
Yea, she who grieves not, neither faints nor fails,
Building the seasons, she will bring again
March with rudening madness of wild gales,
April and her wraiths of tender rain,
And all he loved,—this soul whom memory veils,
Beyond the burden of our strife and pain.

Not his to wake the strident note of song
Nor pierce the deep recesses of the heart,
Those tragic wells, remote, of [r]ight[1] and wrong;
But rather, with those gentler souls apart,
He dreamed like his own summer days along,
Filled with the beauty born of his own heart,
Sufficient in the sweetness of his song.

Outside the prison-house of all our tears,
Enfranchised from our sorrow and our wrong,
Beyond the failure of our days and years,
Beyond the burden of our saddest song,
He moves with those whose music filled his ears,
And claimed his gentle spirit from the throng,—
Wordsworth, Arnold, Keats, high masters of his song.

Like some rare Pan of those old Grecian days,
Here in our hour of deeper stress reborn,
Unfortunate thrown upon life's evil ways,
His inward ear heard ever that satyr horn
From Nature's lips reverberate night and morn,
And fled from men and all their troubled maze,
Standing apart, with sad, incurious gaze.

And now, untimely cut, like some sweet flower
Plucked in the early summer of its prime,
Before it reached the fullness of its dower,
He withers in the morning of our time;
Leaving behind him, like a summer shower,
A fragrance of earth's beauty, and the chime
Of gentle and imperishable rhyme.

Songs in our ears of winds and flowers and buds
And gentle loves and tender memories
Of Nature's sweetest aspects, her pure moods,
Wrought from the inward truth of intimate eyes
And delicate ears of him who harks and broods,
And, nightly pondering, daily grows more wise,
And dreams and sees in mighty solitudes.

Soft fall the February snows, and soft
He sleeps in peace upon the breast of her
He loved the truest; where, by wood and croft,

[1]This word has commonly been printed as "might".

The wintry silence folds in fleecy blur
About his silence, while in glooms aloft
The mighty forest fathers, without stir,
Guard well the rest of him, their rare sweet worshipper.

1899
Toronto Globe, 27 May 1899
Beyond the Hills of Dream, 1899

WALLS OF GREEN

Walls of green where the wind and the sunlight stir,
Rippling windows of light where the sun looks through,
And spaces of day that widen and blur beyond,
Out to the haze-rimmed, purpled edge of the world.

Aisles whose pavements are etched with ghosts of moving
Leaves and phantom branches raftered above;
Wind-swayed arches rocking under the blue,
Breathing under the dim, stirred peace of the world.

Walls of green skirting the high-built heaven,
Dusky pines, poplars clapping their hands,
Arching elms holding the spaces aloft,
Under the wind-swept, argosied dome of the sky.

Walls of green. Under their luminous glooms,
Dim and sweet, the fancies of summer lie,
Sylvan murmurs of sun and leafy shadow,
Music of bird and swaying of tenuous bough.

Under here the haunted heart of summer
Hides in its pensive veilings of tremulous green,
Where the sky peers through and the ruddy eye of the sun,
Letting the world, remote, and its roar go by.

Here is the realm of fancy, the poet's land,
This house of breathing leaves and summer and sun;
Where the eye is keen for beauty, the ear intuned,
And the hushed heart glad for silence and slumber and
  dreams.

And here, chance now and anon when the world is stilled,
And life is afar, and earth of her care swept clean,
Do the gods come back as of old in the gold of the world,
And the elfin creatures dance in their sunbeam dreams:

And the high thoughts wake, and the great ones tread as
  of yore,
In olden majesty under these lofty aisles,
Where the woodshade glooms, or the gossamer sunlight
  smiles,
In the strength of the trees or the wide, blue lift of the sky.

Yea, here they come to the children of earth as of yore,
Bringing their god-gifts, vision and beauty and lore,
Brimming the world with the old-time effort and joy,
And Titan moods of the old world's golden desire.

2 July 1900 (Lorne Pierce Collection MS)
The Collected Poems of Wilfred Campbell, 1905

LOVE

  The truest is the simplest. Why entail
  Whole days of years to some complex pursuit,
  To probe life's flower and analyse its fruit?
O weary student, perplexed, spectre-pale,
Why beat against the granite of thy gaol,
  Self-built; or kill the flower to search the root?
  Doth lore make mankind any less the brute?
Or knowledge alone for godlike flight avail?

'Tis love draws all from earth to heaven's heights.
Not all thy weary lore of sleepless nights
  Hath power to touch like one low daisied sod;—
'Tis love, not lore, whatever come to pass.
We are but child-kin to the birds and grass,—
  And he who yearns, life's heir, and kin to God.

c. 1901 (Lorne Pierce Collection clipping ms)
The Collected Poems of Wilfred Campbell, 1905

THE HIGHER KINSHIP

Life is too grim with anxious, eating care
To cherish what is best. Our souls are scarred
By daily agonies, and our conscience marred
By petty tyrannies that waste and wear.
Why is this human fate so hard to bear?
Could we but live with hill-lakes silver-starred,
Or where the eternal silence leaneth toward
The awful front of nature, waste and bare,

Then might we, brothers to the lofty thought
And inward self-communion of her dream,
Into that closer kin with love be brought,
Where mighty hills and woods and waters, wan,
Moon-paved at midnight, or godlike at dawn,
Hold all earth's aspirations in their gleam.

April 1901
The Collected Poems of Wilfred Campbell, 1905

THE BLIND CARAVAN

I am a slave, both dumb and blind,
Upon a journey dread;
The iron hills lie far behind,
The seas of mist ahead.

Amid a mighty caravan
I toil a sombre track,
The strangest road since time began,
Where no foot turneth back.

Here rosy youth at morning's prime
And weary man at noon
Are crooked shapes at eventime
Beneath the haggard moon.

Faint elfin songs from out the past
   Of some lost sunset land
Haunt this grim pageant drifting, vast,
   Across the trackless sand.

And often for some nightward wind
   We stay a space and hark,
Then leave the sunset lands behind,
   And plunge into the dark.

Somewhere, somewhere, far on in front,
   There strides a lonely man
Who is all strength, who bears the brunt,
   The battle and the ban.

I know not of his face or form,
   His voice or battle-scars,
Or how he fronts the haunted storm
   Beneath the wintry stars;

I know not of his wisdom great
   That leads this sightless host
Beyond the barren hills of fate
   Unto some kindlier coast.

But often 'mid the eerie black
   Through this sad caravan
A strange, sweet thrill is whispered back,
   Borne on from man to man.

A strange, glad joy that fills the night
   Like some far marriage horn,
Till every heart is filled with light
   Of some belated morn.

The way is long, and rough the road,
   And bitter the night, and dread,
And each poor slave is but a goad
   To lash the one ahead.

Evil the foes that lie in wait
   To slay us in the pass,
Bloody the slaughter at the gate,
   And bleak the wild morass;

And I am but a shrivelled thing
   Beneath the midnight sky;
A wasted, wan remembering
   Of days long wandered by.

And yet I lift my sightless face
   Toward the eerie light,
And tread the lonely way we trace
   Across the haunted night.

c. 1904
The Outlook, 4 March 1905
The Collected Poems of Wilfred Campbell, 1905

THE POLITICIAN

Carven in leathern mask or brazen face,
   Were I time's sculptor, I would set this man.
   Retreating from the truth, his hawk-eyes scan
The platforms of all public thought for place.
There wriggling with insinuating grace,
   He takes poor hope and effort by the hand,
   And flatters with half-truths and accents bland,
Till even zeal and earnest love grow base.

Knowing no right, save power's grim right-of-way;
   No nobleness, save life's ignoble praise;
No future, save this sordid day to day;
   He is the curse of these material days:
Juggling with mighty wrongs and mightier lies,
This worshipper of Dagon and his flies!

c. 1904
The Outlook, 5 November 1904
The Collected Poems of Wilfred Campbell, 1905

TO THE CANADIAN PATRIOT

This is the land of the rugged North; these wide,
Life-yielding fields, these inland oceans; these
Vast rivers moving seaward their wide floods,
Majestic music: these sky-bounded plains
And heaven-topping mountains; these iron shores,
Facing toward either ocean; fit home, alone,
For the indomitable and nobly strong.

In that dread hour of evil when thy land
Is rent with strifes and ground with bigotry,
And all looks dark for honour, and poor Truth
Walks cloaked in shadow, alien from her marts,
Go forth alone and view the earth and sky,
And those eternal waters, moving, vast,
In endless duty, ever rendering pure
Those mild or angry airs; the gladdening sun,
Reviving, changing, weaving life from death;
Those elemental uses nature puts
Her patient hours to; and then thou shalt know
A larger vista, glean a greater truth
Than man has put into his partial creeds
Of blinded feud and custom. Thou wilt know
That nature's laws are greater and more sure,
More calm, more patient, wise and tolerant,
Than these poor futile efforts of our dream;
That human life is stronger in its yearning
Than those blind walls our impotence builds between;
And underneath this calloused rind we see,
As the obedient tides the swaying moon,
A mightier law the whole wide world obeys,
And far beyond these mists of human vision
God's great horizon stands out fixed and sure.

c. 1905
The Collected Poems of Wilfred Campbell, 1905

STELLA FLAMMARUM

(An Ode to Halley's Comet)

Strange Wanderer out of the deeps,
  Whence, journeying, come you?
From what far, unsunned sleeps
  Did fate foredoom you,
Returning for ever again
  Through the surgings of man,
A flaming, awesome portent of dread
  Down the centuries' span?

Riddle! from the dark unwrung
  By all earth's sages;
God's fiery torch from His hand outflung,
  To flame through the ages:
Thou Satan of planets eterne,
  'Mid angry path,
Chained, in circlings vast, to burn
  Out ancient wrath.

By what dread hand first loosed
  From fires eternal?
With majesties dire infused
  Of force supernal,
Takest thy headlong way
  O'er the highways of space?
Oh, wonderful, blossoming flower of fear
  On the sky's far face!

What secrets of destiny's will
  In thy wild burning?
What portent dire of humanity's ill
  In thy returning?
Or art thou brand of love
  In masking of bale?
And bringest thou ever some mystical surcease
  For all who wail?

Perchance, O Visitor dread,
  Thou hast thine appointed
Task, thou bolt of the vasts outsped!
  With God's anointed,
Performest some endless toil

In the universe wide:
Feeding or curing some infinite need
Where the vast worlds ride.

Once, only once, thy face
Will I view in this breathing;
Just for a space thy majesty trace
'Mid earth's mad seething:
Ere I go hence to my place,
As thou to thy deeps;
Thou flambent core of a universe dread,
Where all else sleeps.

But thou and man's spirit are one:
Thou poet! Thou flaming
Soul of the dauntless sun,
Past all reclaiming!
One in that red unrest,
That yearning, that surge,
That mounting surf of the infinite dream
O'er eternity's verge.

12-16 April 1910 (Lorne Pierce Collection MS)
Toronto Globe, 17 May 1910
Sagas of Vaster Britain, 1914

THE GRIM BUILDERS

No, you never have thought of, or cared for what happens to others,
But only for gain;
Grasping more firmly cruelty's shears, you note not the quiver
Of the heavenward wings you have slain.

Shut in your iron-bound casing of self,
Impervious, grim;
You seize and grind and ravish and crush,
At your brute will's whim.

All the world is the place of your hideous game,
Where the weak are but mimes;
Pawns to be played with, or thrust rudely aside,
Like a poor poet's rhymes.

And you are the masters, you brutally strong ones,
You men of the hour;
You, who laugh at that thing they call conscience, whose whole thought is self,
Whose whole aim is power.

You scorn all religion and right as but dreams for weak women
And parsons and fools;
For you, in your shouldering rude through the game of existence,
Have no use for the rules.

Yea, you scorn all religion and honour and feeling and truth,
While you patronize all
Those conventional hypocrisies, sleek, that veneer with applause
Your grim crimes that appal.

But what is this monstrous, huge edifice, crude, you have built;
With your demon-like will?
This hideous, shadowing, wall that hems man in with
Its hopeless, pitiless ill?

Where shut in from nature and freedom and God,
And all that redeems;
Man's soul dies out, like a poor spent taper at end,
That flickers and gleams.

A moment in some foul air of some hideous place;
Then panting, o'erthrown,
From the flame of its glory; flashes out in despair,
And to blackness is gone.

And this is your work, grim Builders; you crude senseless agents
Of evil and death;
Where the wrecks of men's hopings, ideals and holiest dreams
Lie your grim walls beneath.

Yet you ride in in your pride, down those ways
Of this money-god hour you have built;
Nor reck you at all of Belshazzar's dread wall,
And that sentence of guilt,

Indignant, divine, that flamed forth,—
  As it shall flame for you;—
In that hour of God's patience, and ultimate triumph of all
  That is holy and true.

1911 (Lorne Pierce Collection MS)
The Complete Poems of Wilfred Campbell, 1981

THE AVENGING ANGEL

(To Flight-Lieutenant Robinson and all the heroic aviators of the Royal Flying Corps)

When the last faint red of the day is dead,
  And the dim, far heaven is lit
    With the silvern cars
    Of the orient stars,
  And the winged winds whimper and flit;

Then I rise through the dome of my aerodrome,
  Like a giant eagle in flight;
    And I take my place
    In the vengeful race
  With the sinister fleets of night.

As I rise and rise in the cloudy skies,
  No sound in the silence is heard,
    Save the lonesome whirr
    Of my engine's purr,
  Like the wings of a monster bird.

And naught is seen save the vault, serene,
  Of the vasty realms of night
    That vanish, aloof
    To eternity's roof,
  As I mount in my ominous flight.

And I float and pause in the fleecy gauze,
  Like a bird in a nest of down;

While 'neath me in deeps
Of blackness, sleeps
The far, vast London town.

But I am not here, like a silvern sphere,
To glory the deeps of space,
But a sentinel, I,
In this tower of the sky,
Scanning the dim deep's face.

For, sudden, afar, like a luminous star,
Or a golden horn of the moon,
Or a yellow leaf
Of the forest's grief,
When the Autumn winds are atune;

There is borne on my sight, down the spaces of night,
By the engines of evilment sped,
That wonderful, rare,
Vast ship of the air,
Beautiful, ominous, dread.

One instant she floats, most magic of boats,
Illusive, implacable, there;
Throned angel of ill,
On her crystal-built hill,
O'er a people's defenceless despair.

Then sudden, I rise, like a bolt through the skies,
To the very dim roofs of the world;
Till down in the grey,
I see my grim prey,
Like a pallid gold leaf, upcurled.

And I hover and swing, until swiftly I spring,
And drop like a falling star;
And again and again,
My death-dealing rain,
Hurl to the deeps afar.

Then I hover and listen, till I see the far glisten
Of a flame-flash blanching the night;
And I know that my hate,
That has lain in wait,
Has won in the grim air-fight.

Then I curve and slant, while my engines pant,
And the wings of my great bird tame;

While the sinister Hun,
In his ill, undone,
Goes out in a blinding flame.

c. 1917
Ottawa Evening Journal, 7 April 1917
"*Langemarck" and Other Poems*, 1918

Charles G.D. Roberts

1860–1943

Born in Douglas, New Brunswick, in 1860, and moving that year to Westock Parsonage, near Sackville, New Brunswick, Roberts grew up near the red-soiled Tantramar Marshes and the southward-looking hills at the top of the Bay of Fundy, an area he repeatedly returned to and represented in his poetry and prose. Roberts' father, an Anglican priest, became Canon of Christ Church Cathedral in Fredericton, where young Roberts attended the University of New Brunswick, graduating in 1879 and becoming headmaster of a high school in Chatham. He married in 1880, and in that year dramatically launched his poetic career with the publication of *Orion and Other Poems*. He gained his M.A. (UNB) in 1881 and left his school post in 1882. In 1883 he was editor of *The Week*, but his income during these years was uncertain, especially as he was a young writer. In 1885 he began a ten-year teaching period at King's College, Windsor, Nova Scotia, where he carried on with his writing, including fiction. He was elected a Fellow of the Royal Society of Canada in 1890 and, in 1893, of the Royal Society of Literature, both honours constituting a measure of the regard in which he was held by an increasingly wide audience. After two more years in Fredericton, he separated from his wife and left to work in New York in 1897; he went to Europe in 1907, settling in England in 1912. He served with the British and Canadian armies during World War I, and resided afterwards in Europe and England until 1925, when he returned to Canada to enjoy a considerable reputation as a writer and a speaker. Living in Toronto, he was knighted in 1935, and he remarried in 1943.

Influenced not only by the Classics but by the Romantic and Victorian poets, Roberts often displays his literary heritage in his portrayals of the Canadian landscape. But what marks his work particularly is his concern for detail—the subtle touches, often involving sensual response, that take a sensitive reader into a scene despite the brevity or apparent generality of the description. Images such as "... One lonely golden ray, /Wherein the dust is dancing ..." ("In an Old Barn") and "The crying knives glide on ..." ("The Mowing") are examples of his ability to give economical voice to his observations. Readers of his prose will discover the same characteristic, coupled with a sure grip on narrative direction and pace. If there are, then, for instance, Wordsworthian touches to "Tantramar Revisited", the voice is very much Roberts' own, just as is his approach to the awesome wonder of the unknown in "The Skater" or the romance and nostalgia in "The Night Watches". Yet a considered survey of his canon defeats the notion that he was simply interested in the landscape and human reaction to it; he was also well able to give expression to the urban scene, the mechanical and sometimes brutal features of his age. "At the Railway Station" and "Going Over (The Somme, 1917)", for example, need to be set alongside his rural poems, as does a poem like "Peace with Dishonour", which offers a trenchant comment on the dubious compromises which failed to halt the chilling march to the second World War. "The Iceberg" stands as a compelling precursor to *The Titanic* of Pratt and to the latter's concern with the conflict between natural forces and modern engineering. If Roberts still seems, on balance, a regional writer, that is not to say that his appeal in his day was not wide-ranging or that it cannot be so in our own: the universality of the experience in his poetry is always inherent, just as it is in the work of the Canadian painters of his era. What often contributes so often to his success is his metrical skill within forms which, if oft-used, nonetheless suit his chosen subjects with propriety and ease.

The definitive edition of Roberts' poetry is *The Collected Poems of Sir Charles G.D. Roberts: A Critical Edition*, ed. Desmond Pacey and Graham Adams (1985). His manuscripts are located in: Charles G.D. Roberts Collection, Lloyd Roberts Collection and Rufus Hathaway Collection, University of New Brunswick, Fredericton; Charles G.D. Roberts

Papers, and the Edith and Lorne Pierce Collection at the Queen's University Archives, Kingston; and McGill University, Montreal.

Works on Roberts include: E.M. Pomeroy, *Sir Charles G.D. Roberts: A Biography* (1943); W.J. Keith, *Charles G.D. Roberts* (1969); John Coldwell Adams, "Sir Charles G.D. Roberts' Later Poetry, 1926-42", *Journal of Canadian Poetry* 1 (Autumn 1978), 2, 43-58; Fred Cogswell, "Charles G.D. Roberts" in *Canadian Writers and their Works, Vol. II*, ed. Robert Lecker, Jack David and Ellen Quigley (1983), 187-234; *Proceedings of the Sir Charles G.D. Roberts Symposium, Mount Allison University*, ed. Carrie MacMillan (1984); *The Sir Charles G.D. Roberts Symposium*, ed. Glenn Clever (1984); John Coldwell Adams, *Sir Charles God Damn* (1986), and Don Precosky, " 'The Need that Irks': Roberts' Sonnets in *Songs of the Common Day*", *Canadian Poetry* 22 (Spring-Summer 1988), 22-31.

EPISTLE TO BLISS CARMAN

(September, 1878)

An azure splendour floats upon the world.
Around my feet the blades of grass, impearled
And diamonded, are changing radiantly.
At every step new wonders do I see
Of fleeting sapphire, gold and amethyst,—
Enchanting magic of the dew sun-kissed.
The felon jay mid golden-russet beeches
Ruffles his crest, and flies with startled screeches.
Ever before me the shy cricket whistles
From underneath the dry, brown, path-side thistles.
His gay note leads me, and I quickly follow
Where dips the path down through a little hollow
Of young fir-seedlings. Then I cross the brook
On two grey logs, whose well-worn barkless look
Tells of the many black-gown-shadowed feet
Which tread them daily, save when high June's heat
Scatters us wide, to roll in cool, salt billows
Of Fundy's make, or under hanging willows
Slide the light birch, and dream, and watch the grasses
Wave on the intervale as the light wind passes,
Puffing a gentle cloud of smoke to scare
The sand-flies, which are ravening everywhere.
Such our enjoyment, Bliss, few weeks ago;
And the remembrance warms me with a glow
Of pleasure, as I cross the track and climb
The rocky lane I've clambered many a time.
On either side, where birch and maples grow,
The young firs stand with eager hands below,
And catch the yellow dropping leaves, and hold
Them fast, as if they thought them dropping gold;
But fairy gold they'll find them on the morrow,
When their possessing joy shall turn to sorrow.
Now thro' the mottled trunks, beneath the boughs,
I see the terrace, and the lower rows
Of windows drinking in the waking air;
While future Freshmen stand around and stare.

Last week the bell cut short my happy strain.
Now half in pleasure, half in a vague pain,
For you I undertake my rhyme again.
Last week in its first youth saw you begin
Your happy three-years' course with us, and win
The highest honours, half of which are due
To your own strength of brain, and half accrue
To that wise master from whose hands you came
Equipped to win, and win yourself a name.
But I,—I have but one quick-slipping year
To spend amid these rooms and faces dear,
And then must quit this fostering roof, these walls
Where from each door some bright-faced memory calls,
And halt outside in sore uncertainty,
Not knowing which way lies the path for me
Through the unlighted, difficult, misty world.
Ah, whither must I go? Thick smoke is curled
Close round my feet, but lifts a little space
Further ahead, and shows to me the face—
Distorted, dim, and glamorous—of Life;
With many ways, all cheerless ways, and rife
With bristling toils crowned with no fitting fruit,—
All songless ways, whose goals are bare and mute.
But *one* path leads out from my very feet,—
The only one which lures me, which is sweet.
Ah! might I follow it, methinketh then
My childhood's brightest dreams would come again.
Indeed, I know they dwell there, and I'd find
Them meeting me, or hastening up behind.
See where it windeth, always bright and clear,
Though over stony places here and there;
Up steep ascents, thro' bitter obstacles,
But interspersed with glorious secret dells;
And vocal with rich promise of delight,
And ever brightening with an inward light
That soothes and blesses all the ways that lie
In reach of its soft light and harmony.
And were this path made for my following,
Then would I work and sing, and work and sing;
And though the songs were cryings now and then
Of me thus singing in the midst of men,—
Where some are weary, some are weeping, some
Are hungering for joys that never come;
And some drive on before a bitter fate
That bends not to their prayers importunate;
Where some say God is deaf and hears not now,

And speaks not now, some that He *is* not now,
Nor ever was, and these in fancied power
See not the mighty workings of each hour,
Or, seeing, read them wrong. Though now and then
My songs were wailings from the midst of men,
Yet would I deem that it were ever best
To sing them out of weariness to rest;
Yet would I cheer them, sharing in their ills,
Weaving them dreams of waves, and skies, and hills;
Yet would I sing of Peace, and Hope, and Truth,
Till softly o'er my song should beam the youth,—
The morning of the world. Ah, yes, there hath
The goal been planted all along that path;
And as the swallow were my heart as free,
Might I but hope that path belonged to me.

I've prated so, I scarce know what I've said.
But you'll not think me to have lost the thread,
Seeing I had none. Do not say I've kept
My promises too amply, and o'erleapt
A letter's bounds; not harshly criticise;
But miss the spots and blots with lenient eyes.
Scan not its outer, but its inner part;
'Twas not the head composed it, but the heart.

September 1878
Orion, and Other Poems, 1880

OFF PELORUS

Crimson swims the sunset over far Pelorus;
Burning crimson tops its frowning crest of pine.
Purple sleeps the shore and floats the wave before us,
Eachwhere from the oar-stroke eddying warm like wine.

Soundless foams the creamy violet wake behind us;
We but *see* the creaking of the laboured oar;
We have stopped our ears,—mad were we not to blind us,
Lest our eyes behold our Ithaca no more.

See the purple splendour o'er the island streaming,
O'er the prostrate sails and equal-sided ship!

Windless hangs the vine, and warm the sands lie gleaming;
Droop the great grape-clusters melting for the lip.

Sweet the golden calm, the glowing light elysian.
Sweet were red-mouthed plenty mindless grown of pain.
Sweeter yet behold—a sore-bewildering vision!
Idly took we thought, and stopped our ears in vain.

Idly took we thought, for still our eyes betray us.
Lo, the white-limbed maids, with love-soft eyes aglow,
Gleaming bosoms bare, loosed hair, sweet hands to slay us,
Warm lips wild with song, and softer throats than snow!

See the King! he hearkens,—hears their song,—strains forward,—
As some mountain snake attends the shepherd's reed.
Now with urgent hand he bids us turn us shoreward,—
Bend the groaning oar now; give the King no heed!

Mark the luring music by his eyes' wild yearning,
Eager lips, and mighty straining at the cords!
Well we guess the song, the subtle words and burning,
Sung to him, the subtle king of burning words.

"Much-enduring Wanderer, wondrous-tongued, come nigher!
Sage of princes, bane of Ilion's lofty walls!
Whatsoe'er in all the populous earth befalls
We will teach thee, to thine uttermost desire."

So, we rise up twain, and make his bonds securer.
Seethes the startled sea now from the surging blade.
Leaps the dark ship forth, as we, with hearts grown surer,
Eyes averse, and war-worn faces made afraid,

O'er the waste warm reaches drive our prow, sea-cleaving,
Past the luring death, into the folding night.
Home shall hold us yet, and cease our wives from grieving,—
Safe from storm, and toil, and flame, and clanging fight.

February 1881
Canadian Monthly, April 1881
Later Poems, 1881

OUT OF POMPEII

Save what the night-wind woke of sweet
And solemn sound, I heard alone
The sleepless ocean's ceaseless beat,
The surge's monotone.

Low down the south a dreary gleam
Of white light smote the sullen swells,
Evasive as a blissful dream,
Or wind-borne notes of bells.

The water's lapping whispers stole
Into my brain, and there effaced
All human memories from my soul,—
An atom in a shifting waste.

Weird fingers, groping, strove to raise
Some numbing horror from my mind;
And ever, as it met my gaze,
The sharp truth struck me blind.

The keen-edged breath of the salt sea
Stung; but a faint, swift, sulphurous smell
Blew past, and I reeled dizzily
As from the brink of hell,

One moment; then the swan-necked prow
Sustained me, and once more I scanned
The unfenced flood, against my brow
Arching my lifted hand.

O'er all the unstable vague expanse
I towered the lord supreme, and smiled;
And marked the hard, white sparkles glance,
The dark vault wide and wild.

Again that faint wind swept my face—
With hideous menace swept my eyes.
I cowered back in my straitened place
And groped with dim surmise,

Not knowing yet. Not knowing why,
I turned, as one asleep might turn,
And noted with half curious eye
The figure crouched astern.

On heaped-up leopard skins she crouched,
   Asleep, and soft skins covered her,
And scarlet stuffs where she was couched,
   Sodden with sea-water,

Burned lurid with black stains, and smote
   My thought with waking pangs; I saw
The white arm drooping from the boat,
   Round-moulded, pure from flaw;

The yellow sandals even-thonged;
   The fair face, wan with haunting pain,—
Then sudden, crowding memories thronged
   Like unpent sudden rain.

Clear-stamped, as by white lightning when
   The swift flame rends the night, wide-eyed
I saw dim streets, and fleeing men,
   And walls from side to side

Reeling, and great rocks fallen; a pall
   Above us, an encumbering shroud
About our feet, and over all
   The awful Form that bowed

Our hearts, the fiery scourge that smote
   The city,—the red Mount. Clear, clear
I saw it,—and this lonely boat,
   And us two drifting here!

With one sharp cry I sprang and hid
   My face among the skins beside
Her feet, and held her safe, and chid
   The tumult till it died.

And crouched thus at her rescued feet,
   Save her low breath, I heard alone
The sleepless ocean's ceaseless beat,
   The surge's monotone.

Begun 1873; first six stanzas finished 1876; completed October 1881
Later Poems, 1881

THE TANTRAMAR REVISITED

Summers and summers have come, and gone with the
flight of the swallow;
Sunshine and thunder have been, storm, and winter, and
frost;
Many and many a sorrow has all but died from
remembrance,
Many a dream of joy fall'n in the shadow of pain.
Hands of chance and change have marred, or moulded,
or broken,
Busy with spirit or flesh, all I most have adored;
Even the bosom of Earth is strewn with heavier shadows—
Only in these green hills, aslant to the sea, no change!
Here where the road that has climbed from the inland
valleys and woodlands,
Dips from the hill-tops down, straight to the base of the
hills—
Here, from my vantage-ground, I can see the scattering
houses,
Stained with time, set warm in orchards, meadows and
wheat,
Dotting the broad bright slopes outspread to southward
and eastward,
Wind-swept all day long, blown by the south-east wind.

Skirting the sunbright uplands stretches a riband of
meadow,
Shorn of the labouring grass, bulwarked well from the sea,
Fenced on its seaward border with long clay dikes from
the turbid
Surge and flow of the tides vexing the Westmoreland
shores.
Yonder, toward the left, lie broad the Westmoreland
marshes—
Miles on miles they extend, level, and grassy, and dim,
Clear from the long red sweep of flats to the sky in the
distance,
Save for the outlying heights, green-rampired Cumberland
Point;
Miles on miles outrolled, and the river-channels divide
them—
Miles on miles of green, barred by the hurtling gusts.

Miles on miles beyond the tawny bay is Minudie.
There are the low blue hills; villages gleam at their feet.
Nearer a white sail shines across the water, and nearer
Still are the slim, grey masts of fishing boats dry on the
flats.

Ah, how well I remember those wide red flats, above
tide-mark
Pale with scurf of the salt, seamed and baked in the sun!
Well I remember the piles of blocks and ropes, and the
net-reels
Wound with beaded nets, dripping and dark from the sea!
Now at this season the nets are unwound; they hang
from the rafters
Over the fresh-stowed hay in upland barns, and the wind
Blows all day through the chinks, with the streaks of
sunlight, and sways them
Softly at will; or they lie heaped in the gloom of a loft.

Now at this season the reels are empty and idle; I see
them
Over the lines of the dikes, over the gossiping grass.
Now at this season they swing in the long strong wind,
thro' the lonesome
Golden afternoon, shunned by the foraging gulls.
Near about sunset the crane will journey homeward
above them;
Round them, under the moon, all the calm night long,
Winnowing soft grey wings of marsh-owls wander and
wander,
Now to the broad, lit marsh, now to the dusk of the dike.
Soon, thro' their dew-wet frames, in the live keen freshness
of morning,
Out of the teeth of the dawn blows back the awakening
wind.
Then, as the blue day mounts, and the low-shot shafts
of the sunlight
Glance from the tide to the shore, gossamers jewelled
with dew
Sparkle and wave, where late sea-spoiling fathoms of
drift-net
Myriad-meshed, uploomed sombrely over the land.
Well I remember it all. The salt raw scent of the margin;
While, with men at the windlass, groaned each reel, and
the net,

Surging in ponderous lengths, uprose and coiled in its station;
Then each man to his home—well I remember it all!

Yet, as I sit and watch, this present peace of the landscape—
Stranded boats, these reels empty and idle, the hush,
One grey hawk slow-wheeling above yon cluster of haystacks—
More than the old-time stir this stillness welcomes me home.
Ah the old-time stir, how once it stung me with rapture—
Old-time sweetness, the winds freighted with honey and salt!
Yet will I stay my steps and not go down to the marsh-land—
Muse and recall far off, rather remember than see—
Lest on too close sight I miss the darling illusion,
Spy at their task even here the hands of chance and change.

1883
The Week, December 1883
In Divers Tones, 1886

THE SOWER

A brown, sad-coloured hillside, where the soil,
Fresh from the frequent harrow, deep and fine,
Lies bare; no break in the remote sky-line,
Save where a flock of pigeons streams aloft,
Startled from feed in some low-lying croft,
Of far-off spires with yellow of sunset shine;
And here the Sower, unwittingly divine,
Exerts the silent forethought of his toil.

Alone he treads the glebe, his measured stride
Dumb in the yielding soil; and though small joy

Dwell in his heavy face, as spreads the blind
Pale grain from his dispensing palm aside,
This plodding churl grows great in his employ—
Godlike, he makes provision for mankind.

1884
Manhattan Magazine, July 1884
In Divers Tones, 1886

AN ODE FOR THE CANADIAN CONFEDERACY

Awake, my country, the hour is great with change!
  Under this gloom which yet obscures the land,
From ice-blue strait and stern Laurentian range
  To where giant peaks our western bounds command,
A deep voice stirs, vibrating in men's ears
  As if their own hearts throbbed that thunder forth,
A sound wherein who hearkens wisely hears
  The voice of the desire of this strong North,—
    This North whose heart of fire
    Yet knows not its desire
Clearly, but dreams, and murmurs in the dream.
The hour of dreams is done. Lo, on the hills the gleam!

Awake, my country, the hour of dreams is done!
  Doubt not, nor dread the greatness of thy fate.
Tho' faint souls fear the keen confronting sun,
  And fain would bid the morn of splendour wait;
Tho' dreamers, rapt in starry visions, cry
  "Lo, yon thy future, yon thy faith, thy fame!"
And stretch vain hands to stars, thy fame is nigh,
  Here in Canadian hearth, and home, and name,—
    This name which yet shall grow
    Till all the nations know
Us for a patriot people, heart and hand
Loyal to our native earth, our own Canadian land!

O strong hearts, guarding the birthright of our glory,
  Worth your best blood this heritage that ye guard!

These mighty streams resplendent with our story,
  These iron coasts by rage of seas unjarred,—
What fields of peace these bulwarks well secure!
  What vales of plenty those calm floods supply!
Shall not our love this rough, sweet land make sure,
  Her bounds preserve inviolate, though we die?
    O strong hearts of the North,
    Let flame your loyalty forth,
And put the craven and base to an open shame,
Till earth shall know the Child of Nations by her name!

Early 1885
In Divers Tones, 1886

THE DEPARTING OF GLUSKÂP

  It is so long ago, and men well-nigh
Forget what gladness was, and how the earth
Gave corn in plenty, and the rivers fish,
And the woods meat, before he went away.
His going was on this wise.

                All the works
And words and ways of men and beasts became
Evil, and all their thoughts continually
Were but of evil. Then he made a feast.
Upon the shore that is beside the sea
That takes the setting sun, he ordered it,
And called the beasts thereto. Only the men
He called not, seeing them evil utterly.
He fed the panther's crafty brood, and filled
The lean wolf's hunger; from the hollow tree
His honey stayed the bear's terrific jaws;
And the brown rabbit couched at peace, within
The circling shadow of the eagle's wings.
And when the feast was done he told them all
That now, because their ways were evil grown,
On that same day he must depart from them,
And they should look upon his face no more.
Then all the beasts were very sorrowful.

It was near sunset, and the wind was still,
And down the yellow shore a thin wave washed
Slowly; and Gluskâp launched his birch canoe,
And spread his yellow sail, and moved from shore,
Though no wind followed, streaming in the sail,
Or roughening the clear waters after him.
And all the beasts stood by the shore, and watched.
Then to the west appeared a long red trail
Over the wave; and Gluskâp sailed and sang
Till the canoe grew little, like a bird,
And black, and vanished in the shining trail.
And when the beasts could see his form no more,
They still could hear him, singing as he sailed,
And still they listened, hanging down their heads
In long row, where the thin wave washed and fled.
But when the sound of singing died, and when
They lifted up their voices in their grief,
Lo! on the mouth of every beast a strange
New tongue! Then rose they all and fled apart,
Nor met again in council from that day.

c. 1886
In Divers Tones, 1886

AUTOCHTHON

I

I am the spirit astir
To swell the grain
When fruitful suns confer
With labouring rain;
I am the life that thrills
In branch and bloom;
I am the patience of abiding hills,
The promise masked in doom.

II

When the sombre lands are wrung
And storms are out,

And giant woods give tongue,
I am the shout;
And when the earth would sleep,
Wrapped in her snows,
I am the infinite gleam of eyes that keep
The post of her repose.

III

I am the hush of calm,
I am the speed,
The flood-tide's triumphing psalm,
The marsh-pool's heed;
I work in the rocking roar
Where cataracts fall;
I flash in the prismy fire that dances o'er
The dew's ephemeral ball.

IV

I am the voice of wind
And wave and tree,
Of stern desires and blind,
Of strength to be;
I am the cry by night
At point of dawn,
The summoning bugle from the unseen height,
In cloud and doubt withdrawn.

V

I am the strife that shapes
The stature of man,
The pang no hero escapes,
The blessing, the ban;
I am the hammer that moulds
The iron of our race,
The omen of God in our blood that a people beholds,
The foreknowledge veiled in our face.

December 1889
University Quarterly Review, February 1890
Songs of the Common Day and Ave, 1893

THE WINTER FIELDS

Winds here, and sleet, and frost that bites like steel.
  The low bleak hill rounds under the low sky.
Naked of flock and fold the fallows lie,
  Thin streaked with meagre drift. The gusts reveal
By fits the dim grey snakes of fence, that steal
  Through the white dusk. The hill-foot poplars sigh,
  While storm and death with winter trample by,
And the iron fields ring sharp, and blind lights reel.

Yet in the lonely ridges, wrenched with pain,
  Harsh solitary hillocks, bound and dumb,
Grave glebes close-lipped beneath the scourge and chain,
  Lurks hid the germ of ecstasy—the sum
Of life that waits on summer, till the rain
  Whisper in April and the crocus come.

c. 1890
The Century Magazine, January 1890
Songs of the Common Day and Ave, 1893

THE MOWING

This is the voice of high midsummer's heat.
  The rasping vibrant clamour soars and shrills
  O'er all the meadowy range of shadeless hills,
As if a host of giant cicadae beat
The cymbals of their wings with tireless feet,
  Or brazen grasshoppers with triumphing note
  From the long swath proclaimed the fate that smote
The clover and timothy-tops and meadowsweet.

The crying knives glide on; the green swath lies.
  And all noon long the sun, with chemic ray,
  Seals up each cordial essence in its cell,

That in the dusky stalls, some winter's day,
   The spirit of June, here prisoned by his spell,
May cheer the herds with pasture memories.

c. 1890
The Independent, 21 August 1890
Songs of the Common Day and Ave, 1893

AVÉ!

An Ode for the Shelley Centenary, 1892

I

O tranquil meadows, grassy Tantramar,
   Wide marshes ever washed in clearest air,
Whether beneath the sole and spectral star
   The dear severity of dawn you wear,
Or whether in the joy of ample day
   And speechless ecstasy of growing June
You lie and dream the long blue hours away
      Till nightfall comes too soon,
Or whether, naked to the unstarred night,
You strike with wondering awe my inward sight,—

II

You know how I have loved you, how my dreams
   Go forth to you with longing, though the years
That turn not back like your returning streams
   And fain would mist the memory with tears,
Though the inexorable years deny
   My feet the fellowship of your deep grass,
O'er which, as o'er another, tenderer sky,
      Cloud phantoms drift and pass,—
You know my confident love, since first, a child,
Amid your wastes of green I wandered wild.

III

Inconstant, eager, curious, I roamed;
  And ever your long reaches lured me on;
And ever o'er my feet your grasses foamed,
  And in my eyes your far horizons shone.
But sometimes would you (as a stillness fell
  And on my pulse you laid a soothing palm)
Instruct my ears in your most secret spell;
    And sometimes in the calm
Initiate my young and wondering eyes
Until my spirit grew more still and wise.

IV

Purged with high thoughts and infinite desire
  I entered fearless the most holy place,
Received between my lips the secret fire,
  The breath of inspiration on my face.
But not for long these rare illumined hours,
  The deep surprise and rapture not for long.
Again I saw the common, kindly flowers,
    Again I heard the song
Of the glad bobolink, whose lyric throat
Pealed like a tangle of small bells afloat.

V

The pounce of mottled marsh-hawk on his prey;
  The flicker of sand-pipers in from sea
In gusty flocks that puffed and fled; the play
  Of field-mice in the vetches,—these to me
Were memorable events. But most availed
  Your strange unquiet waters to engage
My kindred heart's companionship; nor failed
    To grant this heritage,—
That in my veins forever must abide
The urge and fluctuation of the tide.

VI

The mystic river whence you take your name,
  River of hubbub, raucous Tantramar,
Untamable and changeable as flame,
  It called me and compelled me from afar,
Shaping my soul with its impetuous stress.
  When in its gaping channel deep withdrawn

Its waves ran crying of the wilderness
And winds and stars and dawn,
How I companioned them in speed sublime,
Led out a vagrant on the hills of Time!

VII

And when the orange flood came roaring in
From Fundy's tumbling troughs and tide-worn caves,
While red Minudie's flats were drowned with din
And rough Chignecto's front oppugned the waves,
How blithely with the refluent foam I raced
Inland along the radiant chasm, exploring
The green solemnity with boisterous haste;
My pulse of joy outpouring
To visit all the creeks that twist and shine
From Beauséjour to utmost Tormentine.

VIII

And after, when the tide was full, and stilled
A little while the seething and the hiss,
And every tributary channel filled
To the brim with rosy streams that swelled to kiss
The grass-roots all awash and goose-tongue wild
And salt-sap rosemary,—then how well content
I was to rest me like a breathless child
With play-time rapture spent,—
To lapse and loiter till the change should come
And the great floods turn seaward, roaring home.

IX

And now, O tranquil marshes, in your vast
Serenity of vision and of dream,
Wherethrough by every intricate vein have passed
With joy impetuous and pain supreme
The sharp, fierce tides that chafe the shores of earth
In endless and controlless ebb and flow,
Strangely akin you seem to him whose birth
One hundred years ago
With fiery succour to the ranks of song
Defied the ancient gates of wrath and wrong.

X

Like yours, O marshes, his compassionate breast,
Wherein abode all dreams of love and peace,

Was tortured with perpetual unrest.
Now loud with flood, now languid with release,
Now poignant with the lonely ebb, the strife
Of tides from the salt sea of human pain
That hiss along the perilous coasts of life
Beat in his eager brain;
But all about the tumult of his heart
Stretched the great calm of his celestial art.

XI

Therefore with no far flight, from Tantramar
And my still world of ecstasy, to thee,
Shelley, to thee I turn, the avatar
Of Song, Love, Dream, Desire, and Liberty;
To thee I turn with reverent hands of prayer
And lips that fain would ease my heart of praise,
Whom chief of all whose brows prophetic wear
The pure and sacred bays
I worship, and have worshipped since the hour
When first I felt thy bright and chainless power.

XII

About thy sheltered cradle in the green
Untroubled groves of Sussex, brooded forms
That to the mother's eye remained unseen,—
Terrors and ardours, passionate hopes, and storms
Of fierce retributive fury, such as jarred
Ancient and sceptred creeds, and cast down kings,
And oft the holy cause of Freedom marred
With lust of meaner things,
With guiltless blood, and many a frenzied crime
Dared in the face of unforgetful Time.

XIII

The star that burns on revolution smote
Wild heats and change on thine ascendant sphere,
Whose influence thereafter seemed to float
Through many a strange eclipse of wrath and fear,
Dimming awhile the radiance of thy love.
But still supreme in thy nativity,
All dark, invidious aspects far above,
Beamed one clear orb for thee,—
The star whose ministrations just and strong
Controlled the tireless flight of Dante's song.

XIV

With how august contrition, and what tears
  Of penitential, unavailing shame,
Thy venerable foster-mother hears
  The sons of song impeach her ancient name,
Because in one rash hour of anger blind
  She thrust thee forth in exile, and thy feet
Too soon to earth's wild outer ways consigned,—
    Far from her well-loved seat,
Far from her studious halls and storied towers
And weedy Isis winding through his flowers.

XV

And thou, thenceforth the breathless child of change,
  Thine own Alastor, on an endless quest
Of unimagined loveliness didst range,
  Urged ever by the soul's divine unrest.
Of that high quest and that unrest divine
  Thy first immortal music thou didst make,
Inwrought with fairy Alp, and Reuss, and Rhine,
    And phantom seas that break
In soundless foam along the shores of Time,
Prisoned in thine imperishable rhyme.

XVI

Thyself the lark melodious in mid-heaven;
  Thyself the Protean shape of chainless cloud,
Pregnant with elemental fire, and driven
  Through deeps of quivering light, and darkness loud
With tempest, yet beneficent as prayer;
  Thyself the wild west wind, relentless strewing
The withered leaves of custom on the air,
    And through the wreck pursuing
O'er lovelier Arnos, more imperial Romes,
Thy radiant visions to their viewless homes.

XVII

And when thy mightiest creation thou
  Wert fain to body forth,—the dauntless form,
The all-enduring, all-forgiving brow
  Of the great Titan, flinchless in the storm
Of pangs unspeakable and nameless hates,
  Yet rent by all the wrongs and woes of men,
And triumphing in his pain, that so their fates

Might be assuaged,—oh then
Out of that vast compassionate heart of thine
Thou wert constrained to shape the dream benign.

XVIII

—O Baths of Caracalla, arches clad
In such transcendent rhapsodies of green
That one might guess the sprites of spring were glad
For your majestic ruin, yours the scene,
The illuminating air of sense and thought;
And yours the enchanted light, O skies of Rome,
Where the giant vision into form was wrought;
Beneath your blazing dome
The intensest song our language ever knew
Beat up exhaustless to the blinding blue!—

XIX

The domes of Pisa and her towers superb,
The myrtles and the ilexes that sigh
O'er San Giuliano, where no jars disturb
The lonely aziola's evening cry,
The Serchio's sun-kissed waters,—these conspired
With Plato's theme occult, with Dante's calm
Rapture of mystic love, and so inspired
Thy soul's espousal psalm,
A strain of such elect and pure intent
It breathes of a diviner element.

XX

Thou on whose lips the word of Love became
A rapt evangel to assuage all wrong,
Not Love alone, but the austerer name
Of Death engaged the splendours of thy song.
The luminous grief, the spacious consolation
Of thy supreme lament, that mourned for him
Too early haled to that still habitation
Beneath the grass-roots dim,—
Where his faint limbs and pain-o'erwearied heart
Of all earth's loveliness became a part,

XXI

But where, thou sayest, himself would not abide,—
Thy solemn incommunicable joy

Announcing Adonais has not died,
  Attesting death to free but not destroy,
All this was as thy swan-song mystical.
  Even while the note serene was on thy tongue
Thin grew the veil of the Invisible,
    The white sword nearer swung,—
And in the sudden wisdom of thy rest
Thou knewest all thou hadst but dimly guessed.

XXII

Lament, Lerici, mourn for the world's loss!
  Mourn that pure light of song extinct at noon!
Ye waves of Spezzia that shine and toss
  Repent that sacred flame you quenched too soon!
Mourn, Mediterranean waters, mourn
  In affluent purple down your golden shore!
Such strains as his, whose voice you stilled in scorn,
    Our ears may greet no more,
Unless at last to that far sphere we climb
Where he completes the wonder of his rhyme!

XXIII

How like a cloud she fled, thy fateful bark,
  From eyes that watched to hearts that waited, till
Up from the ocean roared the tempest dark—
  And the wild heart Love waited for was still!
Hither and thither in the slow, soft tide,
  Rolled seaward, shoreward, sands and wandering shells
And shifting weeds thy fellows, thou didst hide
    Remote from all farewells,
Nor felt the sun, nor heard the fleeting rain,
Nor heeded Casa Magni's quenchless pain.

XXIV

Thou heedest not? Nay, for it was not thou,
  That blind, mute clay relinquished by the waves
Reluctantly at last, and slumbering now
  In one of kind earth's most compassionate graves!
Not thou, not thou,—for thou wert in the light
  Of the Unspeakable, where time is not.
Thou sawest those tears; but in thy perfect sight
    And thy eternal thought
Were they not even now all wiped away
In the reunion of the infinite day!

XXV

There face to face thou sawest the living God
And worshippedst, beholding Him the same
Adored on earth as Love, the same whose rod
Thou hadst endured as Life, whose secret name
Thou now didst learn, the healing name of Death.
In that unroutable profound of peace,
Beyond experience of pulse and breath,
Beyond the last release
Of longing, rose to greet thee all the lords
Of Thought, with consummation in their words:

XXVI

He of the seven cities claimed, whose eyes,
Though blind, saw gods and heroes, and the fall
Of Ilium, and many alien skies,
And Circe's Isle; and he whom mortals call
The Thunderous, who sang the Titan bound
As thou the Titan victor; the benign
Spirit of Plato; Job; and Judah's crowned
Singer and seer divine;
Omar; the Tuscan; Milton, vast and strong;
And Shakespeare, captain of the host of Song.

XXVII

Back from the underworld of whelming change
To the wide-glittering beach thy body came;
And thou didst contemplate with wonder strange
And curious regard thy kindred flame,
Fed sweet with frankincense and wine and salt,
With fierce purgation search thee, soon resolving
Thee to the elements of the airy vault
And the far spheres revolving,
The common waters, the familiar woods,
And the great hills' inviolate solitudes.

XXVIII

Thy close companions there officiated
With solemn mourning and with mindful tears,—
The pained, imperious wanderer unmated
Who voiced the wrath of those rebellious years;
Trelawney, lion-limbed and high of heart;
And he, that gentlest sage and friend most true,
Whom Adonais loved. With these bore part

One grieving ghost, that flew
Hither and thither through the smoke unstirred
In wailing semblance of a wild white bird.

XXIX

O heart of fire, that fire might not consume,
Forever glad the world because of thee;
Because of thee forever eyes illume
A more enchanted earth, a lovelier sea!
O poignant voice of the desire of life,
Piercing our lethargy, because thy call
Aroused our spirits to a nobler strife
Where base and sordid fall,
Forever past the conflict and the pain
More clearly beams the goal we shall attain!

XXX

And now once more, O marshes, back to you
From whatsoever wanderings, near or far,
To you I turn with joy forever new,
To you, O sovereign vasts of Tantramar!
Your tides are at the full. Your wizard flood,
With every tribute stream and brimming creek,
Ponders, possessor of the utmost good,
With no more left to seek,—
But the hour wanes and passes; and once more
Resounds the ebb with destiny in its roar.

XXXI

So might some lord of men, whom force and fate
And his great heart's unvanquishable power
Have thrust with storm to his supreme estate,
Ascend by night his solitary tower
High o'er the city's lights and cries uplift.
Silent he ponders the scrolled heaven to read
And the keen stars' conflicting message sift,
Till the slow signs recede,
And ominously scarlet dawns afar
The day he leads his legions forth to war.

29 October 1892
Avé! An Ode for the Centenary of the Birth of Percy Bysshe Shelley, 1892

THE HERRING WEIR

Back to the green deeps of the outer bay
   The red and amber currents glide and cringe,
   Diminishing behind a luminous fringe
Of cream-white surf and wandering wraiths of spray.
Stealthily, in the old reluctant way,
   The red flats are uncovered, mile on mile,
   To glitter in the sun a golden while.
Far down the flats, a phantom sharply grey,

The herring weir emerges, quick with spoil.
   Slowly the tide forsakes it. Then draws near,
   Descending from the farm-house on the height,
A cart, with gaping tubs. The oxen toil
   Sombrely o'er the level to the weir,
   And drag a long black trail across the light.

c. 1893
The Independent, 29 June 1893
Songs of the Common Day and Ave, 1893

IN AN OLD BARN

Tons upon tons the brown-green fragrant hay
   O'erbrims the mows beyond the time-warped eaves,
   Up to the rafters where the spider weaves,
Though few flies wander his secluded way.
Through a high chink one lonely golden ray,
   Wherein the dust is dancing, slants unstirred.
   In the dry hush some rustlings light are heard,
Of winter-hidden mice at furtive play.

Far down, the cattle in their shadowed stalls,
   Nose-deep in clover fodder's meadowy scent,

Forget the snows that whelm their pasture streams,
The frost that bites the world beyond their walls.
Warm housed, they dream of summer, well content
In day-long contemplation of their dreams.

c. 1893
Songs of the Common Day and Ave, 1893

MARSYAS

A little grey hill-glade, close-turfed, withdrawn
Beyond resort or heed of trafficking feet,
Ringed round with slim trunks of the mountain ash.
Through the slim trunks and scarlet bunches flash—
Beneath the clear chill glitterings of the dawn—
Far off, the crests, where down the rosy shore
The Pontic surges beat.
The plains lie dim below. The thin airs wash
The circuit of the autumn-coloured hills,
And this high glade, whereon
The satyr pipes, who soon shall pipe no more.
He sits against the beech-tree's mighty bole,—
He leans, and with persuasive breathing fills
The happy shadows of the slant-set lawn.
The goat-feet fold beneath a gnarlèd root;
And sweet, and sweet the note that steals and thrills
From slender stops of that shy flute.
Then to the goat-feet comes the wide-eyed fawn
Hearkening; the rabbits fringe the glade, and lay
Their long ears to the sound;
In the pale boughs the partridge gather round,
And quaint hern from the sea-green river reeds;
The wild ram halts upon a rocky horn
O'erhanging; and, unmindful of his prey,
The leopard steals with narrowed lids to lay
His spotted length along the ground.
The thin airs wash, the thin clouds wander by,
And those hushed listeners move not. All the morn

He pipes, soft-swaying, and with half-shut eye,
In rapt content of utterance,—
nor heeds
The young god standing in his branchy place,
The languor on his lips, and in his face,
Divinely inaccessible, the scorn.

c. 1893
Songs of the Common Day and Ave, 1893

TWILIGHT ON SIXTH AVENUE AT NINTH STREET

Over the tops of the houses
Twilight and sunset meet.
The green, diaphanous dusk
Sinks to the eager street.

Astray in the tangle of roofs
Wanders a wind of June.
The dial shines in the clock-tower
Like the face of a strange-scrawled moon.

The narrowing lines of the houses
Palely begin to gleam,
And the hurrying crowds fade softly
Like an army in a dream.

Above the vanishing faces
A phantom train flares on
With a voice that shakes the shadows,—
Diminishes, and is gone.

And I walk with the journeying throng
In such a solitude
As where a lonely ocean
Washes a lonely wood.

c. 1895
Youth's Companion, 14 February 1895
The Book of the Native, 1896

EARTH'S COMPLINES

Before the feet of the dew
There came a call I knew,
   Luring me into the garden
Where the tall white lilies grew.

I stood in the dusk between
The companies of green,
   O'er whose aërial ranks
The lilies rose serene.

And the breathing air was stirred
By an unremembered word,
   Soft, incommunicable—
And wings not of a bird.

I heard the spent blooms sighing,
The expectant buds replying;
   I felt the life of the leaves,
Ephemeral, yet undying.

The spirits of earth were there,
Thronging the shadowed air,
   Serving among the lilies,
In an ecstasy of prayer.

Their speech I could not tell;
But the sap in each green cell,
   And the pure initiate petals,
They knew that language well.

I felt the soul of the trees—
Of the white, eternal seas—
   Of the flickering bats and night-moths
And my own soul kin to these.

And a spell came out of space
From the light of its starry place,
   And I saw in the deep of my heart
The image of God's face.

c. 1895
The Yellow Book, July 1895
The Book of the Native, 1899

AT THE RAILWAY STATION

Here the night is fierce with light,
  Here the great wheels come and go,
Here are partings, waitings, meetings,
  Mysteries of joy and woe.

Here is endless haste and change,
  Here the ache of streaming eyes,
Radiance of expectant faces,
  Breathless askings, brief replies.

Here the jarred, tumultuous air
  Throbs and pauses like a bell,
Gladdens with delight of greeting,
  Sighs and sorrows with farewell.

Here, ah, here with hungry eyes
  I explore the passing throng.
Restless I await your coming
  Whose least absence is so long.

Faces, faces pass me by,
  Meaningless, and blank, and dumb,
Till my heart grows faint and sickens
  Lest at last you should not come.

Then—I see you. And the blood
  Surges back to heart and brain.
Eyes meet mine,—and Heaven opens.
  Your are at my side again.

c. 1898
Harper's Weekly, 5 February 1898
New York Nocturnes, 1898

THE ROSE'S AVATAR

There grew a rose more wonderful
Than ever Saadi sang.
Its loveliness occult and strange,
A rapture and a pang.
Its petals had the pulsing touch
That shakes the blood with fire.
Its warm deeps were the avatar
Of unassuaged desire.
His scents and hushed seraglio dreams
Were in its subtle breath,
The madness of the Mænad's joy,
The tenderness of death.
Its soul was all the mystic East,
Its heart was all the South,—
Till love and tears transmuted it
To the dark rose of thy mouth.

c. 1901
The Smart Set, February 1901
The Book of the Rose, 1903

THE SKATER

My glad feet shod with the glittering steel
I was the god of the wingèd heel.

The hills in the far white sky were lost;
The world lay still in the wide white frost;

And the woods hung hushed in their long white dream
By the ghostly, glimmering, ice-blue stream.

Here was a pathway, smooth like glass,
Where I and the wandering wind might pass

To the far-off palaces, drifted deep,
Where Winter's retinue rests in sleep.

I followed the lure, I fled like a bird,
Till the startled hollows awoke and heard

A spinning whisper, a sibilant twang,
As the stroke of the steel on the tense ice rang;

And the wandering wind was left behind
As faster, faster I followed my mind;

Till the blood sang high in my eager brain,
And the joy of my flight was almost pain.

Then I stayed the rush of my eager speed
And silently went as a drifting seed,—

Slowly, furtively, till my eyes
Grew big with the awe of a dim surmise,

And the hair of my neck began to creep
At hearing the wilderness talk in sleep.

Shapes in the fir-gloom drifted near.
In the deep of my heart I heard my fear.

And I turned and fled, like a soul pursued,
From the white, inviolate solitude.

c. 1901
Poems, 1901/7

FROM THE HIGH WINDOW OF YOUR ROOM

From the high window of your room,
  Above the roofs, and streets, and cries,
Lying awake and still, I watch
  The wonder of the dawn arise.

Slow tips the world's deliberate rim,
  Descending to the baths of day:
Up floats the pure, ethereal tide
  And floods the outworn dark away.

The city's sprawled, uneasy bulk
  Illumines slowly in my sight.

The crowded roofs, the common walls,
 The grey streets, melt in mystic light.

It passes. Then, with longing sore
 For that veiled light of paradise,
I turn my face,—and find it in
 The wonder of your waking eyes.

23-24 December 1905
New Poems, 1919

GOING OVER

(The Somme, 1917)

A girl's voice in the night troubled my heart
Across the roar of the guns, the crash of the shells,
Low and soft as a sigh, clearly I heard it.

Where was the broken parapet, crumbling about me?
Where my shadowy comrades, crouching expectant?
A girl's voice in the dark troubled my heart.

A dream was the ooze of the trench, the wet clay slipping.
A dream the sudden out-flare of the wide-flung Verys.
I saw but a garden of lilacs, a-flower in the dusk.

What was the sergeant saying?—I passed it along.—
Did *I* pass it along? I was breathing the breath of the lilacs.
For a girl's voice in the night troubled my heart.

Over! How the mud sucks! Vomits red the barrage.
But I am far off in the hush of a garden of lilacs.
For a girl's voice in the night troubled my heart.
Tender and soft as a sigh, clearly I heard it.

20 October 1918
New Poems, 1919

IN THE NIGHT WATCHES

When the little spent winds are at rest in the tamarack tree
In the still of the night,
And the moon in her waning is wan and misshapen,
And out on the lake
The loon floats in a glimmer of light,
And the solitude sleeps,—
Then I lie in my bunk wide awake,
And my long thoughts stab me with longing,
Alone in my shack by the marshes of lone Margaree.

Far, oh so far in the forests of silence they lie,
The lake and the marshes of lone Margaree,
And no man comes my way.
Of spruce logs my cabin is builded securely;
With slender spruce saplings its bark roof is battened down
  surely;
In its rafters the mice are at play,
With rustlings furtive and shy,
In the still of the night.

Awake, wide-eyed, I watch my window-square,
Pallid and grey.
(O Memory, pierce me not! O Longing, stab me not!
O ache of longing memory, pass me by, and spare,
And let me sleep!)
Once and again the loon cries from the lake.
Though no breath stirs
The ghostly tamaracks and the brooding firs,
Something as light as air leans on my door.

Is it an owl's wing brushes at my latch?
Are they of foxes, those light feet that creep
Outside, light as fall'n leaves
On the forest floor?
From the still lake I hear
A feeding trout rise to some small night fly.
The splash, how sharply clear!
Almost I see the wide, slow ripple circling to the shore.

The spent winds are at rest, but my heart, spent and faint,
  is unresting,
Long, long a stranger to peace . . .
O so Dear, O so Far, O so Unforgotten-in-dream,

Somewhere in the world, somewhere beyond reach of my
questing.
Beyond seas, beyond years,
You will hear my heart in your sleep, and you will stir
restlessly;
You will stir at the touch of my hand on your hair;
You will wake with a start,
With my voice in your ears
And an old, old ache at your heart,
(In the still of the night)
And your pillow wet with tears.

10, 22 September 1926
Willison's Monthly, January 1927
The Vagrant of Time, 1927

THE ICEBERG

I was spawned from the glacier,
A thousand miles due north
Beyond Cape Chidley;
And the spawning,
When my vast, wallowing bulk went under,
Emerged and heaved aloft,
Shaking down cataracts from its rocking sides,
With mountainous surge and thunder
Outraged the silence of the Arctic sea.

Before I was thrust forth
A thousand years I crept,
Crawling, crawling, crawling irresistibly,
Hid in the blue womb of the eternal ice,
While under me the tortured rock
Groaned,
And over me the immeasurable desolation slept.

Under the pallid dawning
Of the lidless Arctic day
Forever no life stirred.
No wing of bird—
Of ghostly owl low winnowing

Or fleet-winged ptarmigan fleeing the pounce of death,—
No foot of backward-glancing fox
Half glimpsed, and vanishing like a breath,—
No lean and gauntly stalking bear,
Stalking his prey.
Only the white sun, circling the white sky.
Only the wind screaming perpetually.

And then the night—
The long night, naked, high over the roof of the world,
Where time seemed frozen in the cold of space,—
Now black, and torn with cry
Of unseen voices where the storm raged by,
Now radiant with spectral light
As the vault of heaven split wide
To let the flaming Polar cohorts through,
And close ranked spears of gold and blue,
Thin scarlet and thin green,
Hurtled and clashed across the sphere
And hissed in sibilant whisperings,
And died.
And then the stark moon, swinging low,
Silver, indifferent, serene,
Over the sheeted snow.

But now, an Alp afloat,
In seizure of the surreptitious tide,
Began my long drift south to a remote
And unimagined doom.
Scornful of storm,
Unjarred by thunderous buffeting of seas,
Shearing the giant floes aside,
Ploughing the wide-flung ice-fields in a spume
That smoked far up my ponderous flanks,
Onward I fared,
My ice-blue pinnacles rendering back the sun
In darts of sharp radiance;
My bases fathoms deep in the dark profound.

And now around me
Life and the frigid waters all aswarm.
The smooth wave creamed
With tiny capelin and the small pale squid,—
So pale the light struck through them.
Gulls and gannets screamed
Over the feast, and gorged themselves, and rose,
A clamour of weaving wings, and hid

Momently my face.
The great bull whales
With cavernous jaws agape,
Scooped in the spoil, and slept,
Their humped forms just awash, and rocking softly,—
Or sounded down, down to the deeps, and nosed
Along my ribbed and sunken roots,
And in the green gloom scattered the pasturing cod.

And so I voyaged on, down the dim parallels,
Convoyed by fields
Of countless calving seals
Mild-featured, innocent-eyed, and unforeknowing
The doom of the red flenching knives.
I passed the storm-racked gate
Of Hudson Strait,
And savage Chidley where the warring tides
In white wrath seethe forever.
Down along the sounding shore
Of iron-fanged, many-watered Labrador
Slow weeks I shaped my course, and saw
Dark Mokkowic and dark Napiskawa,
And came at last off lone Belle Isle, the bane
Of ships and snare of bergs.
Here, by the deep conflicting currents drawn,
I hung,
And swung,
The inland voices Gulfward calling me
To ground amid my peers on the alien strand
And roam no more.
But then an off-shore wind,
A great wind fraught with fate,
Caught me and pressed me back,
And I resumed my solitary way.
Slowly I bore
South-east by bastioned Bauld,
And passed the sentinel light far-beaming late
Along the liners' track,
And slanted out Atlanticwards, until
Above the treacherous swaths of fog
Faded from the view the loom of Newfoundland.

Beautiful, ethereal
In the blue sparkle of the gleaming day,
A soaring miracle
Of white immensity,
I was the cynosure of passing ships

That wondered and were gone,
Their wreathed smoke trailing them beyond the verge.
And when in the night they passed—
The night of stars and calm,
Forged up and passed, with churning surge
And throb of huge propellers, and long-drawn
Luminous wake behind,
And sharp, small lights in rows,
I lay a ghost of menace chill and still,
A shape pearl-pale and monstrous, off to leeward,
Blurring the dim horizon line.

Day dragged on day,
And then came fog,
By noon, blind-white,
And in the night
Black-thick and smothering the sight.
Folded therein I waited,
Waited I knew not what
And heeded not,
Greatly incurious and unconcerned.
I heard the small waves lapping along my base,
Lipping and whispering, lisping with bated breath
A casual expectancy of death.
I heard remote
The deep, far carrying note
Blown from the hoarse and hollow throat
Of some lone tanker groping on her course.
Louder and louder rose the sound
In deepening diapason, then passed on,
Diminishing, and dying,—
And silence closed around.
And in the silence came again
Those stealthy voices,
That whispering of death.

And then I heard
The thud of screws approaching.
Near and more near,
Louder and yet more loud,
Through the thick dark I heard it,—
The rush and hiss of waters as she ploughed
Head on, unseen, unseeing,
Toward where I stood across her path, invisible.
And then a startled blare
Of horror close re-echoing,—a glare
Of sudden, stabbing searchlights

That but obscurely pierced the gloom;
And there
I towered, a dim immensity of doom.

A roar
Of tortured waters as the giant screws,
Reversed, thundered full steam astern.
Yet forward still she drew, until,
Slow answering desperate helm,
She swerved, and all her broadside came in view,
Crawling beneath me;
And for a moment I saw faces, blanched,
Stiffly agape, turned upward, and wild eyes
Astare; and one long, quavering cry went up
As a submerged horn gored her through and through,
Ripping her beam wide open;
And sullenly she listed, till her funnels
Crashed on my steep,
And men sprang, stumbling, for the boats.
But now, my deep foundations
Mined by those warmer seas, the hour had come
When I must change.
Slowly I leaned above her,
Slowly at first, then faster,
And icy fragments rained upon her decks.
Then my enormous mass descended on her,
A falling mountain, all obliterating,—
And the confusion of thin, wailing cries,
The Babel of shouts and prayers
And shriek of steam escaping
Suddenly died.
And I rolled over,
Wallowing,
And once more came to rest,
My long hid bases heaved up high in air.

And now, from fogs emerging,
I traversed blander seas,
Forgot the fogs, the scourging
Of sleet-whipped gales, forgot
My austere origin, my tremendous birth,
My journeyings, and that last cataclysm
Of overwhelming ruin.
My squat, pale, alien bulk
Basked in the ambient sheen;
And all about me, league on league outspread,

A gulf of indigo and green.
I laughed in the light waves laced with white,—
Nor knew
How swiftly shrank my girth
Under their sly caresses, how the breath
Of that soft wind sucked up my strength, nor how
The sweet, insidious fingers of the sun
Their stealthy depredations wrought upon me.

Slowly now
I drifted, dreaming.
I saw the flying-fish
With silver gleaming
Flash from the peacock-bosomed wave
And flicker through an arc of sunlit air
Back to their element, desperate to elude
The jaws of the pursuing albacore.

Day after day
I swung in the unhasting tide.
Sometimes I saw the dolphin folk at play,
Their lithe sides iridescent-dyed,
Unheeding in their speed
That long grey wraith,
The shark that followed hungering beneath.
Sometimes I saw a school
Of porpoise rolling by
In ranked array,
Emerging and submerging rhythmically,
Their blunt black bodies heading all one way
Until they faded
In the horizon's dazzling line of light.
Night after night
I followed the low, large moon across the sky,
Or counted the large stars on the purple dark,
The while I wasted, wasted and took no thought,
In drowsed entrancement caught;—
Until one noon a wave washed over me,
Breathed low a sobbing sigh,
Foamed indolently, and passed on;
And then I knew my empery was gone;
As I, too, soon must go.
Nor was I ill content to have it so.

Another night
Gloomed o'er my sight,
With cloud, and flurries of warm, wild rain.

Another day,
Dawning delectably
With amber and scarlet stain,
Swept on its way,
Glowing and shimmering with heavy heat.
A lazing tuna rose
And nosed me curiously,
And shouldered me aside in brusque disdain,
So had I fallen from my high estate.
A foraging gull
Stooped over me, touched me with webbed pink feet,
And wheeled and skreeled away,
Indignant at the chill.

Last I became
A little glancing globe of cold
That slid and sparkled on the slow-pulsed swell.
And then my fragile, scintillating frame
Dissolved in ecstasy
Of many coloured light,
And I breathed up my soul into the air
And merged forever in the all-solvent sea.

February-March 1931; dated 9 March 1931
The University of Toronto Quarterly, October 1931
The Iceberg and Other Poems, 1934

TAORMINA

A little tumbled city on the height,
Basking above the cactus and the sea!
What pale, frail ghosts of memory come to-night!
And call back the forgotten years to me!
Taormina, Taormina,
And the month of the almond blossom.

In an old book I find a withered flower,
And withered dreams awake to their old fire.
How far have danced your feet since that fair hour
That brought us to the land of heart's desire!

Taormina, Taormina,
Oh, the scent of the almond blossom.

The grey-white monastery-garden wall
O'erpeers the white crag, and the flung vines upclamber
In the white sun, and cling and seem to fall,—
Brave bougainvilleas, purple and smoky amber.
Taormina, Taormina,
And the month of the almond blossom.

You caught your breath, as hand in hand we stood
To watch the luminous peak of Aetna there
Soaring above the cloudy solitude,
Enmeshed in the opaline Sicilian air.
Taormina, Taormina,
Oh, the scent of the almond blossom.

We babbled of Battos and brown Corydon,—
Of Amaryllis coiling her dark locks,—
Of the sad-hearted satyr grieving on
The tomb of Helicé among the rocks
O'erhung with the almond blossom,—

Of how the goat-boy wrenched apart the vines
That veiled the slim-limbed Chloe at her bath,
And followed her fleet-foot flight among the pines
And caught her close, and kissed away her wrath.
Taormina, Taormina,
And the month of the almond blossom.

And then—you turned impetuously to me!
We saw the blue hyacinths at our feet; and came
To the battlements, and looked down upon the sea—
And the sea was a blue flame!

The blue flame dies. The ghosts come back to me.
Taormina, Taormina,
Oh, the scent of the almond blossom.

3-5 May 1932
Dalhousie Review, October 1932
The Iceberg and Other Poems, 1934

PEACE WITH DISHONOUR

The red flame of war, the anguish of woman,
The dropped bomb, the gas-choked breath,
The groans of the stricken, or the swift death—
These, alas, are but human!

'Tis not for these my heart sinks—not for these!
Their horrors pass like a sick dream.
Their scars fade in Time's detergent stream.
Oh! not for these!

But oh, for faith betrayed cringes my soul.
For long dishonour brief, cowed peace.
For Freedom stripped and cast to the loud pack.
This stain endures. For this cringes my soul.

18-20 September 1938
Saturday Night, October 1938
Canada Speaks of Britain, 1941

CANADA SPEAKS OF BRITAIN

This is that bastioned rock where dwell the Free,
   That citadel against whose front in vain
Storm up the mad assaults of air and sea
   To shatter down in flaming wreck again.

This, this is Britain, bulwark of our breed,
   Our one sure shield against the hordes of hate.
Smite her, and we are smitten; wound her, we bleed.
   Yet firm she stands and fears no thrust of fate.

Stands she, and shall;—but not by guns alone,
   And ships and planes and ramparts. Her own soul

That knows neither to bend nor break,—her own
   Will, hammered to temper,—keeps her whole.

She calls. And we will answer to our last breath,—
Make light of sacrifice, and jest with Death.

28 July-19 August 1940
Maclean's Magazine, 1 October 1940
Canada Speaks of Britain, 1941

EPITAPH FOR A YOUNG AIRMAN

(Shot down over the Channel)

He who would mount on eager wing
   With morning in his eyes
To climb through cloud and storm, and hurl
   His challenge through the skies,—

Would scale the heights of air too thin
   For toil of labouring breath,
Alone to front the foe and fling
   His dare to flaming death,—

Would plunge through scathing hail of fire
   And blast of screaming shell
To scourge with steel the ravening horde
   Back to their hell,—

He sleeps today, how deep a sleep,
   Beneath the Channel wave,
Nor heeds how well his task was done
   For those he died to save.

c. 1940
Saturday Night, October 1940
Canada Speaks of Britain, 1941

Bliss Carman

1861–1929

Carman was born in Fredericton, New Brunswick in 1861. He was a cousin of Charles G.D. Roberts: his mother, a descendant of the Reverend Daniel Bliss (grandfather of Ralph Waldo Emerson), was Roberts' aunt. Carman attended the University of New Brunswick, graduating in 1884, and though subsequently studying law, philosophy, and engineering in Edinburgh and at Harvard, he determined on a literary career. In the 1890s, he gained editorial and journalistic experience with American periodicals, and established a significant position as a poet in 1893 with the publication of *Low Tide on Grand Pré*, the title of which derives from the well-known poem that draws its setting from the shores of Nova Scotia, near Wolfville. Although he lived from 1908 on in New Canaan, Connecticut, and in the Catskill Mountains, New York, in the winter and summer respectively, Carman could not escape his Canadian and particularly Maritime roots, as his poetry clearly reveals. From 1925 on, prompted by Roberts' return to Canada from England and Europe, Carman frequently visited his own country to offer readings and lectures across the land. Though he died in New Canaan, he was buried in Fredericton in accordance with his wishes.

Like Roberts, Carman was influenced by Classical, Romantic and Victorian writers, as well as by impressionism and transcendentalism. Like his cousin, he tended not to be drawn into the modernist manner. That is not to say that Carman was unaware of new styles and new voices, or even new philosophical trends; rather, the sharper economics of the modernist way simply seem not to have suited him, particularly because of his own singular lyrical gifts. He could be pithy and concise in verse when he wanted, but never, it appears, would he sacrifice his own poetic melody to tenser, more tightly drawn statements. Again, the reader is confronted not only with a writer who finds ready enough inspiration, but one who knows how *he* wants to and *must* write.

Carman employed a wide range of forms, always with a deftness that sometimes catches the reader unawares. In the case of longer poems with fixed stanzaic patterns, the structural repetition is inevitably used to advantage and often emphasized, as in "A Northern Vigil", with its inherent diction in the opening lines of various stanzas. Even in this respect, certain traditional characteristics of song, including the ballad, are not far distant.

Like Roberts, Carman is painterly in his figurative approach, frequently dealing in brighter colours, but always with the greys and darker shades ready at hand, as in "The Eavesdropper". And here, perhaps, is one of the recurring themes in Carman's work. Frequently there is a sense not merely of nostalgia but of loss, such as the problem of the absent beloved. Although a somewhat traditional theme, especially with some of the European Romantics, it is given extensive expression by Carman.

For Carman, what hope there is lies not in the earthly resolution of a lonely state, but in the comfort he derives in his own certainty of divine presence. His apprehension of the spiritual realm is clear enough with Wordsworthian overtones in "Vestigia": "I knew God dwelt within my heart." And it is that point that one needs to keep in mind in coming to terms with what might otherwise seem to be a rather long run of tenacious longing. His poetic credo is clearly expressed in *The Kinship of Nature* (1903), where he is well aware of "... the cadence of [his] lines ...", the "... undefinable magic ...", the "... music of [his] verse".

Carman's major collection of poetry is *The Poems of Bliss Carman*, ed. John Robert Sorfleet; his manuscripts are located in the Hathaway Collection, Bonar Law-Bennett Library, University of New Brunswick, Fredericton.

Works on Carman include: Odell Shepherd, *Bliss Carman* (1923); R.H. Hathaway, "The Poetry of Bliss Carman",

Sewanee Review 33 (October 1925), 467-83; James Cappon, *Bliss Carman and the Literary Currents and Influences of His Time* (1930); Desmond Pacey, "Bliss Carman" in *Ten Canadian Poets* (1958); Donald Stephens, *Bliss Carman* (1966); John Robert Sorfleet, "Transcendentalist, Mystic, Evolutionary Idealist: Bliss Carman, 1886-1894", in *Colony and Confederation: Early Canadian Poets and Their Background*, ed. George Woodcock (1974); D.M.R. Bentley, "Pan and the Confederation Poets", *Canadian Literature* 81 (Summer 1979), 59-71; Terry Whalen, "Bliss Carman", *Canadian Writers and Their Works*, ed. Robert Lecker, Jack David, and Ellen Quigley (1983); Muriel Miller, *Bliss Carman: Quest and Revolt* (1985); Malcolm Ross, "Bliss Carman and the Poetry of Mystery: A Defense of the Personal Fallacy", *The Bicentennial Lectures on New Brunswick Literature* (1985); and *Bliss Carman: A Reappraisal* (1990), ed. Gerald Lynch.

LOW TIDE ON GRAND PRÉ

The sun goes down, and over all
These barren reaches by the tide
Such unelusive glories fall,
I almost dream they yet will bide
Until the coming of the tide.

And yet I know that not for us,
By any ecstasy of dream,
He lingers to keep luminous
A little while the grievous stream,
Which frets, uncomforted of dream—

A grievous stream, that to and fro
Athrough the fields of Acadie
Goes wandering, as if to know
Why one beloved face should be
So long from home and Acadie.

Was it a year or lives ago
We took the grasses in our hands,
And caught the summer flying low
Over the waving meadow lands,
And held it there between our hands?

The while the river at our feet—
A drowsy inland meadow stream—
At set of sun the after-heat
Made running gold, and in the gleam
We freed our birch upon the stream.

There down among the elms at dusk
We lifted dripping blade to drift,
Through twilight scented fine like musk,
Where night and gloom awhile uplift,
Nor sunder soul and soul adrift.

And that we took into our hands
Spirit of life or subtler thing—
Breathed on us there, and loosed the bands
Of death, and taught us, whispering,
The secret of some wonder-thing.

Then all your face grew light, and seemed
  To hold the shadow of the sun;
The evening faltered, and I deemed
  That time was ripe, and years had done
  Their wheeling underneath the sun.

So all desire and all regret,
  And fear and memory, were naught;
One to remember or forget
  The keen delight our hands had caught;
  Morrow and yesterday were naught.

The night has fallen, and the tide . . .
  Now and again comes drifting home,
Across these aching barrens wide,
  A sigh like driven wind or foam:
  In grief the flood is bursting home.

June 1886
The Atlantic Monthly, March 1887
Low Tide on Grand Pré, 1893

A SEA CHILD

The lover of child Marjory
  Had one white hour of life brim full;
Now the old nurse, the rocking sea,
  Hath him to lull.

The daughter of child Marjory
  Hath in her veins, to beat and run,
The glad indomitable sea,
  The strong white sun.

1889
Low Tide on Grand Pré, 1893

THE VAGABONDS

"Such as wake on the night and sleep on the day, and haunt customable taverns and alehouses and routs about, and no man wot from whence they came, nor whither they go."—*Old English Statute*.

We are the vagabonds of time,
  And rove the yellow autumn days,
When all the roads are grey with rime
  And all the valleys blue with haze.

We came unlooked for as the wind
  Trooping across the April hills,
When the brown waking earth had dreams
  Of summer in the Wander Kills.

How far afield we joyed to fare,
  With June in every blade and tree!
Now with the sea-wind in our hair
  We turn our faces to the sea.

We go unheeded as the stream
  That wanders by the hill-wood side,
Till the great marshes take his hand
  And lead him to the roving tide.

The roving tide, the sleeping hills,
  These are the borders of that zone
Where they may fare as fancy wills
  Whom wisdom smiles and calls her own.

It is a country of the sun,
  Full of forgotten yesterdays,
When Time takes Summer in his care,
  And fills the distance of her gaze.

It stretches from the open sea
  To the blue mountains and beyond;
The world is Vagabondia
  To him who is a vagabond.

In the beginning God made man
  Out of the wandering dust, men say;
And in the end his life shall be
  A wandering wind and blown away.

We are the vagabonds of time,
Willing to let the world go by,
With joy supreme, with heart sublime,
And valour in the kindling eye.

We have forgotten where we slept,
And guess not where we sleep to-night,
Whether among the lonely hills
In the pale streamers' ghostly light

We shall lie down and hear the frost
Walk in the dead leaves restlessly,
Or somewhere on the iron coast
Learn the oblivion of the sea.

It matters not. And yet I dream
Of dreams fulfilled and rest somewhere
Before this restless heart is stilled
And all its fancies blown to air.

Had I my will! . . . The sun burns down
And something plucks my garment's hem:
The robins in their faded brown
Would lure me to the south with them.

'Tis time for vagabonds to make
The nearest inn. Far on I hear
The voices of the Northern hills
Gather the vagrants of the year.

Brave heart, my soul! Let longings be!
We have another day to wend.
For dark or waylay what care we
Who have the lords of time to friend?

And if we tarry or make haste,
The wayside sleep can hold no fear.
Shall fate unpoise, or whim perturb,
The calm-begirt in dawn austere?

There is a tavern, I have heard,
Not far, and frugal, kept by One
Who knows the children of the Word,
And welcomes each when day is done.

Some say the house is lonely set
In Northern night, and snowdrifts keep
The silent door; the hearth is cold,
And all my fellows gone to sleep. . . .

Had I my will! I hear the sea
  Thunder a welcome on the shore;
I know where lies the hostelry
  And who should open me the door.

1892
New York Independent, 8 December 1892
Low Tide on Grand Pré, 1893

OVERLORD

πνευμα κυριον επ' εμε.

Lord of the grass and hill,
Lord of the rain,
White Overlord of will,
Master of pain,

I who am dust and air
Blown through the halls of death,
Like a pale ghost of prayer,—
I am thy breath.

Lord of the blade and leaf,
Lord of the bloom,
Sheer Overlord of grief,
Master of doom,

Lonely as wind or snow,
Through the vague world and dim,
Vagrant and glad I go;
I am thy whim.

Lord of the storm and lull,
Lord of the sea,
I am thy broken gull,
Blown far alee.

Lord of the harvest dew,
Lord of the dawn,
Star of the paling blue
Darkling and gone,

Lost on the mountain height
Where the first winds are stirred,
Out of the wells of night
I am thy word.

Lord of the haunted hush,
Where raptures throng,
I am thy hermit thrush,
Ending no song.

Lord of the frost and cold,
Lord of the North,
When the red sun grows old
And day goes forth,

I shall put off this girth,—
Go glad and free,
Earth to my mother earth,
Spirit to thee.

7 August 1892
From the Book of Myths, 1903

THE GRAVE-TREE

(Second Version)

Let me have a scarlet maple
For the grave-tree at my head,
With the quiet sun behind it,
In the years when I am dead.

Let me have it for a signal,
Where the long winds stream and stream,
Clear across the dim blue distance,
Like a horn blown in a dream;

Scarlet when the April vanguard
Bugles up the laggard Spring,
Scarlet when the bannered Autumn,
Marches by unwavering.

It will comfort me with honey
When the shining rifts and showers
Sweep across the purple valley
And bring back the forest flowers.

It will be my leafy cabin,
Large enough when June returns
And I hear the golden thrushes
Flute and hesitate by turns.

And in fall, some yellow morning,
When the stealthy frost has come,
Leaf by leaf it will befriend me
As with comrades going home.

Let me have the Silent Valley
And the hill that fronts the east,
So that I can watch the morning
Redden and the stars released.

Leave me in the Great Lone Country,
For I shall not be afraid
With the shy moose and the beaver
There within my scarlet shade.

I would sleep, but not too soundly,
Where the sunning partridge drums,
Till the crickets hush before him
When the Scarlet Hunter comes.

That will be in warm September,
In the stillness of the year,
When the river-blue is deepest
And the other world is near.

When the apples burn their reddest
And the corn is in the sheaves,
I shall stir and waken lightly
At a footfall in the leaves.

It will be the Scarlet Hunter
Come to tell me time is done;
On the idle hills forever
There will stand the idle sun.

There the wind will stay to whisper
Many wonders to the reeds;
But I shall not fear to follow
Where my Scarlet Hunter leads.

I shall know him in the darkling
Murmur of the river bars,
While his feet are on the mountains
Treading out the smouldering stars.

I shall know him, in the sunshine
Sleeping in my scarlet tree,
Long before he halts beside it
Stooping down to summon me.

Then fear not, my friends, to leave me
In the boding autumn vast;
There are many things to think of
When the roving days are past.

Leave me by the scarlet maple,
When the journeying shadows fail,
Waiting till the Scarlet Hunter
Pass upon the endless trail.

20 August 1892
By the Aurelian Wall and Other Elegies, 1898

THE EAVESDROPPER

In a still room at hush of dawn,
  My Love and I lay side by side
And heard the roaming forest wind
  Stir in the paling autumn-tide.

I watched her earth-brown eyes grow glad
  Because the round day was so fair;
While memories of reluctant night
  Lurked in the blue dusk of her hair.

Outside, a yellow maple tree,
  Shifting upon the silvery blue
With tiny multitudinous sound,
  Rustled to let the sunlight through.

The livelong day the elvish leaves
  Danced with their shadows on the floor;
And the lost children of the wind
  Went straying homeward by our door.

And all the swarthy afternoon
   We watched the great deliberate sun
Walk through the crimsoned hazy world,
   Counting his hilltops one by one.

Then as the purple twilight came
   And touched the vines along our eaves,
Another Shadow stood without
   And gloomed the dancing of the leaves.

The silence fell on my Love's lips;
   Her great brown eyes were veiled and sad
With pondering some maze of dream,
   Though all the splendid year was glad.

Restless and vague as a grey wind
   Her heart had grown, she knew not why.
But hurrying to the open door,
   Against the verge of western sky

I saw retreating on the hills,
   Looming and sinister and black,
The stealthy figure swift and huge
   Of One who strode and looked not back.

1893
The Atlantic Monthly, February 1893
Low Tide on Grand Pré, 1893

EARTH'S LYRIC

April. You hearken, my fellow,
Old slumberer down in my heart?
There's a whooping of ice in the rivers;
The sap feels a start.

The snow-melted torrents are brawling;
The hills, orange-misted and blue,
Are touched with the voice of the rainbird
Unsullied and new.

The houses of frost are deserted,
Their slumber is broken and done,
And empty and pale are the portals
Awaiting the sun.

The bands of Arcturus are slackened;
Orion goes forth from his place
On the slopes of the night, leading homeward
His hound from the chase.

The Pleiades weary and follow
The dance of the ghostly dawn;
The revel of silence is over;
Earth's lyric comes on.

A golden flute in the cedars,
A silver pipe in the swales,
And the slow large life of the forest
Wells back and prevails.

A breath of the woodland spirit
Has blown out the bubble of spring
To this tenuous hyaline glory
One touch sets a-wing.

24 March 1894
More Songs from Vagabondia, 1896

LORD OF MY HEART'S ELATION

Lord of my heart's elation,
Spirit of things unseen,
Be thou my aspiration
Consuming and serene!

Bear up, bear out, bear onward
This mortal soul alone,
To selfhood or oblivion,
Incredibly thine own,—

As the foamheads are loosened
And blown along the sea,
Or sink and merge forever
In that which bids them be.

I, too, must climb in wonder,
Uplift at thy command,—

Be one with my frail fellows
Beneath the wind's strong hand,

A fleet and shadowy column
Of dust or mountain rain,
To walk the earth a moment
And be dissolved again.

Be thou my exaltation
Or fortitude of mien,
Lord of the world's elation,
Thou breath of things unseen!

26 August 1894
From the Green Book of Bards, 1903

BEHIND THE ARRAS

I like the old house tolerably well,
Where I must dwell
Like a familiar gnome;
And yet I never shall feel quite at home.
I love to roam.

Day after day I loiter and explore
From door to door;
So many treasures lure
The curious mind. What histories obscure
They must immure!

I hardly know which room I care for best;
This fronting west,
With the strange hills in view,
Where the great sun goes,—where I may go too,
When my lease is through,—

Or this one for the morning and the east,
Where a man may feast
His eyes on looming sails,
And be the first to catch their foreign hails
Or spy their bales

Then the pale summer twilights towards the pole!
It thrills my soul

With wonder and delight,
When gold-green shadows walk the world at night,
So still, so bright.

There at the window many a time of year,
Strange faces peer,
Solemn though not unkind,
Their wits in search of something left behind
Time out of mind;

As if they once had lived here, and stole back
To the window crack
For a peep which seems to say,
"Good fortune, brother, in your house of clay!"
And then, "Good day!"

I hear their footsteps on the gravel walk,
Their scraps of talk,
And hurrying after, reach
Only the crazy sea-drone of the beach
In endless speech.

And often when the autumn noons are still,
By swale and hill
I see their gipsy signs,
Trespassing somewhere on my border lines;
With what designs?

I forth afoot; but when I reach the place,
Hardly a trace,
Save the soft purple haze
Of smouldering camp-fires, any hint betrays
Who went these ways.

Or tatters of pale aster blue, descried
By the roadside,
Reveal whither they fled;
Or the swamp maples, here and there a shred
Of Indian red.

But most of all, the marvellous tapestry
Engrosses me,
Where such strange things are rife,
Fancies of beasts and flowers, and love and strife,
Woven to the life;

Degraded shapes and splendid seraph forms,
And teeming swarms
Of creatures gauzy dim

That cloud the dusk, and painted fish that swim,
At the weaver's whim;

And wonderful birds that wheel and hang in the air;
And beings with hair,
And moving eyes in the face,
And white bone teeth and hideous grins, who race
From place to place;

They build great temples to their John-a-nod,
And fume and plod
To deck themselves with gold,
And paint themselves like chattels to be sold,
Then turn to mould.

Sometimes they seem almost as real as I;
I hear them sigh;
I see them bow with grief,
Or dance for joy like any aspen leaf;
But that is brief.

They have mad wars and phantom marriages;
Nor seem to guess
There are dimensions still,
Beyond thought's reach, though not beyond love's will,
For soul to fill.

And some I call my friends, and make believe
Their spirits grieve,
Brood, and rejoice with mine;
I talk to them in phrases quaint and fine
Over the wine;

I tell them all my secrets; touch their hands;
One understands
Perhaps. How hard he tries
To speak! And yet those glorious mild eyes,
His best replies!

I even have my cronies, one or two,
My cherished few.
But ah, they do not stay!
For the sun fades them and they pass away,
As I grow grey.

Yet while they last how actual they seem!
Their faces beam;
I give them all their names,

Bertram and Gilbert, Louis, Frank and James,
Each with his aims;

One thinks he is a poet, and writes verse
His friends rehearse;
Another is full of law;
A third sees pictures which his hand can draw
Without a flaw.

Strangest of all, they never rest. Day long
They shift and throng,
Moved by invisible will,
Like a great breath which puffs across my sill,
And then is still;

It shakes my lovely manikins on the wall;
Squall after squall,
Gust upon crowding gust,
It sweeps them willy nilly like blown dust
With glory or lust.

It is the world-ghost, the time-spirit, come
None knows wherefrom,
The viewless draughty tide
And wash of being. I hear it yaw and glide,
And then subside,

Along these ghostly corridors and halls
Like faint footfalls;
The hangings stir in the air;
And when I start and challenge, "Who goes there?"
It answers, "Where?"

The wail and sob and moan of the sea's dirge,
Its plangor and surge;
The awful biting sough
Of drifted snows along some arctic bluff,
That veer and luff,

And have the vacant boding human cry,
As they go by;—
Is it a banished soul
Dredging the dark like a distracted mole
Under a knoll?

Like some invisible henchman old and grey,
Day after day
I hear it come and go,

With stealthy swift unmeaning to and fro,
Muttering low,

Ceaseless and daft and terrible and blind,
Like a lost mind.
I often chill with fear
When I bethink me, What if it should peer
At my shoulder here!

Perchance he drives the merry-go-round whose track
Is the zodiac;
His name is No-man's-friend;
And his gabbling parrot-talk has neither trend,
Beginning, nor end.

A prince of madness too, I'd cry, "A rat!"
And lunge thereat,—
Let out at one swift thrust
The cunning arch-delusion of the dust
I so mistrust,

But that I fear I should disclose a face
Wearing the trace
Of my own human guise,
Piteous, unharmful, loving, sad, and wise
With the speaking eyes.

I would the house were rid of his grim pranks,
Moaning from banks
Of pine trees in the moon,
Startling the silence like a demoniac loon
At dead of noon.

Or whispering his fool-talk to the leaves
About my eaves.
And yet how can I know
'T is not a happy Ariel masking so
In mocking woe?

Then with a little broken laugh I say,
Snatching away
The curtain where he grinned
(My feverish sight thought) like a sin unsinned,
"Only the wind!"

Yet often too he steals so softly by.
With half a sigh,
I deem he must be mild,
Fair as a woman, gentle as a child,
And forest wild.

Passing the door where an old wind-harp swings,
With its five strings,
Contrived long years ago
By my first predecessor bent to show
His handcraft so,

He lay his fingers on the aeolian wire,
As a core of fire
Is laid upon the blast
To kindle and glow and fill the purple vast
Of dark at last.

Weird wise, and low, piercing and keen and glad,
Or dim and sad
As a forgotten strain
Born when the broken legions of the rain
Swept through the plain—

He plays, like some dread veiled mysteriarch,
Lighting the dark,
Bidding the spring grow warm,
The gendering merge and loosing of spirit in form,
Peace out of storm.

For music is the sacrament of love;
He broods above
The virgin silence, till
She yields for rapture shuddering, yearning still
To his sweet will.

I hear him sing, "Your harp is like a mesh,
Woven of flesh
And spread within the shoal
Of life, where runs the tide-race of the soul
In my control.

"Though my wild way may ruin what it bends,
It makes amends
To the frail downy clocks,
Telling their seed a secret that unlocks
The granite rocks.

"The womb of silence to the crave of sound
Is heaven unfound,
Till I, to soothe and slake
Being's most utter and imperious ache,
Bid rhythm awake.

"If with such agonies of bliss, my kin,
I enter in

Your prison house of sense,
With what a joyous freed intelligence
I shall go hence."

I need no more to guess the weaver's name,
Nor ask his aim,
Who hung each hall and room
With swarthy-tinged vermilion upon gloom;
I know that loom.

Give me a little space and time enough,
From ravelings rough
I could revive, reweave,
A fabric of beauty art might well believe
Were past retrieve.

O men and women in that rich design,
Sleep-soft, sun-fine,
Dew-tenuous and free,
A tone of the infinite wind-themes of the sea,
Borne in to me,

Reveals how you were woven to the might
Of shadow and light.
You are the dream of One
Who loves to haunt and yet appears to shun
My door in the sun;

As the white roving sea tern fleck and skim
The morning's rim;
Or the dark thrushes clear
Their flutes of music leisurely and sheer,
Then hush to hear.

I know him when the last red brands of day
Smoulder away,
And when the vernal showers
Bring back the heart to all my valley flowers
In the soft hours.

O hand of mine and brain of mine, be yours,
While time endures,
To acquiesce and learn!
For what we best may dare and drudge and yearn,
Let soul discern.

So, fellows, we shall reach the gusty gate,
Early or late,
And part without remorse,

A cadence dying down unto its source
In music's course;

You to the perfect rhythms of flowers and birds,
Colours and words,
The heart-beats of the earth,
To be remoulded always of one worth
From birth to birth;

I to the broken rhythm of thought and man,
The sweep and span
Of memory and hope
About the orbit where they still must grope
For wider scope,

To be through thousand springs restored, renewed,
With love imbrued,
With increments of will
Made strong, perceiving unattainment still
From each new skill.

Always the flawless beauty, always the chord
Of the Overword,
Dominant, pleading, sure,
No truth too small to save and make endure.
No good too poor!

And since no mortal can at last disdain
That sweet refrain,
But lets go strife and care,
Borne like a strain of bird notes on the air,
The wind knows where;

Some quiet April evening soft and strange,
When comes the change
No spirit can deplore,
I shall be one with all I was before,
In death once more.

11 February 1895
Behind the Arras: A Book of the Unseen, 1895

BY THE AURELIAN WALL

(In Memory of John Keats)

By the Aurelian Wall,
Where the long shadows of the centuries fall
From Caius Cestius' tomb,
A weary mortal seeking rest found room
For quiet burial,

Leaving among his friends
A book of lyrics.
Such untold amends
A traveller might make
In a strange country, bidden to partake
Before he farther wends;

Who shyly should bestow
The foreign reed-flute they had seen him blow
And finger cunningly,
On one of the dark children standing by,
Then lift his cloak and go.

The years pass. And the child
Thoughtful beyond his fellows, grave and mild,
Treasures the rough-made toy,
Until one day he blows it for clear joy,
And wakes the music wild.

His fondness makes it seem
A thing first fashioned in delirious dream,
Some god had cut and tried,
And filled with yearning passion, and cast aside
On some far woodland stream,—

After long years to be
Found by the stranger and brought over sea,
A marvel and delight
To ease the noon and pierce the dark blue night,
For children such as he.

He learns the silver strain
Wherewith the ghostly houses of grey rain
And lonely valleys ring,
When the untroubled whitethroats make the spring
A world without a stain;

Then on his river reed,
With strange and unsuspected notes that plead
Of their own wild accord
For utterances no bird's throat could afford,
Lifts it to human need.

His comrades leave their play,
When calling and compelling far away
By river-slope and hill,
He pipes their wayward footsteps where he will,
All the long lovely day.

Even his elders come.
"Surely the child is elvish," murmur some,
And shake the knowing head;
"Give us the good old simple things instead,
Our fathers used to hum."

Others at open door
Smile when they hear what they have hearkened for
These many summers now,
Believing they should live to learn somehow
Things never known before.

But he can only tell
How the flute's whisper lures him with a spell,
Yet always just eludes
The lost perfection over which he broods;
And how he loves it well.
Till all the country-side,
Familiar with his piping far and wide,
Has taken for its own
That weird enchantment down the evening blown,—
Its glory and its pride.

And so his splendid name,
Who left the book of lyrics and small fame
Among his fellows then,
Spreads through the world like autumn—who knows
when?—
Till all the hillsides flame.

Grand Pré and Margaree
Hear it upbruited from the unresting sea;
And the small Gaspereau,
Whose yellow leaves repeat it, seems to know
A new felicity.

Even the shadows tall,
Walking at sundown through the plain, recall
A mound the grasses keep,
Where once a mortal came and found long sleep
By the Aurelian Wall.

10 February 1896
By the Aurelian Wall and Other Elegies, 1898

WHITE NASSAU

There is fog upon the river, there is mirk upon the town;
You can hear the groping ferries as they hoot each other
down;
From the Battery to Harlem there's seven miles of slush,
Through looming granite canyons of glitter, noise, and rush.

Are you sick of phones and tickers and crazing cable gongs,
Of the theatres, the hansoms, and the breathless Broadway
throngs,
Of Flouret's and the Waldorf and the chilly, drizzly Park,
When there's hardly any morning and five o'clock is dark?

I know where there's a city, whose streets are white and clean,
And sea-blue morning loiters by walls where roses lean,
And quiet dwells; that's Nassau, beside her creaming key,
The queen of the Lucayas in the blue Bahaman sea.

She's ringed with surf and coral, she's crowned with sun and
palm;
She has the old-world leisure, the regal tropic calm;
The trade winds fan her forehead; in everlasting June
She reigns from deep verandas above her blue lagoon.

She has had many suitors,—Spaniard and Buccaneer,—
Who roistered for her beauty and split their blood for her;
But none has dared molest her, since the loyalist Deveaux
Went down from Carolina a hundred years ago.

Unmodern, undistracted, by grassy ramp and fort,
In decency and order she holds her modest court;
She seems to have forgotten rapine and greed and strife,
In that unaging gladness and dignity of life.

Through streets as smooth as asphalt and white as bleaching shell,
Where the slip-shod heel is happy and the naked foot goes well,
In their gaudy cotton kerchiefs, with swaying hips and free,
Go her black folk in the morning to the market of the Sea.

Into her bright sea-gardens the flushing tide-gates lead,
Where fins of chrome and scarlet loll in the lifting weed;
With the long sea-draft behind them, through luring coral groves
The shiny water-people go by in painted droves.

Under her old pink gateways, where Time a moment turns,
Where hang the orange lanterns and the red hibiscus burns,
Live the harmless merry lizards, quickersilver in the sun,
Or still as any image with their shadow on a stone.

Through the lemon-trees at leisure a tiny olive bird
Moves all day long and utters his wise assuring word;
While up in their blue chantry murmur the solemn palms,
At their litanies of joyance, their ancient ceaseless psalms.

There in the endless sunlight, within the surf's low sound,
Peace tarries for a lifetime at doorways unrenowned;
And a velvet air goes breathing across the sea-girt land,
Till the sense begins to waken and the soul to understand.

There's a pier in the East River, where a black Ward Liner lies,
With her wheezy donkey-engines taking cargo and supplies;
She will clear the Hook to-morrow for the Indies of the West,
For the lovely white girl city in the Islands of the Blest.

She'll front the riding winter on the grey Atlantic seas,
And thunder through the surf-heads till her funnels crust and freeze;
She'll grapple the Southeaster, the Thing without a Mind,
Till she drops him, mad and monstrous, with the light ship far behind.

Then out into a morning all summer warmth and blue!
By the breathing of her pistons, by the purring of the screw,
By the springy dip and tremor as she rises, you can tell
Her heart is light and easy as she meets the lazy swell.

With the flying fish before her, and the white wake running aft,
Her smoke-wreath hanging idle, without breeze enough for draft,

She will travel fair and steady, and in the afternoon
Run down the floating palm-tops where lift the Isles of June.

With the low boom of breakers for her only signal gun,
She will anchor off the harbour when her thousand miles are
done,
And there's my love, white Nassau, girt with her foaming key,
The queen of the Lucayas in the blue Bahaman sea!

October 1899
A Winter Holiday, 1899

"I LOVED THEE, ATTHIS, IN THE LONG AGO"

(Sappho XXIII)

I loved thee, Atthis, in the long ago,
When the great oleanders were in flower
In the broad herded meadows full of sun.
And we would often at the fall of dusk
Wander together by the silver stream,
When the soft grass-heads were all wet with dew
And purple-misted in the fading light.
And joy I knew and sorrow at thy voice,
And the superb magnificence of love,—
The loneliness that saddens solitude,
And the sweet speech that makes it durable,—
The bitter longing and the keen desire,
The sweet companionship through quiet days
In the slow ample beauty of the world,
And the unutterable glad release
Within the temple of the holy night.
O Atthis, how I loved thee long ago
In that fair perished summer by the sea!

17 July 1902
Sappho, 1903

SOFTER THAN THE HILL-FOG TO THE FOREST

(Sappho LXV)

Softer than the hill-fog to the forest
Are the loving hands of my dear lover,
When she sleeps beside me in the starlight
And her beauty drenches me with rest.

As the quiet mist enfolds the beech-trees,
Even as she dreams her arms enfold me,
Half awaking with a hundred kisses
On the scarlet lily of her mouth.

11 September 1902
Sappho, 1905

OVER THE ROOFS THE HONEY-COLOURED MOON

(Sappho LXXXII)

Over the roofs the honey-coloured moon,
With purple shadows on the silver grass,

And the warm south-wind on the curving sea,
While we two, lovers past all turmoil now,

Watch from the window the white sails come in,
Bearing what unknown ventures safe to port!

So falls the hour of twilight and of love
With wizardry to loose the hearts of men,

And there is nothing more in this great world
Than thou and I, and the blue dome of dusk.

14 October 1902
Sappho, 1905

MORNING IN THE HILLS

How quiet is the morning in the hills!
The stealthy shadows of the summer clouds
Trail through the cañon, and the mountain stream
Sounds his sonorous music far below
In the deep-wooded wind-enchanted cove.

Hemlock and aspen, chestnut, beech, and fir
Go tiering down from storm-worn crest and ledge,
While in the hollows of the dark ravine
See the red road emerge, then disappear
Towards the wide plain and fertile valley lands.

My forest cabin half-way up the glen
Is solitary, save for one wise thrush,
The sound of falling water, and the wind
Mysteriously conversing with the leaves.

Here I abide unvisited by doubt,
Dreaming of far-off turmoil and despair,
The race of men and love and fleeting time,
What life may be, or beauty, caught and held
For a brief moment at eternal poise.

What impulse now shall quicken and make live
This outward semblance and this inward self?
One breath of being fills the bubble world,
Coloured and frail, with fleeting change on change.

Surely some God contrived so fair a thing
In a vast leisure of uncounted days,
And touched it with the breath of living joy,
Wondrous and fair and wise! It must be so.

Summer 1903
Echoes from Vagabondia, 1912

AT THE GREAT RELEASE

When the black horses from the house of Dis
Stop at my door and the dread charioteer
Knocks at my portal, summoning me to go
On the far solitary unknown way
Where all the race of men fare and are lost,
Fleeting and numerous as the autumnal leaves
Before the wind in Lesbos of the Isles;

Though a chill draught of fear may quell my soul
And dim my spirit like a flickering lamp
In the great gusty hall of some old king,
Only one mordant unassuaged regret,
One passionate eternal human grief,
Would wring my heart with bitterness and tears
And set the mask of sorrow on my face.

Not youth, nor early fame, nor pleasant days,
Nor flutes, nor roses, nor the taste of wine,
Nor sweet companions of the idle hour
Who brought me tender joys, nor the glad sound
Of children's voices playing in the dusk;
All these I could forget and bid good-bye
And pass to my oblivion nor repine.

Nor the green woods that I so dearly love,
Nor summer hills in their serenity,
Nor the great sea mystic and musical,
Nor drone of insects, nor the call of birds,
Nor soft spring flowers, nor the wintry stars;
To all the lovely earth that was my home
Smiling and valiant I could say farewell.

But not, O not to one strong little hand,
To one droll mouth brimming with witty words,
Nor ever to the unevasive eyes
Where dwell the light and sweetness of the world
With all the sapphire sparkle of the sea!
Ah, Destiny, against whose knees we kneel
With prayer at evening, spare me this one woe!

21 January 1904
From the Book of Valentines, 1905

PAN IN THE CATSKILLS

They say that he is dead, and now no more
The reedy syrinx sounds among the hills,
When the long summer heat is on the land.
But I have heard the Catskill thrushes sing,
And therefore am incredulous of death,
Of pain and sorrow and mortality.

In these blue cañons, deep with hemlock shade,
In solitudes of twilight or of dawn,
I have been rapt away from time and care
By the enchantment of a golden strain
As pure as ever pierced the Thracian wild,
Filling the listener with a mute surmise.

At evening and at morning I have gone
Down the cool trail between the beech-tree boles,
And heard the haunting music of the wood
Ring through the silence of the dark ravine,
Flooding the earth with beauty and with joy
And all the ardours of creation old.

And then within my pagan heart awoke
Remembrance of far-off and fabled years
In the untarnished sunrise of the world,
When clear-eyed Hellas in her rapture heard
A slow mysterious piping wild and keen
Thrill though her vales, and whispered, "It is Pan!"

1906
Outing, August 1906
Echoes from Vagabondia, 1912

ON THE PLAZA

One August day I sat beside
A café window open wide
To let the shower-freshened air
Blow in across the Plaza, where
In golden pomp against the dark
Green leafy background of the Park,
St. Gaudens' hero, gaunt and grim,
Rides on with Victory leading him.

The wet, black asphalt seemed to hold
In every hollow pools of gold,
And clouds of gold and pink and grey
Were piled up at the end of day,
Far down the cross street, where one tower
Still glistened from the drenching shower.

A weary, white-haired man went by,
Cooling his forehead gratefully
After the day's great heat. A girl,
Her thin white garments in a swirl
Blown back against her breasts and knees,
Like a Winged Victory in the breeze,
Alive and modern and superb,
Crossed from the circle of the curb.
We sat there watching people pass,
Clinking the ice against the glass
And talking idly—books or art,
Or something equally apart
From the essential stress and strife
That rudely form and further life,
Glad of a respite from the heat,
When down the middle of the street,
Trundling a hurdy-gurdy, gay
In spite of the dull-stifling day,
Three street-musicians came. The man,
With hair and beard as black as Pan,
Strolled on one side with lordly grace,
While a young girl tugged at a trace
Upon the other. And between
The shafts there walked a laughing queen,
Bright as a poppy, strong and free.
What likelier land than Italy

Breeds such abandon? Confident
And rapturous in mere living spent
Each moment to the utmost, there
With broad, deep chest and kerchiefed hair,
With head thrown back, bare throat, and waist
Supple, heroic and free-laced,
Between her two companions walked
This splendid woman, chaffed and talked,
Did half the work, made all the cheer
Of that small company.
No fear
Of failure in a soul like hers
That every moment throbs and stirs
With merry ardour, virile hope,
Brave effort, nor in all its scope
Has room for thought of discontent,
Each day its own sufficient vent
And source of happiness.

Without
A trace of bitterness or doubt
Of life's true worth, she strode at ease
Before those empty palaces,
A simple heiress of the earth
And all its joys by happy birth,
Beneficent as breeze or dew,
And fresh as though the world were new
And toil and grief were not. How rare
A personality was there!

c. 1907
Town Topics, December 1907
A Painter's Holiday, 1911

EASTER EVE

If I should tell you I saw Pan lately down by the shallows of
Silvermine,
Blowing an air on his pipe of willow, just as the moon began
to shine;
Or say that, coming from town on Wednesday, I met Christ
walking in Ponus Street;
You might remark, "Our friend is flighty! Visions, for want of
enough red meat!"

Then let me ask you. Last December, when there was skating
on Wampanaw,
Among the weeds and sticks and grasses under the hard black
ice I saw
An old mud-turtle poking about, as if he were putting his
house to rights,
Stiff with the cold perhaps, yet knowing enough to prepare
for the winter nights.

And here he is on a log this morning, sunning himself as calm
as you please.
But I want to know, when the lock of winter was sprung of a
sudden, who kept the keys?
Who told old nibbler to go to sleep safe and sound with the
lily roots,
And then in the first warm days of April—out to the sun with
the greening shoots?

By night a flock of geese went over, honking north on the
trails of air,
The spring express—but who despatched it, equipped with
speed and cunning care?
Hark to our bluebird down in the orchard trolling his chant of
the happy heart,
As full of light as a theme of Mozart's—but where did he
learn that more than art?

Where the river winds through grassy meadows, as sure as the
south wind brings the rain,
Sounding his reedy note in the alders, the redwing comes back
to his nest again.
Are these not miracles? Prompt you answer: "Merely the
prose of natural fact;

Nothing but instinct plain and patent, born in the creatures,
that bids them act."

Well, I have an instinct as fine and valid, surely, as that of the
beasts and birds,
Concerning death and the life immortal, too deep for logic,
too vague for words.
No trace of beauty can pass nor perish, but other beauty is
somewhere born;
No seed of truth or good be planted, but the yield must grow
as the growing corn.

Therefore this ardent mind and spirit I give to the glowing
days of earth,
To be wrought by the Lord of life to something of lasting
import and lovely worth.
If the toil I give be without self-seeking, bestowed to the limit
of will and power,
To fashion after some form ideal the instant task and the
waiting hour,

It matters not though defeat undo me, though faults betray
me and sorrows scar,
Already I share the life eternal with the April buds and the
evening star.
The slim new moon is my sister now; the wind, my brother;
the rain, my friend.
Is it not well with these forever? Can the soul of man fare ill
in the end?

1909
Colliers, 10 April 1909
The Rough Rider and Other Poems, 1909

THE GIVERS OF LIFE

I

Who called us forth out of darkness and gave us the gift of
life,
Who set our hands to the toiling, our feet in the field of strife?

Darkly they mused, predestined to knowledge of viewless
things,
Sowing the seed of wisdom, guarding the living springs.

Little they reckoned privation, hunger or hardship or cold,
If only the life might prosper, and the joy that grows not old.

With sorceries subtler than music, with knowledge older than speech,
Gentle as wind in the wheat-field, strong as the tide on the beach,

Out of their beauty and longing, out of their raptures and tears,
In patience and pride they bore us, to war with the warring years.

II

Who looked on the world before them, and summoned and chose our sires,
Subduing the wayward impulse to the will of their deep desires?

Sovereigns of ultimate issues under the greater laws,
Theirs was the mystic mission of the eternal cause;

Confident, tender, courageous, leaving the low for the higher,
Lifting the feet of the nations out of the dust and the mire,

Luring civilization on to the fair and new,
Given God's bidding to follow, having God's business to do.

III

Who strengthened our souls with courage, and taught us the ways of Earth?
Who gave us our patterns of beauty, our standards of flawless worth?

Mothers, unmilitant, lovely, moulding our manhood then,
Walked in their woman's glory, swaying the might of men.

They schooled us to service and honour, modest and clean and fair,—
The code of their worth of living, taught with the sanction of prayer.

They were our sharers of sorrow, they were our makers of joy,
Lighting the lamp of manhood in the heart of the lonely boy.

Haloed with love and with wonder, in sheltered ways they trod,
Seers of sublime divination, keeping the truce of God.

IV

Who called us from youth and dreaming, and set ambition
alight,
And made us fit for the contest,—men, by their tender rite?

Sweethearts above our merit, charming our strength and skill
To be the pride of their living, to be the means of their will.

If we be the builders of beauty, if we be the masters of art,
Theirs were the gleaming ideals, theirs the uplift of the heart.

Truly they measure the lightness of trappings and ease and
fame,
For the teeming desire of their yearning is ever and ever the
same:

To crown their lovers with gladness, to clothe their sons with
delight,
And see the men of their making lords in the best man's right.

Lavish of joy and labour, broken only by wrong,
These are the guardians of being, spirited, sentient and strong.

Theirs is the starry vision, theirs the inspiriting hope,
Since Night, the brooding enchantress, promised that day
should ope.

V

Lo, we have built and invented, reasoned, discovered and
planned,
To rear us a palace of splendour, and make us a heaven by
hand.

We are shaken with dark misgiving, as kingdoms rise and fall;
But the women who went to found them are never counted
at all.

Versed in the soul's traditions, skilled in humanity's lore,
They wait for their crown of rapture, and weep for the sins
of war.

And behold they turn from our triumphs, as it was in the first
of days,
For a little heaven of ardour and a little heartening of praise.

These are the rulers of kingdoms beyond the domains of state,
Martyrs of all men's folly, over-rulers of fate.

These we will love and honour, these we will serve and
defend,
Fulfilling the pride of nature, till nature shall have an end.

VI

This is the code unwritten, this is the creed we hold,
Guarding the little and lonely, gladdening the helpless and
old,—

Apart from the brunt of the battle our wondrous women shall
bide,
For the sake of a tranquil wisdom and the need of a spirit's
guide.

Come they into assembly, or keep they another door,
Our makers of life, shall lighten the days as the years of yore.

The lure of their laughter shall lead us, the lilt of their words
shall sway.
Though life and death should defeat us, their solace shall be
our stay.

Veiled in mysterious beauty, vested in magical grace,
They have walked with angels at twilight and looked upon
glory's face.

Life we will give for their safety, care for their fruitful ease,
Though we break at the toiling benches or go down in the
smoky seas.

This is the gospel appointed to govern a world of men,
Till love has died, and the echoes have whispered the last
Amen.

1912
The American, September 1912
April Airs: A Book of New England Lyrics, 1916

EARTH VOICES

I

I heard the spring wind whisper
Above the brushwood fire,
"The world is made forever
Of transport and desire.

"I am the breath of being,
The primal urge of things;

I am the whirl of star dust,
I am the lift of wings.

"I am the splendid impulse
That comes before the thought,
The joy and exaltation
Wherein the life is caught.

"Across the sleeping furrows
I call the buried seed,
And blade and bud and blossom
Awaken at my need.

"Within the dying ashes
I blow the sacred spark,
And make the hearts of lovers
To leap against the dark."

II

I heard the spring light whisper
Above the dancing stream,
"The world is made forever
In likeness of a dream.

"I am the law of planets,
I am the guide of man;
The evening and the morning
Are fashioned to my plan.

"I tint the dawn with crimson,
I tinge the sea with blue;
My track is in the desert,
My trail is in the dew.

"I paint the hills with colour,
And in my magic dome
I light the star of evening
To steer the traveller home.

"Within the house of being,
I feed the lamp of truth
With tales of ancient wisdom
And prophecies of youth."

III

I heard the spring rain murmur
Above the roadside flower,
"The world is made forever
In melody and power.

"I keep the rhythmic measure
That marks the steps of time,
And all my toil is fashioned
To symmetry and rhyme.

"I plow the untilled upland,
I ripe the seeding grass,
And fill the leafy forest
With music as I pass.

"I hew the raw, rough granite
To loveliness of line,
And when my work is finished,
Behold, it is divine!

"I am the master-builder
In whom the ages trust.
I lift the lost perfection
To blossom from the dust."

IV

Then Earth to them made answer,
As with a slow refrain
Born of the blended voices
Of wind and sun and rain,

"This is the law of being
That links the threefold chain:
The life we give to beauty
Returns to us again."

May 1913
April Airs: A Book of New England Lyrics, 1916

SORCERY

Under grey skies the mirror of the lake
Reflects the misty flush of the young leaves.
From its smooth lip the pastel woodlands rise
In the soft-tinted loveliness of May
Over the dark-stemmed brushwood Spring has thrown
Her impalpable veil of changing green and red,
Like an elusive sorceress who lays
Her spell of wonder on a waiting world.

And all her lovers who had half forgot
Her beauty must arise and follow her,
Enthralled as ever by her witchery.
A breath of wind comes ruffling the smooth lake
And strews the white plum-blossoms on the grass,
Stirring old transports, and is still again.

24 May 1917
Sanctuary, 1929

VESTIGIA

I took a day to search for God,
And found Him not. But as I trod
By rocky ledge, through woods untamed,
Just where one scarlet lily flamed,
I saw His footprint in the sod.

Then suddenly, all unaware,
Far off in the deep shadows, where
A solitary hermit thrush
Sang through the holy twilight hush—
I heard His voice upon the air.

And even as I marvelled how
God gives us Heaven here and now,
In a stir of wind that hardly shook
The poplar leaves beside the brook—
His hand was light upon my brow.

At last with evening as I turned
Homeward, and thought what I had learned
And all that there was still to probe—
I caught the glory of His robe
Where the last fires of sunset burned.

Back to the world with quickening start
I looked and longed for any part

In making saving Beauty be . . .
And from that kindling ecstasy
I knew God dwelt within my heart.

20 July 1920
Later Poems, 1921

THE SHIPS OF SAINT JOHN[1]

(Second Version)

Where are the ships I used to know,
That came to port on the Fundy tide
Half a century ago,
In beauty and stately pride?

In they would come past the beacon light,
With the sun on gleaming sail and spar,
Folding their wings like birds in flight
From countries strange and far.

Schooner and brig and barkentine,
I watched them slow as the sails were furled,
And wondered what cities they must have seen
On the other side of the world.

Frenchman and Britisher and Dane,
Yankee, Spaniard and Portugee,
And many a home ship back again
With her stories of the sea.

Calm and victorious, at rest
From the relentless, rough sea-play,
The wild duck on the river's breast
Was not more sure than they.

[1]The first version, titled "The Ships of St. John", written on 29 August 1893 (with a different final stanza), appeared in *Canadian Magazine,* December 1893, and in *Ballads of Lost Haven: A Book of the Sea* (1897); the poem was revised in July 1921.

The creatures of a passing race,
The dark spruce forests made them strong,
The sea's lore gave them magic grace,
The great winds taught them song.

And God endowed them each with life—
His blessing on the craftsman's skill—
To meet the blind unreasoned strife
And dare the risk of ill.

Not mere insensate wood and paint
Obedient to the helm's command,
But often restive as a saint
Beneath the Heavenly hand.

All the beauty and mystery
Of life were there, adventure bold,
Youth, and the glamour of the sea
And all its sorrows old.

And many a time I saw them go
Out on the flood at morning brave,
As the little tugs had them in tow,
And the sunlight danced on the wave.

There all day long you could hear the sound
Of the caulking iron, the ship's bronze bell,
And the clank of the capstan going round
As the great tides rose and fell.

The sailors' songs, the Captain's shout,
The boatswain's whistle piping shrill,
And the roar as the anchor chain runs out,—
I often hear them still.

I can see them still, the sun on their gear,
The shining streak as the hulls careen,
And the flag at the peak unfurling,—clear
As a picture on a screen.

The fog still hangs on the long tide-rips,
The gulls go wavering to and fro,
But where are all the beautiful ships
I knew so long ago?

July 1921
Later Poems, 1921

A MIRAGE OF THE PLAINS

As I stood on the bank of the river that runs by Saskatoon,
I saw the incredible happen in the sober light of noon.

I looked out over the prairie as far as the eye could see,
And never a stone as big as your hand, and never the sign of a
tree;
Only the golden stubble with the first light snow between,
In the fairy light of a primal world where beauty first was
seen.

Then far on the dipped horizon where the sailing cloud-tops
show,
I saw, like a ghost in the sunlight, a prairie schooner go.
And after her laboured others in a trailing caravan—
Lumbering, crude, ill-fitted—but they carried the hope of
man.

A marvellous train unnumbered, swinging before my gaze,
They passed on into the sundown, and were lost in the lilac
haze.
I cleared my eyes of the vision—or the tremor of
sunlit-glare—
Only the golden stubble and the sailing clouds were there.

Again I looked to the Northward as far as the eye could
range,
And never a rise nor a foothill, never a hint of change,
Till a picture rose before me like a mirage at sea,
Or those wonders of incantation from Indian jugglery.

And I beheld no longer the voyaging clouds hull-down,
But towers of beautiful cities and homes of many a town,
And over them all was gladness and peace and freedom from
care,
And I heard the laughter of children ring on the frosty air.

And over the whispering snowdrift a clear far-off voice said,
"No man shall injure his neighbour, and none shall make you
afraid.
Lo, I am with you always unto the end of the world."
Then, as the vision faded, the sails of the clouds were furled.

And there, all round about me, real in the noonday sun,
Stood Houses of Learning and Beauty—the vision's
fulfillment begun.

1 March 1922
Far Horizons, 1925

MAY IN THE SELKIRKS

Up the Illecillewaet and down the Yellow Beaver,
Over skyward passes, where snow-peaks touch the blue;
Shining silver rivers dropping down from heaven,
With the spring-call of the wilderness waking life anew.
Far gleaming glaciers, like the gates of glory,
And the hosts in new green marching up the slopes,
Organ-voiced torrents singing through the gorges,
Songs for the high trail and visions for our hopes.
Hints of light supernal on the rocky ledges,
Echoes of wild music from the valley floors,
And the tall evergreens watching at the threshold—
Keeping the silence of the Lord of out-of-doors.
Balm out of Paradise blown across the canyons,
From the balsam-poplar buds and bronze leaves uncurled,
Soul in her wonder lifts a new magnificat,
Alight with the rapture of the morning of the world.

c. 1929
Saturday Evening Post, 29 May 1929
The Music of the Earth and *Bliss Carman's Poems*, both 1931

Archibald Lampman

1861–1899

Of United Empire Loyalist stock, Lampman was, like Campbell and Roberts, the son of an Anglican priest. Born in Morpeth, Canada West (Ontario), he grew up in eastern Ontario. In 1868 he suffered an attack of rheumatic fever. At the University of Toronto he studied classics, graduating in 1882, and in the following year he obtained a clerkship in the Post Office Department in Ottawa, where he worked until his early death in 1899. Married in 1887, he had two children. In Ottawa, he formed a firm friendship with W.W. Campbell and D.C. Scott, with whom he collaborated on "At the Mermaid Inn", a column in the *Toronto Globe* (1892-3). It was Scott who was to edit a collection of Lampman's poems in 1900. The Ottawa region provided him with much of his poetic inspiration and happiness experienced on various canoe trips, and it formed the background for many of his poems, which display a considerable degree of influence of the English Romantics.

Lampman's first book (*Among the Millet*, 1888) did much to establish his reputation as a poet of considerable sensitivity and skill. Certainly, the volume contains much in the Romantic vein, such as in "Heat", "Among the Timothy", and "Frogs"; but even to those there is more than simple Canadian ruralism and a one-sided view that perceives only the more sublime and comforting side of the natural world. "Among the Timothy", for instance, makes reference to an urban world that prompts escape to the pastoral realm: "The echoing city towers,/ The blind grey streets, the jingle of the throng ..." where one finds "... barren search and toil that beareth nought". These touches herald the darker and far more socially critical view that permeates some of his later works, for example, "The City of the End of Things". "The Railway Station", with its urban realism, acknowledges the presence of "dark distresses" as well as "passionate dreams". "The Modern Politician", which speaks tellingly of "the transit age" and "unnumbered broken hearts" reminiscent of Campbell's "The Politician", also offers a clear indication of Lampman's sober strain.

Thus it is unwise to generalise about Lampman's romanticism by suggesting that what might appear to be a quasi-Arnoldian view only came with growing maturity in his last years, along with a rejection of the notion of the restorative powers of the natural world. In "Alcyone", for instance, contemplation of the celestial realm offers "... shelter and a peace majestical" despite the earthly ties, the "half-blind toils", "little aims", and "little span", and even the chilling narrative of "At the Long Sault: May 1660" ends in pastoral repose. What becomes clear is Lampman's sense of the spiritual world, divine benevolence, and a goodness which will emerge beyond all the temporal strife; read, for example, "The Clearer Self".

Aside from thematic issues, one characteristic of much of Lampman's work is an apparent easy control over forms, especially—but not exclusively—the sonnet. There are those who might argue that, in terms of metrics, he is a conservative, a traditionalist; but it is productive to consider how well he worked within his chosen structures. His diction and imagery, often remarkably striking for their incisive simplicity, display genuine strength. And poems like "Alcyone", "The City of the End of Things", and "At the Long Sault" clearly demonstrate that he was comfortable with the long poem form. It is tantalising to imagine what might have come from his pen over another decade, yet what we have is of considerable impact and importance, well demonstrating the growing vitality of the Canadian poetic craft.

A scholarly edition of Lampman's poetry is being prepared; the definitive works to date remain *The Poems of Archibald Lampman*, ed. Duncan Campbell Scott (1900) and *The Poems of Archibald Lampman*, with an introduction by Margaret Coulby Whitridge (1974; reprint of the 1900 edition, including *At the Long Sault and Other New Poems*). "Twenty-Five Fugitive Poems by Archibald Lampman", edited by L.R. Early, were published in *Canadian Poetry* 12 (Spring-Summer 1983), 46-70. A fine selection of his poetry is Michael Gnarowski's *Selected Poetry of Archibald Lampman* (1990). Major manuscript holdings may be found at: Library of Parliament, Ottawa; The Lampman Papers, Public Archives of Canada, Ottawa; Queen's University, Kingston; and Simon Fraser University, Burnaby. Early poetry is located at Trinity College, University of Toronto, Toronto.

Works on Lampman include: Carl Y. Connor, *Archibald Lampman: Canadian Poet of Nature* (1920); E.K. Brown, "Archibald Lampman" in *On Canadian Poetry* (1944), 88-118; Michael Gnarowski, ed., *Archibald Lampman* (1970); *The Lampman Symposium* (1976), ed. Lorraine McMullen; D.M.R. Bentley, "Watchful Dreams and Sweet Unrest: An Essay on the Vision of Archibald Lampman", *Studies in Canadian Literature* 6 (1981), 188-210, and 7 (1982), 5-26; L.R. Early, *Archibald Lampman and His Works* (1983) and *Archibald Lampman* (1986); Eric Ball, "Life 'Only Sweet': The Significance of the Sequence in Lampman's *Lyrics of Earth*", *Canadian Poetry* 25 (Fall-Winter 1989), 1-20, and 26 (Spring Summer 1990), 19-42.

APRIL

Pale season, watcher in unvexed suspense,
Still priestess of the patient middle day,
Betwixt wild March's humoured petulance
And the warm wooing of green kirtled May,
Maid month of sunny peace and sober grey,
Weaver of flowers in sunward glades that ring
With murmur of libation to the spring:

As memory of pain, all past, is peace,
And joy, dream-tasted, hath the deepest cheer,
So art thou sweetest of all months that lease
The twelve short spaces of the flying year.
The bloomless days are dead, and frozen fear
No more for many moons shall vex the earth,
Dreaming of summer and fruit laden mirth.

The grey song-sparrows full of spring have sung
Their clear thin silvery tunes in leafless trees;
The robin hops, and whistles, and among
The silver-tasseled poplars the brown bees
Murmur faint dreams of summer harvestries;
The creamy sun at even scatters down
A gold-green mist across the murmuring town.

By the slow streams the frogs all day and night
Dream without thought of pain or heed of ill,
Watching the long warm silent hours take flight,
And ever with soft throats that pulse and thrill,
From the pale-weeded shallows trill and trill,
Tremulous sweet voices, flute-like, answering
One to another glorying in the spring.

All day across the ever-cloven soil,
Strong horses labour, steaming in the sun,
Down the long furrows with slow straining toil,
Turning the brown clean layers; and one by one
The crows gloom over them till daylight done
Finds them asleep somewhere in duskèd lines
Beyond the wheatlands in the northern pines.

The old year's cloaking of brown leaves, that bind
The forest floor-ways, plated close and true—
The last love's labour of the autumn wind—
Is broken with curled flower buds white and blue

In all the matted hollows, and speared through
With thousand serpent-spotted blades up-sprung,
Yet bloomless, of the slender adder-tongue.

In the warm noon the south wind creeps and cools,
Where the red-budded stems of maples throw
Still tangled etchings on the amber pools,
Quite silent now, forgetful of the slow
Drip of the taps, the troughs, and trampled snow,
The keen March mornings, and the silvering rime
And mirthful labour of the sugar prime.

Ah, I have wandered with unwearied feet,
All the long sweetness of an April day,
Lulled with cool murmurs and the drowsy beat
Of partridge wings in secret thickets grey,
The marriage hymns of all the birds at play,
The faces of sweet flowers, and easeful dreams
Beside slow reaches of frog-haunted streams;

Wandered with happy feet, and quite forgot
The shallow toil, the strife against the grain,
Near souls, that hear us call, but answer not,
The loneliness, perplexity and pain,
And high thoughts cankered with an earthly stain
And then the long draught emptied to the lees,
I turn me homeward in slow pacing ease,

Cleaving the cedar shadows and the thin
Mist of grey gnats that cloud the river shore,
Sweet even choruses, that dance and spin
Soft tangles in the sunset; and once more
The city smites me with its dissonant roar.
To its hot heart I pass, untroubled yet,
Fed with calm hope, without desire or fret.

So to the year's first altar step I bring
Gifts of meek song, and make my spirit free
With the blind working of unanxious spring,
Careless with her, whether the days that flee
Pale drouth or golden-fruited plenty see,
So that we toil, brothers, without distress,
In calm-eyed peace and godlike blamelessness.

May 1884
Among the Millet and Other Poems, 1888

IN OCTOBER

Along the waste, a great way off, the pines,
Like tall slim priests of storm, stand up and bar
The low long strip of dolorous red that lines
The under west, where wet winds moan afar.
The cornfields all are brown, and brown the meadows
With the blown leaves' wind-heapèd traceries,
And the brown thistle stems that cast no shadows,
And bear no bloom for bees.

As slowly earthward leaf by red leaf slips,
The sad trees rustle in chill misery,
A soft strange inner sound of pain-crazed lips,
That move and murmur incoherently;
As if all leaves, that yet have breath, were sighing,
With pale hushed throats, for death is at the door,
So many low soft masses for the dying
Sweet leaves that live no more.

Here I will sit upon this naked stone,
Draw my coat closer with my numbèd hands,
And hear the ferns sigh, and the wet woods moan,
And send my heart out to the ashen lands;
And I will ask myself what golden madness,
What balmèd breaths of dreamland spicery,
What visions of soft laughter and light sadness
Were sweet last month to me.

The dry dead leaves flit by with thin weird tunes,
Like failing murmurs of some conquered creed,
Graven in mystic markings with strange runes,
That none but stars and biting winds may read;
Here I will wait a little; I am weary,
Not torn with pain of any lurid hue,
But only still and very grey and dreary,
Sweet sombre lands, like you.

c. 1884
Among the Millet and Other Poems, 1888

AMONG THE TIMOTHY

Long hours ago, while yet the morn was blithe,
  Nor sharp athirst had drunk the beaded dew,
A reaper came, and swung his cradled scythe
  Around this stump, and, shearing slowly, drew
  Far round among the clover, ripe for hay,
    A circle clean and grey;
And here among the scented swathes that gleam,
  Mixed with dead daisies, it is sweet to lie
  And watch the grass and the few-clouded sky,
    Nor think but only dream.

For when the noon was turning, and the heat
  Fell down most heavily on field and wood,
I too came hither, borne on restless feet,
  Seeking some comfort for an aching mood.
  Ah, I was weary of the drifting hours,
    The echoing city towers,
The blind grey streets, the jingle of the throng,
  Weary of hope that like a shape of stone
  Sat near at hand without a smile or moan,
    And weary most of song.

And those high moods of mine that sometime made
  My heart a heaven, opening like a flower,
A sweeter world where I in wonder strayed,
  Begirt with shapes of beauty and the power
  Of dreams that moved through that enchanted clime
    With changing breaths of rhyme,
Were all gone lifeless now like those white leaves
  That hang all winter, shivering dead and blind
  Among the sinewy beeches in the wind,
    That vainly calls and grieves.

Ah! I will set no more mine overtaskèd brain
  To barren search and toil that beareth nought,
Forever following with sorefooted pain
  The crossing pathways of unbournèd thought;
  But let it go, as one that hath no skill,
    To take what shape it will,
An ant slow-burrowing in the earthy gloom,
  A spider bathing in the dew at morn,
  Or a brown bee in wayward fancy borne
    From hidden bloom to bloom.

Hither and thither o'er the rocking grass
  The little breezes, blithe as they are blind,
Teasing the slender blossoms pass and pass,
  Soft-footed children of the gipsy wind,
  To taste of every purple-fringèd head
    Before the bloom is dead;
And scarcely heed the daisies that, endowed
  With stems so short they cannot see, up-bear
  Their innocent sweet eyes distressed, and stare
    Like children in a crowd.

Not far to fieldward in the central heat,
  Shadowing the clover, a pale poplar stands
With glimmering leaves that, when the wind comes, beat
  Together like innumerable small hands,
  And with the calm, as in vague dreams astray,
    Hang wan and silver-grey;
Like sleepy maenads, who in pale surprise,
  Half-wakened by a prowling beast, have crept
  Out of the hidden covert, where they slept,
    At noon with languid eyes.

The crickets creak, and through the noonday glow,
  That crazy fiddler of the hot mid-year,
The dry cicada plies his wiry bow
  In long-spun cadence, thin and dusty sere:
  From the green grass the small grasshoppers' din
    Spreads soft and silvery thin:
And ever and anon a murmur steals
  Into mine ears of toil that moves away,
  The crackling rustle of the pitch-forked hay
    And lazy jerk of wheels.

As so I lie and feel the soft hours wane,
  To wind and sun and peaceful sound laid bare,
That aching dim discomfort of the brain
  Fades off unseen, and shadowy-footed care
  Into some hidden corner creeps at last
    To slumber deep and fast;
And gliding on, quite fashioned to forget,
  From dream to dream I bid my spirit pass
  Out into the pale green ever-swaying grass
    To brood, but no more fret.

And hour by hour among all shapes that grow
  Of purple mints and daisies gemmed with gold
In sweet unrest my visions come and go;
  I feel and hear and with quiet eyes behold;

And hour by hour, the ever-journeying sun,
In gold and shadow spun,
Into mine eyes and blood, and through the dim
Green glimmering forest of the grass shines down,
Till flower and blade, and every cranny brown,
And I are soaked with him.

5 August 1885
Among the Millet and Other Poems, 1888

THE FROGS

I

Breathers of wisdom won without a quest,
Quaint uncouth dreamers, voices high and strange,
Flutists of lands where beauty hath no change,
And wintery grief is a forgotten guest,
Sweet murmurers of everlasting rest,
For whom glad days have ever yet to run,
And moments are as aeons, and the sun
But ever sunken half-way toward the west.

Often to me who heard you in your day,
With close wrapt[1] ears, it could not choose but seem
That earth, our mother, searching in what way,
Men's hearts might know her spirit's inmost dream,
Ever at rest beneath life's change and stir,
Made you her soul, and bade you pipe for her.

II

In those mute days when spring was in her glee,
And hope was strong, we knew not why or how,
And earth, the mother, dreamed with brooding brow,
Musing on life, and what the hours might be,
When love should ripen to maternity,

[1]Lampman uses this spelling to mean "enveloped". It was changed to "rapt" by D.C. Scott in his 1900 edition of Lampman's poems (Gnarowski, *Selected Poetry of Archibald Lampman*, 1990; p. 106).

Then like high flutes in silvery interchange
Ye piped with voices still and sweet and strange,
And ever as ye piped, on every tree

The great buds swelled; among the pensive woods
The spirits of first flowers awoke and flung
From buried faces the close fitting hoods,
And listened to your piping till they fell,
The frail spring-beauty with her perfumed bell,
The wind-flower, and the spotted adder-tongue.

III

All the day long, wherever pools might be
Among the golden meadows, where the air
Stood in a dream, as it were moorèd there
Forever in a noon-tide reverie,
Or where the birds made riot of their glee
In the still woods, and the hot sun shone down,
Crossed with warm lucent shadows on the brown
Leaf-paven pools, that bubbled dreamily,

Or far away in whispering river meads
And watery marshes where the brooding noon,
Full with the wonder of its own sweet boon,
Nestled and slept among the noiseless reeds,
Ye sat and murmured, motionless as they,
With eyes that dreamed beyond the night and day.

IV

And when day passed and over heaven's height,
Thin with the many stars and cool with dew,
The fingers of the deep hours slowly drew
The wonder of the ever-healing night,
No grief or loneliness or wrapt delight
Or weight of silence ever brought to you
Slumber or rest; only your voices grew
More high and solemn; slowly with hushed flight

Ye saw the echoing hours go by, long-drawn,
Nor ever stirred, watching with fathomless eyes,
And with your countless clear antiphonies
Filling the earth and heaven, even till dawn,
Last-risen, found you with its first pale gleam,
Still with soft throats unaltered in your dream.

V

And slowly as we heard you, day by day,
The stillness of enchanted reveries
Bound brain and spirit and half-closed eyes,
In some divine sweet wonder-dream astray;
To us no sorrow or upreared dismay
Nor any discord came, but evermore
The voices of mankind, the outer roar,
Grew strange and murmurous, faint and far away.

Morning and noon and midnight exquisitely,
Wrapt with your voices, this alone we knew,
Cities might change and fall, and men might die,
Secure were we, content to dream with you,
That change and pain are shadows faint and fleet,
And dreams are real, and life is only sweet.

May 1887
Among the Millet and Other Poems, 1888

FREEDOM

Out of the heart of the city begotten
Of the labour of men and their manifold hands,
Whose souls, that were sprung from the earth in her morning,
No longer regard or remember her warning,
Whose hearts in the furnace of care have forgotten
Forever the scent and the hue of her lands;

Out of the heat of the usurer's hold,
From the horrible crash of the strong man's feet;
Out of the shadow where pity is dying;
Out of the clamour where beauty is lying,
Dead in the depth of the struggle for gold;
Out of the din and the glare of the street;

Into the arms of our mother we come,
Our broad strong mother, the innocent earth,
Mother of all things beautiful, blameless,
Mother of hopes that her strength makes tameless,

Where the voices of grief and of battle are dumb,
And the whole world laughs with the light of her mirth.

Over the fields, where the cool winds sweep,
Black with the mould and brown with the loam,
Where the thin green spears of the wheat are appearing,
And the high-ho shouts from the smoky clearing;
Over the widths where the cloud shadows creep;
Over the fields and the fallows we come;

Over the swamps with their pensive noises,
Where the burnished cup of the marigold gleams;
Skirting the reeds, where the quick winds shiver
On the swelling breast of the dimpled river,
And the blue of the king-fisher hangs and poises,
Watching a spot by the edge of the streams;

By the miles of the fences warped and dyed
With the white-hot noons and their withering fires,
Where the rough bees trample the creamy bosoms
Of the hanging tufts of the elder blossoms,
And the spiders weave, and the grey snakes hide,
In the crannied gloom of the stones and the briers;

Over the meadow lands sprouting with thistle,
Where the humming wings of the blackbirds pass,
Where the hollows are banked with the violets flowering,
And the long-limbed pendulous elms are towering,
Where the robins are loud with their voluble whistle,
And the ground sparrow scurries away through the grass,

Where the restless bobolink loiters and woos
Down in the hollows and over the swells,
Dropping in and out of the shadows,
Sprinkling his music about the meadows,
Whistles and little checks and coos,
And the tinkle of glassy bells;

Into the dim woods full of the tombs
Of the dead trees soft in their sepulchres,
Where the pensive throats of the shy birds hidden,
Pipe to us strangely entering unbidden,
And tenderly still in the tremulous glooms
The trilliums scatter their white-winged stars;

Up to the hills where our tired hearts rest,
Loosen, and halt, and regather their dreams;
Up to the hills, where the winds restore us,
Clearing our eyes to the beauty before us,

Earth with the glory of life on her breast,
Earth with the gleam of her cities and streams.

Here we shall commune with her and no other;
Care and the battle of life shall cease;
Men her degenerate children behind us,
Only the might of her beauty shall bind us,
Full of rest, as we gaze on the face of our mother,
Earth in the health and the strength of her peace.

June 1887
Among the Millet and Other Poems, 1888

HEAT

From plains that reel to southward, dim,
The road runs by me white and bare;
Up the steep hill it seems to swim
Beyond, and melt into the glare.
Upward half way, or it may be
Nearer the summit, slowly steals
A hay-cart, moving dustily
With idly clacking wheels.

By his cart's side the wagoner
Is slouching slowly at his ease,
Half-hidden in the windless blur
Of white dust puffing to his knees.
This wagon on the height above,
From sky to sky on either hand,
Is the sole thing that seems to move
In all the heat-held land.

Beyond me in the fields the sun
Soaks in the grass and hath his will;
I count the marguerites one by one;
Even the buttercups are still.
On the brook yonder not a breath
Disturbs the spider or the midge.
The water-bugs draw close beneath
The cool gloom of the bridge.

Where the far elm-tree shadows flood
  Dark patches in the burning grass,
The cows, each with her peaceful cud,
  Lie waiting for the heat to pass.
From somewhere on the slope near by
  Into the pale depth of the noon
A wandering thrush slides leisurely
  His thin revolving tune.

In intervals of dreams I hear
  The cricket from the droughty ground;
The grass-hoppers spin into mine ear
    A small innumerable sound.
I lift mine eyes sometimes to gaze:
  The burning sky-line blinds my sight:
The woods far off are blue with haze:
  The hills are drenched in light.

And yet to me not this or that
  Is always sharp or always sweet;
In the sloped shadow of my hat
  I lean at rest, and drain the heat;
Nay more, I think some blessèd power
  Hath brought me wandering idly here:
In the full furnace of this hour
  My thoughts grow keen and clear.

July 1887
Among the Millet and Other Poems, 1888

THE RAILWAY STATION

The darkness brings no quiet here, the light
  No waking: ever on my blinded brain
  The flare of lights, the rush, and cry, and strain,
The engines' scream, the hiss and thunder smite:
I see the hurrying crowds, the clasp, the flight,
  Faces that touch, eyes that are dim with pain:

I see the hoarse wheels turn, and the great train
Move labouring out into the bourneless night.

So many souls within its dim recesses,
So many bright, so many mournful eyes:
Mine eyes that watch grow fixed with dreams and guesses;
What threads of life, what hidden histories,
What sweet or passionate dreams and dark distresses,
What unknown thoughts, what various agonies!

c. 1887
The Week, 22 December 1887
Among the Millet and Other Poems, 1888

WINTER EVENING

To-night the very horses springing by
Toss gold from whitened nostrils. In a dream
The streets that narrow to the westward gleam
Like rows of golden palaces; and high
From all the crowded chimneys tower and die
A thousand aureoles. Down in the west
The brimming plains beneath the sunset rest,
One burning sea of gold. Soon, soon shall fly
The glorious vision, and the hours shall feel
A mightier master; soon from height to height,
With silence and the sharp unpitying stars,
Stern creeping frosts, and winds that touch like steel,
Out of the depth beyond the eastern bars,
Glittering and still shall come the awful night.

4 January 1888
Scribner's, December 1888
Alcyone, 1899

COMFORT OF THE FIELDS

What would'st thou have for easement after grief,
    When the rude world hath used thee with despite,
    And care sits at thine elbow day and night,
Filching thy pleasures like a subtle thief?
To me, when life besets me in such wise,
'Tis sweetest to break forth, to drop the chain,
    And grasp the freedom of this pleasant earth,
    To roam in idleness and sober mirth,
Through summer airs and summer lands, and drain
The comfort of wide fields unto tired eyes.

By hills and waters, farms and solitudes,
    To wander by the day with wilful feet;
    Through fielded valleys wide with yellowing wheat;
Along grey roads that run between deep woods,
Murmurous and cool; through hallowed slopes of pine,
    Where the long daylight dreams, unpierced, unstirred,
    And only the rich-throated thrush is heard;
By lonely forest brooks that froth and shine
    In bouldered crannies buried in the hills;
By broken beeches tangled with wild vine,
    And log-strewn rivers murmurous with mills.

In upland pastures, sown with gold, and sweet
    With the keen perfume of the ripening grass,
    Where wings of birds and filmy shadows pass,
Spread thick as stars with shining marguerite;
To haunt old fences overgrown with brier,
    Muffled in vines, and hawthorns, and wild cherries,
    Rank poisonous ivies, red-bunched elderberries,
And pièd blossoms to the heart's desire,
    Grey mullein towering into yellow bloom,
    Pink-tasseled milkweed, breathing dense perfume,
And swarthy vervain, tipped with violet fire.

To hear at eve the bleating of far flocks,
    The mud-hen's whistle from the marsh at morn;
    To skirt with deafened ears and brain o'erborne
Some foam-filled rapid charging down its rocks
With iron roar of waters; far away
    Across side-reeded meres, pensive with noon,
    To hear the querulous outcry of the loon;

To lie among deep rocks, and watch all day
        On liquid heights the snowy clouds melt by;
Or hear from wood-capped mountain-brows the jay
        Pierce the bright morning with his jibing cry.

To feast on summer sounds; the jolted wains,
        The thrasher humming from the farm near by,
        The prattling cricket's intermittent cry,
The locust's rattle from the sultry lanes;
Or in the shadow of some oaken spray,
        To watch, as through a mist of light and dreams,
        The far-off hay-fields, where the dusty teams
Drive round and round the lessening squares of hay,
        And hear upon the wind, now loud, now low,
With drowsy cadence half a summer's day,
        The clatter of the reapers come and go.

Far violet hills, horizons filmed with showers,
        The murmur of cool streams, the forest's gloom,
        The voices of the breathing grass, the hum
Of ancient gardens overbanked with flowers:
Thus, with a smile as golden as the dawn,
        And cool fair fingers radiantly divine,
        The mighty mother brings us in her hand,
For all tired eyes and foreheads pinched and wan,
Her restful cup, her beaker of bright wine:
    Drink, and be filled, and ye shall understand!

July 1889
Scribner's, February 1892
Lyrics of Earth, 1895

IN NOVEMBER

With loitering step and quiet eye,
Beneath the low November sky,
I wandered in the woods, and found
A clearing, where the broken ground
Was scattered with black stumps and briers,
And the old wreck of forest fires.
It was a bleak and sandy spot,
And, all about, the vacant plot
Was peopled and inhabited
By scores of mulleins long since dead.
A silent and forsaken brood
In that mute opening of the wood,
So shrivelled and so thin they were,
So grey, so haggard, and austere,
Not plants at all they seemed to me,
But rather some spare company
Of hermit folk, who long ago,
Wandering in bodies to and fro,
Had chanced upon this lonely way,
And rested thus, till death one day
Surprised them at their compline prayer,
And left them standing lifeless there.

There was no sound about the wood
Save the wind's secret stir. I stood
Among the mullein-stalks as still
As if myself had grown to be
One of their sombre company,
A body without wish or will.
And as I stood, quite suddenly,
Down from a furrow in the sky
The sun shone out a little space
Across that silent sober place,
Over the sand heaps and brown sod,
The mulleins and dead goldenrod,
And passed beyond the thickets grey,
And lit the fallen leaves that lay,
Level and deep within the wood,
A rustling yellow multitude.

And all around me the thin light,
So sere, so melancholy bright,

Fell like the half-reflected gleam
Or shadow of some former dream;
A moment's golden reverie
Poured out on every plant and tree
A semblance of weird joy, or less,
A sort of spectral happiness;
And I, too, standing idly there,
With muffled hands in the chill air,
Felt the warm glow about my feet,
And shuddering betwixt cold and heat,
Drew my thoughts closer, like a cloak,
While something in my blood awoke,
A nameless and unnatural cheer,
A pleasure secret and austere.

November 1889
Harper's, November 1890
Lyrics of Earth, 1895

AFTER RAIN

For three whole days across the sky,
In sullen packs that loomed and broke,
With flying fringes dim as smoke,
The columns of the rain went by;
At every hour the wind awoke;
    The darkness passed upon the plain;
    The great drops rattled at the pane.

Now piped the wind, or far aloof
Fell to a sough remote and dull;
And all night long with rush and lull
The rain kept drumming on the roof:
I heard till ear and sense were full
    The clash or silence of the leaves,
    The gurgle in the creaking eaves.

But when the fourth day came—at noon,
The darkness and the rain were by;
The sunward roofs were steaming dry;
And all the world was flecked and strewn

With shadows from a fleecy sky.
    The haymakers were forth and gone,
    And every rillet laughed and shone.

Then, too, on me that loved so well
The world, despairing in her blight,
Uplifted with her least delight,
On me, as on the earth, there fell
New happiness of mirth and might;
    I strode the valleys pied and still;
    I climbed upon the breezy hill.

I watched the grey hawk wheel and drop,
Sole shadow on the shining world;
I saw the mountains clothed and curled,
With forest ruffling to the top;
I saw the river's length unfurled,
    Pale silver down the fruited plain,
    Grown great and stately with the rain.

Through miles of shadow and soft heat,
Where field and fallow, fence and tree,
Were all one world of greenery,
I heard the robin ringing sweet,
The sparrow piping silverly,
    The thrushes at the forest's hem;
    And as I went I sang with them.

c. 1889
Lyrics of Earth, 1895

A JANUARY MORNING

The glittering roofs are still with frost; each worn
Black chimney builds into the quiet sky
Its curling pile to crumble silently.
Far out to westward on the edge of morn,
The slender misty city towers up-borne
Glimmer faint rose against the pallid blue;
And yonder on those northern hills, the hue

Of amethyst, hang fleeces dull as horn.
And here behind me come the woodmen's sleighs
With shouts and clamorous squeakings; might and main
Up the steep slope the horses stamp and strain,
Urged on by hoarse-tongued drivers—cheeks ablaze,
Iced beards and frozen eyelids—team by team,
With frost-fringed flanks, and nostrils jetting steam.

c. 1889
The Poems of Archibald Lampman, 1900

THE MODERN POLITICIAN

What manner of soul is his to whom high truth
Is but the plaything of a feverish hour,
A dangling ladder to the ghost of power!
Gone are the grandeurs of the world's iron youth,
When kings were mighty, being made by swords.
Now comes the transit age, the age of brass,
When clowns into the vacant empires pass,
Blinding the multitude with specious words.
To them faith, kinship, truth and verity,
Man's sacred rights and very holiest thing,
Are but the counters at a desperate play,
Flippant and reckless what the end may be,
So that they glitter, each his little day,
The little mimic of a vanished king.

1 December 1890
The Week, 30 November 1894
The Poems of Archibald Lampman, 1900

VOICES OF EARTH

We have not heard the music of the spheres,
The song of star to star, but there are sounds
More deep than human joy and human tears,
That Nature uses in her common rounds;
The fall of streams, the cry of winds that strain
The oak, the roaring of the sea's surge, might
Of thunder breaking afar off, or rain
That falls by minutes in the summer night.
These are the voices of earth's secret soul,
Uttering the mystery from which she came.
To him who hears them grief beyond control,
Or joy inscrutable without a name,
Wakes in his heart thoughts bedded there, impearled,
Before the birth and making of the world.

March 1891
Scribner's, October 1891
Alcyone, 1899

ON THE COMPANIONSHIP WITH NATURE

Let us be much with Nature; not as they
That labour without seeing, that employ
Her unloved forces, blindly without joy;
Nor those whose hands and crude delights obey
The old brute passion to hunt down and slay;
But rather as children of one common birth,
Discerning in each natural fruit of earth
Kinship and bond with this diviner clay.
Let us be with her wholly at all hours,
With the fond lover's zest, who is content

If his ear hears, and if his eye but sees;
So shall we grow like her in mould and bent,
Our bodies stately as her blessèd trees,
Our thoughts as sweet and sumptuous as her flowers.

June 1892
Youth's Companion, 1 December 1892
The Poems of Archibald Lampman, 1900

THE CITY OF THE END OF THINGS

Beside the pounding cataracts
Of midnight streams unknown to us
'Tis builded in the leafless tracts
And valleys huge of Tartarus.
Lurid and lofty and vast it seems;
It hath no rounded name that rings,
But I have heard it called in dreams
The City of the End of Things.

Its roofs and iron towers have grown
None knoweth how high within the night,
But in its murky streets far down
A flaming terrible and bright
Shakes all the stalking shadows there,
Across the walls, across the floors,
And shifts upon the upper air
From out a thousand furnace doors;
And all the while an awful sound
Keeps roaring on continually,
And crashes in the ceaseless round
Of a gigantic harmony.
Through its grim depths re-echoing
And all its weary height of walls,
With measured roar and iron ring,
The inhuman music lifts and falls.
Where no thing rests and no man is,
And only fire and night hold sway;
The beat, the thunder and the hiss

Cease not, and change not, night nor day.
And moving at unheard commands,
The abysses and vast fires between,
Flit figures that with clanking hands
Obey a hideous routine;
They are not flesh, they are not bone,
They see not with the human eye,
And from their iron lips is blown
A dreadful and monotonous cry;
And whoso of our mortal race
Should find that city unaware,
Lean Death would smite him face to face,
And blanch him with its venomed air:
Or caught by the terrific spell,
Each thread of memory snapt and cut,
His soul would shrivel and its shell
Go rattling like an empty nut.

It was not always so, but once,
In days that no man thinks upon,
Fair voices echoed from its stones,
The light above it leaped and shone:
Once there were multitudes of men,
That built that city in their pride,
Until its might was made, and then
They withered age by age and died.
But now of that prodigious race,
Three only in an iron tower,
Set like carved idols face to face,
Remain the masters of its power;
And at the city gate a fourth,
Gigantic and with dreadful eyes,
Sits looking toward the lightless north,
Beyond the reach of memories;
Fast rooted to the lurid floor,
A bulk that never moves a jot,
In his pale body dwells no more,
Or mind, or soul,—an idiot!
But sometime in the end those three
Shall perish and their hands be still,
And with the master's touch shall flee
Their incommunicable skill.
A stillness absolute as death
Along the slacking wheels shall lie,
And, flagging at a single breath,
The fires shall moulder out and die.

The roar shall vanish at its height,
And over that tremendous town
The silence of eternal night
Shall gather close and settle down.
All its grim grandeur, tower and hall,
Shall be abandoned utterly,
And into rust and dust shall fall
From century to century;
Nor ever living thing shall grow,
Or trunk of tree, or blade of grass;
No drop shall fall, no wind shall blow,
Nor sound of any foot shall pass:
Alone of its accursèd state,
One thing the hand of Time shall spare,
For the grim Idiot at the gate
Is deathless and eternal there.

August 1892
The Atlantic Monthly, March 1894
Alcyone, 1899

THE SETTLER'S TALE

You say you have thought of me day by day,
And wondered why I am grim and grey,

So drawn of mouth and so hard of eye:
You are kind, you are good, I will tell you why.

By the tender light and the motherly grace
That win my eyes to your gentle face,

By the little fingers that cling to your hand,
I know you will hear me, and understand.

In a long past year, ere the spring was awake,
I built me a hut by a northern lake.

The logs I measured and hauled and hewed,
Ere the leaves were aflame in the autumn wood.

I raised and mortised them close and well,
And I finished the roof, when the first snow fell.

While the light of the wintry sun was thin,
I carved and fitted it fair within.

Though the drifts were like hills in the frost-white hours,
In my heart there was summer with birds and flowers;

For I thought of the girl I had wooed and won,
And I whistled and sang till my task was done.

I took my paddle when spring began,
And many a gusty rapid I ran.

By lake and river I journeyed down,
Till I came in the mills in a far-off town;

And my love—I found her as fair and true,
As she was in the year when our love was new.

By rapid and pool in my paddle's wake,
I brought her back to my northern lake.

She was all in the world that my heart held dear,
And our days were filled with content and cheer.

A twelve-month long without shadow of dread,
We laboured and planned for the years ahead.

And then in the hour of my hope and pride
She bore me a beautiful child, and died.

I went to the clearing with pick and spade,
And a long, deep grave in the mould I made;

And I bore her and laid her tenderly there,
With her sad white cheeks and her nut-brown hair,

My beautiful one, with her gentle smile.
I lay in the earth at her feet awhile,

With never a moan and never a tear,
For my heart was benumbed with horror and fear.

I rose from the grave, and with silent care
I filled and rounded it smooth and fair;

And then to my motherless babe I turned,
And wept, and the wildness of grief I learned.

As softly and deftly as mothers may,
I tended my little one night and day,

The one thing left that my heart held dear,
I watched her with joy and shuddering fear,

The fairest of delicate baby girls,
With her mother's eyes and her mother's curls.

Winter or summer, whatever befell,
I kept and guarded her safe and well;

And still as she grew, in my gathering joy
I made her many a curious toy,

Seeking ever for some new thing
To make her musical laughter ring.

But I fought in vain with the fate in store,
For the thing I dreaded was there at my door.

In the hush of one sultry summer night
I sprang from my bed in a dark affright.

I called upon God, and my heart beat wild,
For a horrible sickness had seized my child.

I worked as I would, but ere morning was red,
My beautiful baby was cold and dead.

I went to the clearing with pick and spade,
And a small deep grave in the mould I made.

I softened its floor with an otter's skin,
And I laid my little one low therein.

And everything there from the first to the least,
That her hands had touched, or her lips had kissed—

The toys that had been her delight and pride—
I gathered and laid by my little one's side.

I knelt in the mould and I kissed her brow,
And her cheeks and shoulders as cold as snow.

I smoothed her locks on the otter's skin,
And I rose from the grave and covered it in.

I covered it in, and with patient care
I heaped and rounded it smooth and fair.

I wept not, nor moaned, nor uttered her name,
For my heart was dry, as with living flame.

And again I laboured with pick and spade,
And a long, deep grave in the mould I made.

I made it deep and I made it wide,
And I sat in the silent night by its side.

A new day dawned and a second and third,
But I know not if ever I spake or stirred,

For thought with the wreck of my love had fled;
My body still lived, but my soul was dead.

Only one thing in the dark I knew—
The presence of Death that grew and grew.

I saw not its form, for it stretched away,
Miles upon miles, beyond night, beyond day.

But its eyes I saw, yea, I saw its eyes,
That were fixed upon mine with a pale surmise,

With a veiled, impalpable, ceaseless stare,
Till my life ebbed low, and my bones grew bare.

And then in the midnight a tempest came,
With the crash of wind and the stroke of flame,

And I reeled at the end of my life and fell
Into the grave I had dug so well.

I would that the rain with its tempest blow
Had crumbled the earth of its sides, and so

Buried me there, but it heeded me not,
For still I live to recount my lot.

An Indian found me at break of morn,
With limbs rain-sodden, wasted and worn,

And bore me away to his tent, and there
With wild-woods wisdom and rugged care

Nursed me through fever that fought and burned,
Till the fires died low and the life returned.

You see I am bred in a bitter school:
I am not as other men are, a pool

That shrieks in the onrush of every blast,
But smiles and is still, when the tempest is past.

My joy went forth as a word that is said;
It is gone, and forever; my heart is dead.

June 1893
Canadian Magazine, December 1913
Canadian Poetry 12, Spring/Summer 1983

PERSONALITY

O differing human heart,
Why is it that I tremble when thine eyes,
Thy human eyes and beautiful human speech,
Draw me, and stir within my soul
That subtle ineradicable longing
For tender comradeship?
It is because I cannot all at once,
Through the half-lights and phantom-haunted mists
That separate and enshroud us life from life,
Discern the nearness or the strangeness of thy paths
Nor plumb thy depths.
I am like one that comes alone at night
To a strange stream, and by an unknown ford
Stands, and for a moment yearns and shrinks,
Being ignorant of the water, though so quiet it is,
So softly murmurous,
So silvered by the familiar moon.

9 September 1893
Cosmopolitan, April 1895
Alcyone, 1899

ALCYONE

In the silent depth of space,
Immeasurably old, immeasurably far,
Glittering with a silver flame
Through eternity,
Rolls a great and burning star,
With a noble name,
    Alcyone!

In the glorious chart of heaven
It is marked the first of seven;
'Tis a Pleiad:

And a hundred years of earth
With their long-forgotten deeds have come and gone,
Since that tiny point of light,
Once a splendour fierce and bright,
Had its birth
In the star we gaze upon.

It has travelled at that time—
Thought has not a swifter flight—
Through a region where no faintest gust
Of life comes ever, but the power of night
Dwells stupendous and sublime,
Limitless and void and lonely,
A region mute with age, and peopled only
With the dead and ruined dust
Of worlds that lived eternities ago.

Man! when thou dost think of this,
And what our earth and its existence is,
The half-blind toils since life began,
The little aims, the little span,
With what passion and what pride,
And what hunger fierce and wide,
Thou dost break beyond it all,
Seeking for the spirit unconfined
In the clear abyss of mind
A shelter and a peace majestical.
For what is life to thee,
Turning toward the primal light,
With that stern and silent face,
If thou canst not be
Something radiant and august as night,
Something wide as space?

Therefore with a love and gratitude divine
Thou shalt cherish in thine heart for sign
A vision of the great and burning star,
Immeasurably old, immeasurably far,
Surging forth its silver flame
Through eternity;
And thine inner heart shall ring and cry
With the music strange and high,
The grandeur of its name
    Alcyone!

1 November 1893
The Atlantic Monthly, January 1895
Alcyone, 1899

THE CLEARER SELF

Before me grew the human soul,
And after I am dead and gone,
Through grades of effort and control
The marvellous work shall still go on.

Each mortal in his little span
Hath only lived, if he have shown
What greatness there can be in man
Above the measured and the known;

How through the ancient layers of night,
In gradual victory secure,
Grows ever with increasing light
The Energy serene and pure:

The Soul, that from a monstrous past,
From age to age, from hour to hour,
Feels upward to some height at last
Of unimagined grace and power

Though yet the sacred fire be dull,
In folds of thwarting matter furled,
Ere death be nigh, while life is full,
O Master Spirit of the world,

Grant me to know, to seek, to find,
In some small measure though it be,
Emerging from the waste and blind,
The clearer self, the grander me!

January 1894
Alcyone, 1899

WAR

By the Nile, the sacred river,
  I can see the captive hordes
Strain beneath the lash and quiver
  At the long papyrus cords,
While in granite rapt and solemn,
Rising over roof and column,
  Amen-hotep dreams, or Ramses,
    Lord of Lords.

I can hear the trumpets waken
  For a victory old and far—
Carchemish or Kadesh taken—
  I can see the conquerer's car
Bearing down some Hittite valley,
Where the bowmen break and sally,
  Sargina or Esarhaddon,
    Grim with war!

From the mountain streams that sweeten
  Indus, to the Spanish foam,
I can feel the broad earth beaten
  By the serried tramp of Rome;
Through whatever foes environ
Onward with the might of iron—
  Veni, vidi; veni, vici—
    Crashing home!

I can see the kings grow pallid
  With astonished fear and hate,
As the hosts of Amr or Khaled
  On their cities fall like fate;
Like the heat-wind from its prison
In the desert burst and risen—
  La ilaha illah 'llahu—
    God is great!

I can hear the iron rattle,
  I can see the arrows sting
In some far-off northern battle,
  Where the long swords sweep and swing;
I can hear the scalds declaiming,
I can see their eyeballs flaming,

Gathered in a frenzied circle
    Round the king.

I can hear the horn of Uri
  Roaring in the hills enorm;
Kindled at its brazen fury,
  I can see the clansmen form;
In the dawn in misty masses,
Pouring from the silent passes
  Over Granson or Morgarten
    Like the storm.

On the lurid anvil ringing
  To some slow fantastic plan,
I can hear the sword-smith singing
  In the heart of old Japan—
Till the cunning blade grows tragic
With his malice and his magic—
  Tenka tairan! Tenka tairan!
    War to man!

Where a northern river charges
  By a wild and moonlit glade,
From the murky forest marges,
  Round a broken palisade,
I can see the red men leaping,
See the sword of Daulac sweeping,
  And the ghostly forms of heroes
    Fall and fade.

I can feel the modern thunder
  Of the cannon beat and blaze,
When the lines of men go under
  On your proudest battle-days;
Through the roar I hear the lifting
Of the bloody chorus drifting
  Round the burning mill at Valmy—
    Marseillaise!

I can see the ocean rippled
  With the driving shot like rain,
While the hulls are crushed and crippled,
  And the guns are piled with slain;
O'er the blackened broad sea-meadow
Drifts a tall and titan shadow,
  And the cannon of Trafalgar
    Startle Spain.

Still the tides of fight are booming,
And the barren blood is spilt;
Still the banners are up-looming,
And the hands are on the hilt;
But the old world waxes wiser,
From behind the bolted visor
It descries at last the horror
And the guilt.

Yet the eyes are dim, nor wholly
Open to the golden gleam,
And the brute surrenders slowly
To the godhead and the dream.
From his cage of bar and girder,
Still at moments mad with murder,
Leaps the tiger, and his demon
Rules supreme.

One more war with fire and famine
Gathers—I can hear its cries—
And the years of might and Mammon
Perish in a world's demise;
When the strength of man is shattered,
And the powers of earth are scattered,
From beneath the ghastly ruin
Peace shall rise!

8 February 1895
Cosmopolitan, March 1896
The Poems of Archibald Lampman, 1900

MAN

I know that thou art of the world, O man,
And in thy moulding and ordaining breast abides,
Some glimmer of the insight that made the stars
A portion of the universal energy.
The shield of earth and of time and life,
A visible and aggressive, concrete form,
Thou has strength, movement, will.
In thy sheer presence, therefore, I

Who have not either strength or will or movement,
Who am but a net of magical desires,
Of swift perceptions and uncaptained dreams—
A thing out of the ordered way of life,
Not marked nor portioned in the eternal chart—
Shrink, even as on a rhubarb leaf at noon
A globe of dew dissolves, and so become
The impalpable luminous dream mist that I am.

c. 1895
Lampman's Kate: Late Love Poems of Archibald Lampman, 1975

ON LAKE TEMISCAMINGUE

A single dreamy elm, that stands between
   The sombre forest and the wan-lit lake,
Halves with its slim grey stem and pendent green
   The shadowed point. Beyond it without break
Bold brows of pine-topped granite bend away,
   Far to the southward, fading off in grand
Soft folds of looming purple. Cool and grey,
   The point runs out, a blade of thinnest sand.
Two rivers meet beyond it: wild and clear,
   Their deepening thunder breaks upon the ear—
The one descending from its forest home
   By many an eddied pool and murmuring fall—
The other cloven through the mountain wall,
   A race of tumbled rocks, a roar of foam.

25 November 1896
The Poems of Archibald Lampman, 1900

AT THE LONG SAULT: MAY, 1660

Under the day-long sun there is life and mirth
  In the working earth,
And the wonderful moon shines bright
  Through the soft spring night,
The innocent flowers in the limitless woods are springing
  Far and away
  With the sound and the perfume of May,
And ever up from the south the happy birds are winging,
  The waters glitter and leap and play
  While the grey hawk soars.

But far in an open glade of the forest set
  Where the rapid plunges and roars,
Is a ruined fort with a name that men forget,—
  A shelterless pen
  With its broken palisade,
  Behind it, musket in hand,
  Beyond message or aid
  In this savage heart of the wild,
  Mere youngsters, grown in a moment to men,
  Grim and alert and arrayed,
  The comrades of Daulac stand.
  Ever before them, night and day,
  The rush and skulk and cry
  Of foes, not men but devils, panting for prey;
  Behind them the sleepless dream
Of the little frail-walled town, far away by the plunging
    stream,
  Of maiden and matron and child,
With ruin and murder impending, and none but they
To beat back the gathering horror
Deal death while they may,
  And then die.

Day and night they have watched while the little plain
Grew dark with the rush of the foe, but their host
Broke ever and melted away, with no boast
But to number their slain;
And now as the days renew
Hunger and thirst and care
Were they never so stout, so true,

Press at their hearts; but none
Falters or shrinks or utters a coward word,
Though each setting sun
Brings from the pitiless wild new hands to the Iroquois horde,
And only to them despair.

Silent, white-faced, again and again
Charged and hemmed round by furious hands,
Each for a moment faces them all and stands
In his little desperate ring; like a tired bull moose
Whom scores of sleepless wolves, a ravening pack,
Have chased all night, all day
Through the snow-laden woods, like famine let loose;
And he turns at last in his track
Against a wall of rock and stands at bay;
Round him with terrible sinews and teeth of steel
They charge and recharge; but with many a furious plunge
and wheel,
Hither and thither over the trampled snow,
He tosses them bleeding and torn;
Till, driven, and ever to and fro
Harried, wounded and weary grown,
His mighty strength gives way
And all together they fasten upon him and drag him down.

So Daulac turned him anew
With a ringing cry to his men
In the little raging forest glen,
And his terrible sword in the twilight whistled and slew.
And all his comrades stood
With their backs to the pales, and fought
Till their strength was done;
The thews that were only mortal flagged and broke
Each struck his last wild stroke,
And they fell one by one,
And the world that had seemed so good
Passed like a dream and was naught.

And then the great night came
With the triumph-songs of the foe and the flame
Of the camp-fires.
Out of the dark the soft wind woke,
The song of the rapid rose alway
And came to the spot where the comrades lay,
Beyond help or care,
With none but the red men round them
To gnash their teeth and stare.

All night by the foot of the mountain
   The little town lieth at rest,
The sentries are peacefully pacing;
   And neither from East nor from West

Is there rumour of death or of danger;
   None dreameth tonight in his bed
That ruin was near and the heroes
   That met it and stemmed it are dead.

But afar in the ring of the forest,
   Where the air is so tender with May
And the waters are wild in the moonlight,
   They lie in their silence of clay.

The numberless stars out of heaven
   Look down with a pitiful glance;
And the lilies asleep in the forest
   Are closed like the lilies of France.

c. August 1898-January 1899
At the Long Sault and Other New Poems, 1943

Duncan Campbell Scott

1862–1947

Scott, the son of a Methodist minister, was born in Ottawa in 1862. He grew up in towns in Ontario and Quebec in which his father served, moving back to Ottawa at seventeen to become a clerk in the Department of Indian Affairs. In 1913, he became Deputy Superintendent-General and finally retired in 1932. Scott's professional life clearly influenced his writing; his interest in and understanding of native Canadians and their history and way of life were to emerge frequently in his poetry and throughout his canon. He also wrote a good deal of prose and some drama as well. His early poetry was certainly prompted by his friendship with Campbell and Lampman, a collection of whose poetry he edited in 1900. With both these men, he wrote "At the Mermaid Inn", a column in the *Toronto Globe* (1892-1893). He had studied the piano in his early years, and his wife, whom he married in 1894, was a gifted violinist. They had one daughter, born in 1895, whose early death in 1907 caused him considerable and protracted grief, reflected in "The Closed Door". His wife died in 1929 and he remarried in 1931. From the time of his first book of poetry, *The Magic House and Other Poems* (1893), his output was considerable. The honours bestowed on him, including two honorary doctorates and the Lorne Pierce Medal (1927), reflect the significant reputation he had gained over the years.

Even in the somewhat romantic *The Magic*

House and Other Poems (1893), Scott displays one of his hallmarks: his ability to control a narrative in a dramatic and exciting way, as demonstrated in "At the Cedars", one of his most anthologised poems. In this poem, he shapes structure and metre to the demands of his subject, a trait which was to become especially obvious, for example, in *New World Lyrics and Ballads* (1905) and poignantly demonstrated in "The Forsaken". "The Onandaga Madonna", in *Labour and the Angel* (1898) reflects, on the one hand, his ability to work powerfully with a conventional form— in this case, the sonnet—and, on the other, the impact that his work with native people had on his choice of themes. This poem also reflects his very real concern for and sensitivity to native Canadians. Recent critics may find Scott's poetic stance in this area controversial, for it seems at variance with some of the results of his own Department's policies. It is significant that Scott may not have foreseen that particular programmes were potentially detrimental to the native culture. Hindsight, however, frequently offers a chilling perspective on actions perceived as appropriate at the time they were carried out, and it would certainly be unjustifiable to suggest that Scott compartmentalised his poetic and official opinions. Very early in his literary career, he produced three volumes of commanding poetry that contained pieces often reprinted, on which much of his fame frequently rests, although many more books were to follow. The tendency to experiment with form and metre, even in these volumes, offers an interesting prelude to the modernist movement that was shortly to affect the literary scene, echoing developments in both the music and painting of the era (consider the work of Paul Kane, for instance).

Scott was by no means a hidebound traditionalist; nor, for that matter, was he simply a romantic portrayer of the natural world. Anything more than a cursory glance at his work reveals a range of form, mood, and content that includes the descriptive, the narrative, the contemplative, and the historical; and this variety carries through his career. The same degree of intensity, moreover, that marks "On the Way to the Mission" (1901) can be found in "At Gull Lake, 1810" (1934); the vividness of imagery and potent sensuality in "Night Hymns on Lake Nipigon" (1899) are also present in "Powassan's Drum" (1925) and later pieces. Scott's strength as a writer remained his fascination with the nature of the world and of humankind's path, so marked by glory and greed. His work, whether in extended narrative or crafted miniature of classical economy as in "At Delos" (1939), has the power to move the reader.

To date, the 1926 edition of Scott's poetry, *The Poems of Duncan Campbell Scott*, remains the definitive collection. Selected editions of his poetry include: E.K. Brown, *Selected Poems of Duncan Campbell Scott* (1951); Glenn Clever, *Selected Poetry of Duncan Campbell Scott* (1974), and *Powassan's Drum: Poems of Duncan Campbell Scott*, ed. Raymond Souster and Douglas Lochhead (1985). Manuscript locations include: Lorne Pierce papers and George Herbert Clarke papers at the Queen's University Archives, Kingston; W. Sherwood Fox Papers at the University of Western Ontario Treasure Room, London, Ontario; W.D. Lighthall papers at the McGill University Archives, Montreal; Carleton University Library, Ottawa; National Library, Ottawa; Robert Borden Papers, Public Archives of Canada, Ottawa; William Archer Deacon Papers, Thomas Fisher Rare Book Library, University of Toronto, Toronto; and the Victoria University Library, University of Toronto, Toronto.

Works on Scott include: W.J. Sykes, "The Poetry of Duncan Campbell Scott", *Queen's Quarterly* 46 (February 1939), 51-64; William Paul Denham, "Music and Painting in the Poetry of Duncan Campbell Scott", (M.A. Thesis, University of Western Ontario, 1964); Stan Dragland, ed., *Duncan Campbell Scott: A Book of Criticism* (1974); K.P. Stich, ed., *The Duncan Campbell Scott Symposium* (1980); Patricia Welage, "The Divided Worlds of Duncan Campbell Scott" (microform, 1981); George Johnston, "Duncan Campbell Scott", *Canadian Writers and Their Works*, ed. Robert Lecker, Jack David, and Ellen Quigley (1983); E. Brian Titley, *A Narrow Vision: Duncan Campbell Scott and the Administration of Indian Affairs in Canada* (1986); Tracy Ware, "The Beginnings of Duncan Campbell Scott's Poetic Career", *English Studies in Canada* 26 (June 1990) 2, 215-31; and Stan Dragland, " 'Byron on Wordsworth': Light and Occasional Verse in the Scott/Aylen Papers", *Canadian Poetry* 22 (Spring-Summer 1990), 29-67.

THE MAGIC HOUSE

In her chamber, wheresoe'er
   Time shall build the walls of it,
Melodies shall minister,
   Mellow sounds shall flit
Through a dusk of musk and myrrh.

Lingering in the spaces vague,
   Like the breath within a flute,
Winds shall move along the stair;
   When she walketh mute
Music meet shall greet her there.

Time shall make a truce with Time,
   All the languid dials tell
Irised hours of gossamer,
   Eve perpetual
Shall the night or light defer.

From her casement she shall see
   Down a valley wild and dim,
Swart with woods of pine and fir;
   Shall the sunsets swim
Red with untold gold to her.

From her terrace she shall see
   Lines of birds like dusky motes
Falling in the heated glare;
   How an eagle floats
In the wan unconscious air.

From her turret she shall see
   Vision of a cloudy place,
Like a group of opal flowers
   On the verge of space,
Or a town, or crown of towers.

From her garden she shall hear
   Fall the cones between the pines;
She shall seem to hear the sea,
   Or behind the vines
Some small noise, a voice may be.

But no thing shall habit there,
  There no human foot shall fall,
No sweet word the silence stir,
  Naught her name shall call,
Nothing come to comfort her.

But about the middle night,
  When the dusk is loathèd most,
Ancient thoughts and words long said,
  Like an alien host,
There shall come unsummonèd.

With her forehead on her wrist
  She shall lean against the wall
And see all the dream go by;
  In the interval
Time shall turn Eternity.

But the agony shall pass—
  Fainting with unuttered prayer,
She shall see the world's outlines
  And the weary glare
And the bare unvaried pines.

c. 1890
Scribner's, June 1890
The Magic House and Other Poems, 1893

AT THE CEDARS

You had two girls—Baptiste—
One is Virginie—
Hold hard—Baptiste!
Listen to me.

The whole drive was jammed
In that bend at the Cedars,
The rapids were dammed
With the logs tight rammed
And crammed; you might know
The Devil had clinched them below.

We worked three days—not a budge,
"She's as tight as a wedge, on the ledge,"
Says our foreman;
"Mon Dieu! boys, look here,
We must get this thing clear."
He cursed at the men
And we went for it then;
With our cant-dogs arow,
We just gave he-yo-ho;
When she gave a big shove
From above.

The gang yelled and tore
For the shore,
The logs gave a grind
Like a wolf's jaws behind,
And as quick as a flash,
With a shove and a crash,
They were down in a mash,
But I and ten more,
All but Isaàc Dufour,
Were ashore.

He leaped on a log in the front of the rush,
And shot out from the bind
While the jam roared behind;
As he floated along
He balanced his pole
And tossed us a song.
But just as we cheered,
Up darted a log from the bottom,

Leaped thirty feet square and fair,
And came down on his own.

He went up like a block
With the shock,
And when he was there
In the air,
Kissed his hand
To the land;
When he dropped
My heart stopped,
For the first logs had caught him
And crushed him;
When he rose in his place
There was blood on his face.

There were some girls, Baptiste,
Picking berries on the hillside,
Where the river curls, Baptiste,
You know—on the still side
One was down by the water,
She saw Isaàc
Fall back.

She did not scream, Baptiste,
She launched her canoe;
It did seem, Baptiste,
That she wanted to die too,
For before you could think
The birch cracked like a shell
In that rush of hell,
And I saw them both sink—

Baptiste!—
He had two girls,
One is Virginie,
What God calls the other
Is not known to me.

c. 1893
The Magic House and Other Poems, 1893

THE ONONDAGA MADONNA AND CHILD

She stands full-throated and with careless pose,
This woman of a weird and waning race,
The tragic savage lurking in her face,
Where all her pagan passion burns and glows;
Her blood is mingled with her ancient foes,
And thrills with war and wildness in her veins;
Her rebel lips are dabbled with the stains
Of feuds and forays and her father's woes.

And closer in the shawl about her breast,
The latest promise of her nation's doom,
Paler than she her baby clings and lies,
The primal warrior gleaming from his eyes;
He sulks, and burdened with his infant gloom,
He draws his heavy brows and will not rest.

c. 1894
The Atlantic Monthly, September 1894
Labour and the Angel, 1898

LABOUR AND THE ANGEL

The wind plunges—then stops;
And a column of leaves in a whirl,
Like a dervish that spins—drops,
With a delicate rustle,
Falls into a circle that thins;
The leaves creep away one by one,
Hiding in hollows and ruts;
Silence comes down on the lane:
The light wheels slow from the sun,
And glints where the corn stood,
And strays over the plain,
Touching with patches of gold,

The knolls and the hollows,
Crosses the lane,
And slips into the wood;
Then flashes a mile away on the farm,
A moment of brightness fine;
Then the gold glimmers and wanes,
And is swept by a clouding of grey,
For cheek by jowl, arm in arm,
The shadow's afoot with the shine.
The wind roars out from the elm,
Then leaps tiger-sudden;—the leaves
Shudder up into heaps and are caught
High as the branch where they hung
Over the oriole's nest.
Down in the sodden field,
A blind man is gathering his roots,
Guided and led by a girl;
Her gold hair blows in the wind,
Her garments with flutter and furl
Leap like a flag in the sun;
And whenever he stoops, she stoops,
And they heap the dark coloured beets
In the barrow, row upon row.
When it is full to the brim,
He wheels it patiently, slow,
Something oppressive and grim
Clothing his figure, but she
Beautifully light at his side,
Touches his arm with her hand,
Ready to help or to guide:
Power and comfort at need
In the flex of her figure lurk,
The fire at the heart of the deed
The angel that watches o'er work.

This is her visible form,
Heartening the labour she lives,
Keeping the breath of it warm,
Warm as a nestling of doves.
Humble or high or sublime,
Hers no reward of degrees,
Ditching as precious as rhyme,
If only the spirit be true.
"Effort and effort," she cries,
"This is the heart-beat of life,
Up with the lark and the dew,

Still with the dew and the stars,
Feel it athrob in the earth."

When labour is counselled by love,
You may see her splendid, serene,
Bending and brooding above,
With the justice and power of her mien;
Where thought has its passionate birth,
Her smile is the sweetest renown,
For the stroke and the derring-do
Her crown is the starriest crown.
When tears at the fountain are dry,
Bares she the round of her breast,
Soft to the cicatrized cheek,
Lulls this avatar of rest;
Strength is her arm for the weak;
Courage the wells of her eyes;
What is the power of their deeps,
Only the baffled can guess;
Nothing can daunt the emprise
When she sets hand to the hilt;
Victory is she—not less.
And oh! in the cages and dens
Where women work down to the bone,
Where men never laugh but they curse,
Think you she leaves them alone?
She the twin-sister of Love!
There, where the pressure is worst,
Of this hell-palace built to the skies
Upon hearts too crushed down to burst,
There, she is wiser than wise,
Giving no vistas sublime
Of towers in the murmurous air,
With gardens of pleasaunce and pride
Lulling the fleetness of time,
With doves alight by the side
Of a fountain that veils and drips;
She offers no tantalus-cup
To the shrunken, the desperate lips;
But she calms them with lethe and love,
And deadens the throb and the pain,
And evens the heart-beat wild,
Whispering again and again,
"Work on, work on, work on,
My broken, my agonized child,"
With her tremulous, dew-cool lips,

At the whorl of the tortured ear,
Till the cry is the presage of hope,
The trample of succour near.

And for those whose desperate day
Breeds night with a leaguer of fears,
(Night, that on earth brings the dew,
With stars at the window, and wind
In the maples, and rushes of balm,)
She pours from their limitless stores
Her sacred, ineffable tears.
When a soul too weary of life
Sets to its madness an end,
Then for a moment her eyes
Lighten, and thunder broods dark,
Heavy and strong at her heart;
But for a moment, and then
All her imperious wrath
Breaks in a passion of tears,
With the surge of her grief outpoured,
She sinks on the bosom of Love,
Her sister of infinite years,
And is wrapped, and enclosed, and restored.

So we have come with the breeze,
Up to the height of the hill,
Lost in the valley trees,
The old blind man and the girl;
But deep in the heart is the thrill
Of the image of counselling love;
The shape of the soul in the gloom,
And the power of the figure above,
Stand for the whole world's need:
For labour is always blind,
Unless as the light of the deed
The angel is smiling behind.

Now on the height of the hill,
The wind is fallen to a breath;
But down in the valley still,
It stalks in the shadowy wood,
And angers the river's breast;
The fields turn into the dark
That plays on the round of the sphere;
A star leaps sharp in the clear
Line of the sky, clear and cold;
But a cloud in the warmer west

Holds for a little its gold;
Like the wing of a seraph who sinks
Into antres afar from the earth,
Reluctant he flames on the brinks
Of the circles of nebulous stars,
Reluctant he turns to the rest,
From the planet whose ideal is love,
And then as he sweeps to the void
Vivid with tremulous light,
He gives it his translucent wing,
An emblem of pity unfurled,
Then falls to the uttermost ring,
And is lost to the world.

c. 1898
Labour and the Angel, 1898

WATKWENIES

Vengeance was once her nation's lore and law:
When the tired sentry stooped above the rill,
Her long knife flashed, and hissed, and drank its fill;
Dimly below her dripping wrist she saw,
One wild hand, pale as death and weak as straw,
Clutch at the ripple in the pool; while shrill
Sprang through the dreaming hamlet on the hill,
The war-cry of the triumphant Iroquois.

Now clothed with many an ancient flap and fold,
And wrinkled like an apple kept till May,
She weighs the interest-money in her palm,
And, when the Agent calls her valiant name,
Hears, like the war-whoops of her perished day,
The lads playing snow-snake in the stinging cold.

c. 1898
Labour and the Angel, 1898

NIGHT HYMNS ON LAKE NIPIGON

Here in the midnight, where the dark mainland and island
Shadows mingle in shadow deeper, profounder,
Sing we the hymns of the churches, while the dead water
Whispers before us.

Thunder is travelling slow on the path of the lightning;
One after one the stars and the beaming planets
Look serene in the lake from the edge of the storm-cloud,
Then have they vanished.

While our canoe, that floats dumb in the bursting thunder,
Gathers her voice in the quiet and thrills and whispers,
Presses her prow in the star-gleam, and all her ripple
Lapses in blackness.

Sing we the sacred ancient hymns of the churches,
Chanted first in old-world nooks of the desert,
While in the wild, pellucid Nipigon reaches
Hunted the savage.

Now have the ages met in the Northern midnight,
And on the lonely, loon-haunted Nipigon reaches
Rises the hymn of triumph and courage and comfort,
Adeste Fideles.

Tones that were fashioned when the faith brooded in darkness,
Joined with sonorous vowels in the noble Latin,
Now are married with the long-drawn Ojibwa,
Uncouth and mournful.

Soft with the silver drip of the regular paddles
Falling in rhythm, timed with the liquid, plangent
Sounds from the blades where the whirlpools break and are carried
Down into darkness;

Each long cadence, flying like a dove from her shelter
Deep in the shadow, wheels for a throbbing moment,
Poises in utterance, returning in circles of silver
To nest in the silence.

All wild nature stirs with the infinite, tender
Plaint of a bygone age whose soul is eternal,

Bound in the lonely phrases that thrill and falter
    Back into quiet.

Back they falter as the deep storm overtakes them,
Whelms them in splendid hollows of booming thunder,
Wraps them in rain, that, sweeping, breaks and onrushes
    Ringing like cymbals.

c. 1900
The Atlantic Monthly, August 1900
New World Lyrics and Ballads, 1905

ON THE WAY TO THE MISSION

They dogged him all one afternoon,
Through the bright snow,
Two whitemen servants of greed;
He knew that they were there,
But he turned not his head;
He was an Indian trapper;
He planted his snow-shoes firmly,
He dragged the long toboggan
Without rest.

The three figures drifted
Like shadows in the mind of a seer;
The snow-shoes were whisperers
On the threshold of awe;
The toboggan made the sound of wings,
A wood-pigeon sloping to her nest.

The Indian's face was calm.
He strode with the sorrow of fore-knowledge,
But his eyes were jewels of content
Set in circles of peace.

They would have shot him;
But momently in the deep forest,
They saw something flit by his side:
Their hearts stopped with fear.
Then the moon rose.
They would have left him to the spirit,

But they saw the long toboggan
Rounded well with furs,
With many a silver fox-skin,
With the pelts of mink and of otter.
They were the servants of greed;
When the moon grew brighter
And the spruces were dark with sleep,
They shot him.
When he fell on a shield of moonlight
One of his arms clung to his burden;
The snow was not melted:
The spirit passed away.

Then the servants of greed
Tore off the cover to count their gains;
They shuddered away into the shadows,
Hearing each the loud heart of the other.
Silence was born.

There in the tender moonlight,
   As sweet as they were in life,
Glimmered the ivory features,
   Of the Indian's wife.

In the manner of Montagnais women
   Her hair was rolled with braid;
Under her waxen fingers
   A crucifix was laid.

He was drawing her down to the Mission,
   To bury her there in spring,
When the bloodroot comes and the windflower
   To silver everything.

But as a gift of plunder
   Side by side were they laid,
The moon went on to her setting
   And covered them with shade.

c. 15 September 1901
New World Lyrics and Ballads, 1905

THE FORSAKEN

I

Once in the winter
Out on a lake
In the heart of the north-land,
Far from the Fort
And far from the hunters,
A Chippewa woman
With her sick baby,
Crouched in the last hours
Of a great storm.
Frozen and hungry,
She fished through the ice
With a line of the twisted
Bark of the cedar,
And a rabbit-bone hook
Polished and barbed;
Fished with the bare hook
All through the wild day,
Fished and caught nothing;
While the young chieftain
Tugged at her breasts,
Or slept in the lacings
Of the warm *tikanagan*.
All the lake-surface
Streamed with the hissing
Of millions of iceflakes
Hurled by the wind;
Behind her the round
Of a lonely island
Roared like a fire
With the voice of the storm
In the deeps of the cedars.
Valiant, unshaken,
She took of her own flesh,
Baited the fish-hook,
Drew in a grey-trout,
Drew in his fellows,
Heaped them beside her,
Dead in the snow.
Valiant, unshaken,

She faced the long distance,
Wolf-haunted and lonely,
Sure of her goal
And the life of her dear one:
Tramped for two days,
On the third in the morning,
Saw the strong bulk
Of the Fort by the river,
Saw the wood-smoke
Hang soft in the spruces,
Heard the keen yelp
Of the ravenous huskies
Fighting for whitefish:
Then she had rest.

II

Years and years after,
When she was old and withered,
When her son was an old man
And his children filled with vigour,
They came in their northern tour on the verge of winter,
To an island in a lonely lake.
There one night they camped, and on the morrow
Gathered their kettles and birch-bark
Their rabbit-skin robes and their mink-traps,
Launched their canoes and slunk away through the islands,
Left her alone forever,
Without a word of farewell,
Because she was old and useless,
Like a paddle broken and warped,
Or a pole that was splintered.
Then, without a sigh,
Valiant, unshaken,
She smoothed her dark locks under her kerchief,
Composed her shawl in state,
Then folded her hands ridged with sinews and corded with veins,
Folded them across her breasts spent with the nourishing of children,
Gazed at the sky past the tops of the cedars,
Saw two spangled nights arise out of the twilight,
Saw two days go by filled with the tranquil sunshine,
Saw, without pain, or dread, or even a moment of longing:
Then on the third great night there came thronging and thronging

Millions of snowflakes out of a windless cloud;
They covered her close with a beautiful crystal shroud,
Covered her deep and silent.
But in the frost of the dawn,
Up from the life below,
Rose a column of breath
Through a tiny cleft in the snow,
Fragile, delicately drawn,
Wavering with its own weakness,
In the wilderness a sign of the spirit,
Persisting still in the sight of the sun
Till day was done.
Then all light was gathered up by the hand of God and
hid in His breast,
Then there was born a silence deeper than silence,
Then she had rest.

c. 1902
The Outlook, 25 April 1903
New World Ballads and Lyrics, 1905

NIGHT

The night is old, and all the world
Is wearied out with strife;
A long grey mist lies heavy and wan
Above the house of life.

Four stars burn up and are unquelled
By the low, shrunken moon;
Her spirit draws her down and down—
She shall be buried soon.

There is a sound that is no sound,
Yet fine it falls and clear,
The whisper of the spinning earth
To the tranced atmosphere.

An odour lives where once was air,
A strange, unearthly scent,
From the burning of the four great stars
Within the firmament.

The universe, deathless and old,
   Breathes, yet is void of breath:
As still as death that seems to move
   And yet is still as death.

c. 1905
The Smart Set, 1905
Lundy's Lane and Other Poems, 1916

THE HALF-BREED GIRL

She is free of the trap and the paddle,
   The portage and the trail,
But something behind her savage life
   Shines like a fragile veil.

Her dreams are undiscovered,
   Shadows trouble her breast,
When the time for resting cometh
   Then least is she at rest.

Oft in the morns of winter,
   When she visits the rabbit snares,
An appearance floats in the crystal air
   Beyond the balsam firs.

Oft in the summer mornings
   When she strips the nets of fish,
The smell of the dripping net-twine
   Gives to her heart a wish.

But she cannot learn the meaning
   Of the shadows in her soul,
The lights that break and gather,
   The clouds that part and roll,

The reek of rock-built cities,
   Where her fathers dwelt of yore,
The gleam of loch and shealing,
   The mist on the moor,

Frail traces of kindred kindness,
   Of feud by hill and strand,

The heritage of an age-long life
  In a legendary land.

She wakes in the stifling wigwam,
  Where the air is heavy and wild,
She fears for something or nothing
  With the heart of a frightened child.

She sees the stars turn slowly
  Past the tangle of the poles,
Through the smoke of the dying embers,
  Like the eyes of dead souls.

Her heart is shaken with longing
  For the strange, still years,
For what she knows and knows not,
  For the wells of ancient tears.

A voice calls from the rapids,
  Deep, careless and free,
A voice that is larger than her life
  Or than her death shall be.

She covers her face with her blanket,
  Her fierce soul hates her breath,
As it cries with a sudden passion
  For life or death.

26 July 1906
The Smart Set, 1906
Via Borealis, 1906

THE BATTLE OF LUNDY'S LANE

(Rufus Gale speaks—1852)

Yes,—in the Lincoln Militia,—in the war of eighteen-twelve;
Many's the day I've had since then to dig and delve—
But those are the years I remember as the brightest years of
  all,
When we left the plow in the furrow to follow the bugle's
  call.

Why, even our son Abner wanted to fight with the men!
"Don't you go, d'ye hear, sir!"—I was angry with him then.
"Stay with your mother!" I said, and he looked so old and grim—
He was just sixteen that April—I couldn't believe it was him;
But I didn't think—I was off—and we met the foe again,
Five thousand strong and ready, at the hill by Lundy's Lane.
There as the night came on we fought them from six to nine,
Whenever they broke our line we broke their line,
They took our guns and we won them again, and around the levels
Where the hill sloped up—with the Eighty-ninth,—we fought like devils
Around the flags; and on they came and we drove them back,
Until with its very fierceness the fight grew slack.
It was then about nine and dark as a miser's pocket,
When up came Hercules Scott's brigade swift as a rocket,
And charged,—and the flashes sprang in the dark like a lion's eyes;
The night was full of fire—groans, and cheers, and cries;
Then through the sound and the fury another sound broke in—
The roar of a great old duck-gun shattered the rest of the din;
It took two minutes to charge it and another to set it free.
Every time I heard it an angel spoke to me;
Yes, the minute I heard it I felt the strangest tide
Flow in my veins like lightning, as if, there, by my side,
Was the very spirit of Valour. But 'twas dark—you couldn't see—
And the one who was firing the duck-gun fell against me
And slid down to the clover, and lay there still;
Something went through me—piercing—with a strange, swift thrill;
The noise fell away into silence, and I heard as clear as thunder
The long, slow roar of Niagara: O the wonder
Of that deep sound. But again the battle broke
And the foe, driven before us desperately—stroke upon stroke,
Left the field to his master, and sullenly down the road
Sounded the boom of his guns, trailing the heavy load
Of his wounded men and his shattered flags, sullen and slow,
Setting fire in his rage to Bridgewater mills, and the glow
Flared in the distant forest. We rested as we could,
And for a while I slept in the dark of a maple wood:
But when the clouds in the east were red all over,

I came back there to the place we made the stand in the
clover;
For my heart was heavy then with a strange, deep pain,
As I thought of the glorious fight, and again and again
I remembered the valiant spirit and the piercing thrill;
But I knew it all when I reached the top of the hill,—
For there, there with the blood on his dear, brave head,
There on the hill in the clover lay our Abner—dead!—
No—thank you—no, I don't need it; I'm solid as granite
rock,
But every time that I tell it I feel the old, cold shock,
I'm eighty-one my next birthday—do you breed such fellows
now?
There he lay with the dawn cooling his broad fair brow,
That was no dawn for him; and there was the old duck-gun
That many and many's the time,—just for the fun,
We together, alone, would take to the hickory rise,
And bring home more wild pigeons than ever you saw with
your eyes.
Up with Hercules Scott's brigade, just as it came on night—
He was the angel beside me in the thickest of the fight—
Wrote a note to his mother—He said, "I've got to go;
Mother, what would home be under the heel of the foe!"
Oh! she never slept a wink, she would rise and walk the floor;
She'd say this over and over, "I knew it all before!"
I'd try to speak of the glory to give her a little joy.
"What is the glory to me when I want my boy, my boy!"
She'd say, and she'd wring her hands; her hair grew white as
snow—
And I'd argue with her up and down, to and fro,
Of how she had mothered a hero, and his was a glorious fate,
Better than years of grubbing to gather an estate.
Sometimes I'd put it this way: "If God was to say to me now
'Take him back as he once was helping you with the plow,'
I'd say, 'No, God, thank You kindly; 'twas You that he
obeyed;
You told him to fight and he fought, and he wasn't afraid;
You wanted to prove him in battle, You sent him to Lundy's
Lane,
'Tis well!' " But she only would answer over and over again,
"Give me back my Abner—give me back my son!"
It was so all through the winter until the spring had begun,
And the crocus was up in the dooryard, and the drift by the
fence was thinned,
And the sap drip-dropped from the branches wounded by the
wind,

And the whole earth smelled like a flower,—then she came to
me one night—
"Rufus!" she said, with a sob in her throat,—"Rufus, you're
right."
I hadn't cried till then, not a tear—but then I was torn in
two—
There, it's all right—my eyes don't see as they used to do!
But O the joy of that battle—it was worth the whole of life,
You felt immortal in action with the rapture of the strife,
There in the dark by the river, with the flashes of fire before,
Running and crashing along, there in the dark, and the roar
Of the guns, and the shrilling cheers, and the knowledge that
filled your heart
That there was a victory making and you must do your part,
But—there's his grave in the orchard where the headstone
glimmers white:
We could see it, we thought, from our window even on the
darkest night;
It is set there for a sign that what one lad could do
Would be done by a hundred hundred lads whose hearts were
stout and true.
And when in the time of trial you hear the recreant say,
Shooting his coward lips at us, "You shall have had your day:
For all your state and glory shall pass like a cloudy wrack,
And here some other flag shall fly where flew the Union
Jack,"—
Why tell him a hundred thousand men would spring from
these sleepy farms,
To tie that flag in its ancient place with the sinews of their
arms;
And if they doubt you and put you to scorn, why you can
make it plain,
With the tale of the gallant Lincoln men and the fight at
Lundy's Lane.

1908
Lundy's Lane and Other Poems, 1916

FRAGMENT OF AN ODE TO CANADA

This is the land!
It lies outstretched a vision of delight,
Bent like a shield between the silver seas
It flashes back the hauteur of the sun;
Yet teems with humblest beauties, still a part
Of its Titanic and ebullient heart.

Land of the glacial, lonely mountain ranges,
Where nothing haps save vast Æonian changes,
The slow moraine, the avalanche's wings,
Summer and Sun,—the elemental things,
Pulses of Awe,—Winter and Night and the lightnings.
Land of the pines that rear their dusky spars
A ready midnight for the earliest stars.
The land of rivers, rivulets, and rills,
Straining incessant everyway to the sea,
With their white thunder harnessed in the mills,
Turning one wealth to another wealth perpetually;
Spinning the lightning with dynamic spindles,
Till some far city dowered with fire enkindles.
The land of fruit, fine-flavoured with the frost,
Land of the cattle, the deep-chested host,
The happy-souled, that contemplate the hours,
Their dew-laps buried in the grass and flowers.
And, O! the myriad-miracle of the grain
Cresting the hill, brimming the level plain,
The miracle of the flower and milk and kernel,
Nurtured by sun-fire and frost-fire supernal,
Until the farmer turns it in his hand,
The million-millioned miracle of the land.
And yet with all these pastoral and heroic graces,
Our simplest flowers wear the loveliest faces;
The sparrows are our most enraptured singers,
And round their songs the fondest memory lingers;
Our forests tower and tremble, star-enchanted,
Their roots are by the timid spirits haunted
Of hermit thrushes,—trancèd is the air,
Ever in doubt when they shall sing or where;
The mountains may with ice and avalanche wrestle,
Far down their rugged steeps dimple and nestle
The still, translucent, turquoise-hearted tarns.

And Thou, O Power, that 'stablishest the Nation,
Give wisdom in the midst of our elation;
Who are so free that we forget we are—
That freedom brings the deepest obligation:
Grant us this presage for a guiding star,
To lead the van of Peace, not with a craven spirit,
But with the consciousness that we inherit
What built the Empire out of blood and fire,
And can smite, too, in passion and with ire.
Purge us of Pride, who are so quick in vaunting
Thy gift, this land, that is in nothing wanting;
Give Mind to match the glory of the gift,
Give great Ideals to bridge the sordid rift
Between our heritage and our use of it.
Then in some day of terror for the world,
When all the flags of the Furies are unfurled,
When Truth and Justice, wildered and unknit,
Shall turn for help to this young, radiant land,
We shall be quick to see and understand:
What shall we answer in that stricken hour?
Shall the deep thought be pregnant then with power?
Shall the few words spring swift and grave and clear?
Use well the present moment. They shall hear.

August 1911
Manitoba Free Press, 1918
Lundy's Lane and Other Poems, 1916

LINES IN MEMORY OF EDMUND MORRIS

Dear Morris—here is your letter—
Can my answer reach you now?
Fate has left me your debtor,
You will remember how;
For I went away to Nantucket,
And you to the Isle of Orleans,

And when I was dawdling and dreaming
Over the ways and means
Of answering, the power was denied me,
Fate frowned and took her stand;
I have your unanswered letter
Here in my hand.
This—in your famous scribble,
It was ever a cryptic fist,
Cuneiform or Chaldaic
Meanings held in a mist.

Dear Morris, (now I'm inditing
And poring over your script)
I gather from the writing,
The coin that you had flipt,
Turned tails; and so you compel me
To meet you at Touchwood Hills:
Or, mayhap, you are trying to tell me
The sum of a painter's ills:
Is that Phimister Proctor
Or something about a doctor?
Well, nobody knows, but Eddie,
Whatever it is I'm ready.

For our friendship was always fortunate
In its greetings and adieux,
Nothing flat or importunate,
Nothing of the misuse
That comes of the constant grinding
Of one mind on another.
So memory has nothing to smother,
But only a few things captured
On the wing, as it were, and enraptured.
Yes, Morris, I am inditing—
Answering at last it seems,
How can you read the writing
In the vacancy of dreams?

I would have you look over my shoulder
Ere the long, dark year is colder,
And mark that as memory grows older,
The brighter it pulses and gleams.
And if I should try to render
The tissues of fugitive splendour
That fled down the wind of living,
Will they read it some day in the future,
And be conscious of an awareness
In our old lives, and the bareness

Of theirs, with the newest passions
In the last fad of the fashions?

How often have we risen without daylight
When the day star was hidden in mist,
When the dragon-fly was heavy with dew and sleep,
And viewed the miracle pre-eminent, matchless,
The prelusive light that quickens the morning.
O crystal dawn, how shall we distill your virginal freshness
When you steal upon a land that man has not sullied with his
  intrusion,
When the aboriginal shy dwellers in the broad solitudes
Are asleep in their innumerable dens and night haunts
Amid the dry ferns, in the tender nests
Pressed into shape by the breasts of the Mother birds?

How shall we simulate the thrill of announcement
When lake after lake lingering in the starlight
Turn their faces towards you,
And are caressed with the salutation of colour?
How shall we transmit in tendril-like images,
The tenuous tremor in the tissues of ether,
Before the round of colour buds like the dome of a shrine,
The preconscious moment when love has fluttered in the
  bosom,
Before it begins to ache?

How often have we seen the even
Melt into the liquidity of twilight,
With passages of Titian splendour,
Pellucid preludes, exquisitely tender,
Where vanish and revive, thro' veils of the ashes of roses,
The crystal forms the breathless sky discloses.

The new moon a slender thing,
In a snood of virgin light,
She seemed all shy on venturing
Into the vast night.

Her own land and folk were afar,
She must have gone astray,
But the gods had given a silver star,
To be with her on the way.

I can feel the wind on the prairie
And see the bunch-grass wave,

And the sunlights ripple and vary
The hill with Crowfoot's grave,
Where he "pitched off" for the last time
In sight of the Blackfoot Crossing,
Where in the sun for a pastime
You marked the site of his tepee
With a circle of stones. Old Napiw
Gave you credit for that day.
And well I recall the weirdness
Of that evening at Qu'Appelle,
In the wigwam with old Sakimay,
The keen, acrid smell,
As the kinnikinick was burning;
The planets outside were turning,
And the little splints of poplar
Flared with a thin, gold flame.
He showed us his painted robe
Where in primitive pigments
He had drawn his feats and his forays,
And told us the legend
Of the man without a name,
The hated Blackfoot,
How he lured the warriors,
The young men, to the foray
And they never returned.
Only their ghosts
Goaded by the Blackfoot
Mounted on stallions:
In the night time
He drove the stallions
Reeking into the camp;
The women gasped and whispered,
The children cowered and crept,
And the old men shuddered
Where they slept.
When Sakimay looked forth
He saw the Blackfoot,
And the ghosts of the warriors,
And the black stallions
Covered by the night wind
As by a mantle.

I remember well a day,
When the sunlight had free play,

When you worked in happy stress,
While grave Ne-Pah-Pee-Ness
Sat for his portrait there,
In his beaded coat and his bare
Head, with his mottled fan
Of hawk's feathers, A Man!
Ah Morris, those were the times
When you sang your inconsequent rhymes
Sprung from a careless fountain:

"He met her on the mountain,
He gave her a horn to blow,
And the very last words he said to her
Were, 'Go 'long, Eliza, go.'"

Foolish,—but life was all,
And under the skilful fingers
Contours came at your call—
Art grows and time lingers;—
But now the song has a change
Into something wistful and strange.
And one asks with a touch of ruth
What became of the youth
And where did Eliza go?
He met her on the mountain,
He gave her a horn to blow,
The horn was a silver whorl
With a mouthpiece of pure pearl,
And the mountain was all one glow,
With gulfs of blue and summits of rosy snow.
The cadence she blew on the silver horn
Was the meaning of life in one phrase caught,
And as soon as the magic notes were born,
She repeated them once in an afterthought.
They heard in the crystal passes,
The cadence, calling, calling,
And faint in the deep crevasses,
The echoes falling, falling.
They stood apart and wondered;
Her lips with a wound were aquiver,
His heart with a sword was sundered,
For life was changed forever
When he gave her the horn to blow:
But a shadow arose from the valley,
Desolate, slow and tender,
It hid the herdsmen's chalet,
Where it hung in the emerald meadow,

(Was death driving the shadow?)
It quenched the tranquil splendour
Of the colour of life on the glow-peaks,
Till at the end of the even,
The last shell-tint on the snow-peaks
Had passed away from the heaven.
And yet, when it passed, victorious,
The stars came out on the mountains,
And the torrents gusty and glorious,
Clamoured in a thousand fountains,
And even far down in the valley,
A light re-discovered the chalet.
The scene that was veiled had a meaning,
So deep that none might know;
Was it here in the morn on the mountain,
That he gave her the horn to blow?

Tears are the crushed essence of this world,
The wine of life, and he who treads the press
Is lofty with imperious disregard
Of the burst grapes, the red tears and the murk.
But nay! that is a thought of the old poets,
Who sullied life with the passional bitterness
Of their world-weary hearts. We of the sunrise,
Joined in the breast of God, feel deep the power
That urges all things onward, not to an end,
But in an endless flow, mounting and mounting,
Claiming not overmuch for human life,
Sharing with our brothers of nerve and leaf
The urgence of the one creative breath,—
All in the dim twilight—say of morning,
Where the florescence of the light and dew
Haloes and hallows with a crown adorning
The brows of life with love; herein the clue,
The love of life—yea, and the peerless love
Of things not seen, that leads the least of things
To cherish the green sprout, the hardening seed;
Here leans all nature with vast Mother-love,
Above the cradled future with a smile.
Why are there tears for failure, or sighs for weakness,
While life's rhythm beats on? Where is the rule
To measure the distance we have circled and clomb?
Catch up the sands of the sea and count and count
The failures hidden in our sum of conquest.
Persistence is the master of this life;

The master of these little lives of ours;
To the end—effort—even beyond the end.

Here, Morris, on the plains that we have loved,
Think of the death of Akoose, fleet of foot,
Who, in his prime, a herd of antelope
From sunrise, without rest, a hundred miles
Drove through rank prairie, loping like a wolf,
Tired them and slew them, ere the sun went down.
Akoose, in his old age, blind from the smoke
Of tepees and the sharp snow light, alone
With his great-grandchildren, withered and spent,
Crept in the warm sun along a rope
Stretched for his guidance. Once when sharp autumn
Made membranes of thin ice upon the sloughs,
He caught a pony on a quick return
Of prowess and, all his instincts cleared and quickened,
He mounted, sensed the north and bore away
To the Last Mountain Lake where in his youth
He shot the sand-hill-cranes with his flint arrows.
And for these hours in all the varied pomp
Of pagan fancy and free dreams of foray
And crude adventure, he ranged on entranced,
Until the sun blazed level with the prairie,
Then paused, faltered and slid from off his pony.
In a little bluff of poplars, hid in the bracken,
He lay down; the populace of leaves
In the lithe poplars whispered together and trembled,
Fluttered before a sunset of gold smoke,
With interspaces, green as sea water,
And calm as the deep water of the sea.

There Akoose lay, silent amid the bracken,
Gathered at last with the Algonquin Chieftains.
Then the tenebrous sunset was blown out,
And all the smoky gold turned into cloud wrack.
Akoose slept forever amid the poplars,
Swathed by the wind from the far-off Red Deer
Where dinosaurs sleep, clamped in their rocky tombs.
Who shall count the time that lies between
The sleep of Akoose and the dinosaurs?
Innumerable time, that yet is like the breath
Of the long wind that creeps upon the prairie
And dies away with the shadows at sundown.

What we may think, who brood upon the theme,
Is, when the old world, tired of spinning, has fallen
Asleep, and all the forms, that carried the fire
Of life, are cold upon her marble heart—
Like ashes on the altar—just as she stops,
That something will escape of soul or essence,—
The sum of life, to kindle otherwhere:
Just as the fruit of a high sunny garden,
Grown mellow with autumnal sun and rain,
Shrivelled with ripeness, splits to the rich heart,
And looses a gold kernel to the mould,
So the old world, hanging long in the sun,
And deep enriched with effort and with love,
Shall, in the motions of maturity,
Wither and part, and the kernel of it all
Escape, a lovely wraith of spirit, to latitudes
Where the appearance, throated like a bird,
Winged with fire and bodied all with passion,
Shall flame with presage, not of tears, but joy.

c. 1913
Privately printed by the author, 1915
Lundy's Lane and Other Poems, 1916

THE HEIGHT OF LAND

Here is the height of land:
The watershed on either hand
Goes down to Hudson Bay
Or Lake Superior;
The stars are up, and far away
The wind sounds in the wood, wearier
Than the long Ojibwa cadence
In which Potàn the Wise
Declares the ills of life
And Chees-que-ne-ne makes a mournful sound
Of acquiescence. The fires burn low
With just sufficient glow
To light the flakes of ash that play
At being moths, and flutter away

To fall in the dark and die as ashes:
Here there is peace in the lofty air,
And Something comes by flashes
Deeper than peace;—
The spruces have retired a little space
And left a field of sky in violet shadow
With stars like marigolds in a water-meadow.

Now the Indian guides are dead asleep;
There is no sound unless the soul can hear
The gathering of the waters in their sources.
We have come up through the spreading lakes
From level to level,—
Pitching our tents sometimes over a revel
Of roses that nodded all night,
Dreaming within our dreams,
To wake at dawn and find that they were captured
With no dew on their leaves;
Sometimes mid sheaves
Of bracken and dwarf-cornel, and again
On a wide blueberry plain
Brushed with the shimmer of a bluebird's wing;
A rocky islet followed
With one lone poplar and a single nest
Of white-throat-sparrows that took no rest
But sang in dreams or woke to sing,—
To the last portage and the height of land—:
Upon one hand
The lonely north enlaced with lakes and streams,
And the enormous targe of Hudson Bay,
Glimmering all night
In the cold arctic light;
On the other hand
The crowded southern land
With all the welter of the lives of men.
But here is peace, and again
That Something comes by flashes
Deeper than peace,—a spell
Golden and inappellable
That gives the inarticulate part
Of our strange being one moment of release
That seems more native than the touch of time,
And we must answer in chime;
Though yet no man may tell
The secret of that spell
Golden and inappellable.

Now are there sounds walking in the wood,
And all the spruces shiver and tremble,
And the stars move a little in their courses.
The ancient disturber of solitude
Breathes a pervasive sigh,
And the soul seems to hear
The gathering of the waters at their sources;
Then quiet ensues and pure starlight and dark;
The region-spirit murmurs in meditation,
The heart replies in exaltation
And echoes faintly like an inland shell
Ghost tremors of the spell;
Thought reawakens and is linked again
With all the welter of the lives of men.
Here on the uplands where the air is clear
We think of life as of a stormy scene,—
Of tempest, of revolt and desperate shock;
And here, where we can think, on the bright uplands
Where the air is clear, we deeply brood on life
Until the tempest parts, and it appears
As simple as to the shepherd seems his flock:
A Something to be guided by ideals—
That in themselves are simple and serene—
Of noble deed to foster noble thought,
And noble thought to image noble deed,
Till deed and thought shall interpenetrate,
Making life lovelier, till we come to doubt
Whether the perfect beauty that escapes
Is beauty of deed or thought or some high thing
Mingled of both, a greater boon than either:
Thus we have seen in the retreating tempest
The victor-sunlight merge with the ruined rain,
And from the rain and sunlight spring the rainbow.

The ancient disturber of solitude
Stirs his ancestral potion in the gloom,
And the dark wood
Is stifled with the pungent fume
Of charred earth burnt to the bone
That takes the place of air.
Then sudden I remember when and where,—
The last weird lakelet foul with weedy growths
And slimy viscid things the spirit loathes,
Skin of vile water over viler mud
Where the paddle stirred unutterable stenches,
And the canoes seemed heavy with fear,

Not to be urged toward the fatal shore
Where a bush fire, smouldering, with sudden roar
Leaped on a cedar and smothered it with light
And terror. It had left the portage-height
A tangle of slanted spruces burned to the roots,
Covered still with patches of bright fire
Smoking with incense of the fragrant resin
That even then began to thin and lessen
Into the gloom and glimmer of ruin.
'Tis overpast. How strange the stars have grown;
The presage of extinction glows on their crests
And they are beautied with impermanence;
They shall be after the race of men
And mourn for them who snared their fiery pinions,
Entangled in the meshes of bright words.

A lemming stirs the fern and in the mosses
Eft-minded things feel the air change, and dawn
Tolls out from the dark belfries of the spruces.
How often in the autumn of the world
Shall the crystal shrine of dawning be rebuilt
With deeper meaning! Shall the poet then,
Wrapped in his mantle on the height of land,
Brood on the welter of the lives of men
And dream of his ideal hope and promise
In the blush sunrise? Shall he base his flight
Upon a more compelling law than Love
As Life's atonement; shall the vision
Of noble deed and noble thought immingled
Seem as uncouth to him as the pictograph
Scratched on the cave side by the cave-dweller
To us of the Christ-time? Shall he stand
With deeper joy, with more complex emotion,
In closer commune with divinity,
With the deep fathomed, with the firmament charted,
With life as simple as a sheep-boy's song,
What lies beyond a romaunt that was read
Once on a morn of storm and laid aside
Memorious with strange immortal memories?
Or shall he see the sunrise as I see it
In shoals of misty fire the deluge-light
Dashes upon and whelms with purer radiance,
And feel the lulled earth, older in pulse and motion,
Turn the rich lands and the inundant oceans
To the flushed colour, and hear as now I hear
The thrill of life beat up the planet's margin

And break in the clear susurrus of deep joy
That echoes and reëchoes in my being?
O Life is intuition the measure of knowledge
And do I stand with heart entranced and burning
At the zenith of our wisdom when I feel
The long light flow, the long wind pause, the deep
Influx of spirit, of which no man may tell
The Secret, golden and inappellable?

1915
Lundy's Lane and Other Poems, 1916

BY A CHILD'S BED

She breathèd deep,
And stepped from out life's stream
Upon the shore of sleep;
And parted from the earthly noise,
Leaving her world of toys,
To dwell a little in a dell of dream.

Then brooding on the love I hold so free,
My fond possessions come to be
Clouded with grief;
These fairy kisses,
This archness innocent,
Sting me with sorrow and disturbed content:
I think of what my portion might have been,
A dearth of blisses,
A famine of delights,
If I had never had what now I value most;
Till all I have seems something I have lost;
A desert underneath the garden shows,
And in a mound of cinders roots the rose.

Here then I linger by the little bed,
Till all my spirit's sphere,
Grows one half brightness and the other dead,
One half all joy, the other vague alarms;
And, holding each the other half in fee,
Floats like the growing moon

That bears implicitly
Her lessening pearl of shadow
Clasped in the crescent silver of her arms.

c. 1916
Lundy's Lane and Other Poems, 1916

THE CLOSED DOOR

The dew falls and the stars fall,
The sun falls in the west,
Through the closed door,
But never more
Through the closed door,
Shall the one that I loved best
Return to me:
A salt tear is the sea,
All earth's air is a sigh,
But they never can mourn for me
With my heart's cry,
For the one that I loved best
Who caressed me with her eyes,
And every morning came to me,
With the beauty and sunrise,
Who was health and wealth and all,
Who never shall answer my call,
While the sun falls in the west,
The dew falls and the stars fall.

c. 1916
Lundy's Lane and Other Poems, 1916

TO THE CANADIAN MOTHERS

(1914-1918)

Why mourn thy dead, that are the world's possessions?
These, our Immortals—Shall we give them up
To the complaint of private loss and dole?
Nay—mourn for them, if mourn thou must,—
Grief is thy private treasure;
Thy soul alone can count its weight or measure.
But we who know they saved the world
Think of them joined to that unwithering throng,
Who in the long dread strife
Have thought and fought for Liberty:
When she was but a faint pulsation in the mind,
The faintest rootlet of a growing thought,
They nourished her with tears
And gave their dreams to add depth to her foliage;
And when the enemy ravaged her bright blossoms,
Drenched her with their rich blood
To prove she lived and was the ever-living.
These are the true Immortals,
The deathless ones that saved the world.

Nay, weep, if weep thou must
And think upon thy lad, onetime in trust
To fortune; of his gallant golden head
And all the wayward sanctities of childhood;
Of how he crowned thy life with confidences;
Of the odour of his body, lulled with sleep,
Confusing thy dim prayers for some best future
With the sheer love that is the deepest:
False fortune has destroyed her hostages!
Old joys are bitter, bitter as very death!
Let break thy heart and so be comforted.

Be comforted, for we have claimed the child
And taken him to be with light and glory;
Not as we knew him in his earthly days
The lovely one, the virtuous, the dauntless,—
Or one who was a boaster, thick with faults
Perchance,—but as the index of the time,
The stay and nurture of the world's best hope,
The peerless seed of valour and victory.

Here in a realm beyond the fading world,
We garner them and hold them in abeyance
Ere we deliver them to light and silence—
The vestiges of battle fallen away—
Fragments of storm parting about the moon,—
Here in the dim rock-chambers, garlanded
With frail sea-roses perfumed by the sea
That mumurs of renown, and murmuring,
Scatters the cool light won by the ripple
From the stormless moon, cloistered with memory,
Whose dim caves front the immortal vistas
Plangent with renown, here they await
The light, the glory and the ultimate rest.

Be comforted,—nay sob, if sob thou must,
Cover thy face and dim thy hair with dust,
And we who know they live
Gather thy dead in triumph—
Exalted from the caves of memory,
Purified from the least assoil of time,—
And lay them with all that is most living,
In light transcendent,
In the ageless aisles of silence,
With the Immortals that have saved the world.

c. 1917
To the Canadian Mothers and Three Other Poems, 1917

TO A CANADIAN AVIATOR WHO DIED FOR HIS COUNTRY IN FRANCE

Tossed like a falcon from the hunter's wrist,
A sweeping plunge, a sudden shattering noise,
And thou hast dared, with a long spiral twist,
The elastic stairway to the rising sun.
Peril below thee and above, peril
Within thy car; but peril cannot daunt
Thy peerless heart: gathering wing and poise,
Thy plane transfigured, and thy motor-chant
Subduèd to a whisper—then a silence,—

And thou art but a disembodied venture
In the void.

But Death, who has learned to fly,
Still matchless when his work is to be done,
Met thee between the armies and the sun;
Thy speck of shadow faltered in the sky;
Then thy dead engine and thy broken wings
Drooped through the arc and passed in fire,
A wreath of smoke—a breathless exhalation.
But ere that came a vision sealed thine eyes,
Lulling thy senses with oblivion;
And from its sliding station in the skies
Thy dauntless soul upward in circles soared
To the sublime and purest radiance whence it sprang.

In all their eyries, eagles shall mourn thy fate,
And leaving on the lonely crags and scaurs
Their unprotected young, shall congregate
High in the tenuous heaven and anger the sun
With screams, and with a wild audacity
Dare all the battle danger of thy flight;
Till weary with combat one shall desert the light,
Fall like a bolt of thunder and check his fall
On the high ledge, smoky with mist and cloud,
Where his neglected eaglets shriek aloud,
And drawing the film across his sovereign sight
Shall dream of thy swift soul immortal
Mounting in circles, faithful beyond death.

c. 1917
To the Canadian Mothers and Three Other Poems, 1917

ON THE DEATH OF CLAUDE DEBUSSY

(March 26th 1918)

Then Death who was watching
Raised him more tenderly
Than the forms of other men,
And wrapped him in her hair,
Her mouth drooped to his mouth,
And they became one
Forever—

Then arose around them
A confusion of light and sound,
The complaint of the wind
In the plane-trees,
The far away pulse of a horn,
Ripples of fairy colour,
Rhythms of Spain,
The overtones of cymbals,
The sobs of tormented souls,
Cries of delight and their echoes,
The crystal stroke of goat-bells,
The tremor of temple gongs,
The robes of Melisande,
Trailing vague glories;
Fauns' eyes in the vapour,
Flutes of Dionysus,
Haunting his ruined fane,
Veils of rain, quenching the tulip gardens,
Sea-light at the roots of islands,
The Spirit of Puck
With the ghost of a humming-bird,
The chords of boys' voices,
The open organ tones;
And under all the pedal-point
Of the deep-based ocean,
Hidden under the mists,
Chanting, infinitely remote,
At the foot of enchanted cliffs.
Then with a turn of illumination,
An enharmonic change of vision,
Death and Debussy
Become France and her heroes,

As if all her sacred heroes
Were in that one form,
Clasped in the bosom of France,
Enfolded with her ideals and inspirations.

Then the group loses outline,
Firmness dissolves,
And surrounded by light and sound,
Shadows, they drift away
Into the shadow.

c. 1918
Beauty and Life, 1921

IN THE SELKIRKS

The old grey shade of the Mountain
   Stands in the open sky,
Counting, as if at his leisure,
   The days of Eternity.

The Stream comes down from its Sources,
   Afar in the glacial height,
Rushing along through the valley
   In loops of silver light.

"What is my duty, O Mountain,
   Is it to stand like thee?
Is it, O flashing torrent,
   Like thee—to be free?"

The Man utters the questions,
   He breathes—he is gone!
The Mountain stands in the heavens,
   The Stream rushes on.

c. 1921
Beauty and Life, 1921

BYRON ON WORDSWORTH
Being discovered stanzas of Don Juan

(To My Friend Colonel Henry C. Osborne for the Byron Centenary
1824 April Nineteenth 1924)

Our old Lake Poet, so the tale is set,
When his young northern blood was sharp and eager,
Along with a young person called Annette
Vallon, (later a royalist intriguer,)
Managed somehow and somewhere to beget
A daughter, tho' the detail's somewhat meager,
The outcome "of an innocent flirtation,
Not quite adultery, but adulteration."

For she was French and William was a Briton,
And a chaste youth, if ever youth was chaste,
At least in after life he chose to sit on
A lofty righteous throne and live encased
In a dull code; perhaps he said, "Once bitten
Twice shy". Perhaps no virgin English waist
Was quite so tempting? But 'tis no conjecture
He was past-master of the moral lecture.

Not that I blame him for this charming bastard,
Got in the lusty plain of sunny France,
The best of us at times are overmastered
By a fine woman and a happy chance,
But when I think of that Old Poet plastered
And whited o'er with praise, it makes me dance
That he could pose and smirk and safely do it,
'Twas quite all right so long as no one knew it.

No, I don't blame him, that is not the point,
I never sat in judgment on my neighbours.
I must confess, tho', that I liked to anoint
With acid those who loved me and whose labours
Were bent to show the time was out of joint,
Because that I preferred strings, pipes and tabors
And light and dance and song and wine and women
To their damned cant and most infernal trimmin'.

No, I don't blame him, but the effect on me
Has been most undeniably disturbing,

For all these years I've lived in Purgatory,
And hoped, by constant penitential curbing
Of all my native deviltry, to see
At last the gate of heaven and not perturbing
Saint Peter in the least to let me through
To walk with Wordsworth, Coleridge and their crew.

I was about to renovate Don Juan,
Before I left for Heaven, and recant,
And swear by all the gods the social ruin
I sought to create was merely so much rant,
A naughty lad a teapot-tempest brewing,
Just to disturb the folk that cant and chant
That men were angels all and women purer,
That was the fact and nothing could be surer,

But now I am cast down and quite dejected
And my clear spirit is stirred up and riled,
Tho' the great Goethe said, when I reflected,
That I was nothing but a little child,
I am convinced the next time I'm inspected
"This reformation is entirely spiled"
Will be the verdict of my guardian hoary
Because of William Wordsworth's moral story.

"The child is father of the man";—that was his plaint,
But some men do not linger in society
Quite long enough—I might have been a Saint;
My famed concupiscence and inebriety
Might have developed into something quaint,
If I'd matured the seeds of "natural piety",
But they were burnt up and destroyed, Fate harsh is,
By fever in the Missolonghi marshes.

Thus far I wrote when I was called to Heaven
And rushed thro' ether like a rebel star.
They heard from Purgatory I had seven
New stanzas to Don Juan—I went to par—
The prettiest female angels and eleven
Apostles waiting for me at the bar!
St. Peter said, "I really hope, dear Byron,
"That you won't find it damp here, we've no fire on."

Heaven was a disappointment from the first,
It lacks distinction, leisure and variety,
The place is overcrowded, dulled and cursed
With flatulent folk who bore one to satiety;
The best would side with Peter, if they durst,

Who whispered me one day with frank impiety,
When I was lounging with him at the portal,
"'Twas a mistake to make the soul immortal."

Of all the spirits I like Heine best,
Who looked me up the moment that I landed.
He keeps alive his bright and bitter zest;
He scorns to do whatever is commanded.
"To put *us* here was but a sorry jest,
A verdict fair," he said, "to be quite candid,
Would send us down to Hell with our own set,
Described in Aucassin and Nicolette."

c. 1924
Privately published by the author, 1924

POWASSAN'S DRUM

Throb—throb—throb—throb;—
Is this throbbing a sound
Or an ache in the air?
Pervasive as light,
Measured and inevitable,
It seems to float from no distance,
But to live in the listening world—
Throb—throb—throb—throb—throbbing
The sound of Powassan's Drum.

He crouches in his dwarf wigwam
Wizened with fasting,
Fierce with thirst,
Making great medicine
In memory of hated things dead
Or in menace of hated things to come,
And the universe listens
To the throb—throb—throb—throb—
Throbbing of Powassan's Drum.

The world seems lost and shallow,
Seems sunken and filled with water,
With shores lightly moving

Of marish grass and slender reeds.
Through it all goes
The throbbing of Powassan's Drum.

Has it gone on forever,
As the pulse of Being?
Will it last till the world's end
As the pulse of Being?
He crouches under the poles
Covered with strips of birchbark
And branches of poplar and pine,
Piled for shade and dying
In dense perfume,
With closed eyelids
With eyes so fierce,
Burning under and through
The ancient worn eyelids,
He crouches and beats his drum.

The morning star formed
Like a pearl in the shell of darkness;
Light welled like water from the springs of morning;
The stars in the earth shadow
Caught like whitefish in a net;
The sun, the fisherman,
Pulling the net to the shore of night,
Flashing with the fins of the caught stars;—
All to the throbbing of Powassan's Drum.

The live things in the world
Hear it and are silent.
They hide silent and charmed
As if guarding a secret;
Charmed and silent hiding a rich secret,
Throbbing all to the
Throb—throb—throbbing of Powassan's Drum.

Stealthy as death the water
Wanders in the long grass,
And spangs of sunlight
Slide on the slender reeds
Like beads of bright oil.
The sky is a bubble blown so tense
The blue has gone grey
Stretched to the throb—throb—throb—throb—
Throbbing of Powassan's Drum.

Is it a memory of hated things dead
That he beats—famished—
Or a menace of hated things to come
That he beats—parched with anger
And famished with hatred—?

The sun waited all day.
There was no answer.
He hauled his net
And the glint of the star-fins
Flashed in the water of twilight;
There was no answer.
But in the northeast
A storm cloud reaches like a hand
Out of the half darkness.
The spectral fingers of cloud
Grope in the heavens,
And at moments, sharp as pain,
A bracelet of bright fire
Plays on the wrist of the cloud.
Thunder from the hollow of the hand
Comes almost soundless, like an air pressure,
And the cloud rears up
To the throbbing of Powassan's Drum.
An infusion of bitter darkness
Stains the sweet water of twilight.

Then from the reeds stealing,
A shadow noiseless,
A canoe moves noiseless as sleep,
Noiseless as the trance of deep sleep
And an Indian still as a statue,
Moulded out of deep sleep,
Headless, still as a headless statue
Moulded out of deep sleep,
Sits modelled in full power,
Haughty in manful power,
Headless and impotent in power.
The canoe stealthy as death
Drifts to the throbbing of Powassan's Drum.
The Indian fixed like bronze
Trails his severed head
Through the dead water
Holding it by the hair,
By the plaits of hair,

Wound with sweet grass and tags of silver.
The face looks through the water
Up to its throne on the shoulders of power,
Unquenched eyes burning in the water,
Piercing beyond the shoulders of power
Up to the fingers of the storm cloud.
Is this the meaning of the magic—
The translation into sight
Of the viewless hate?
Is this what the world waited for
As it listened to the throb—throb—throb—throb—
Throbbing of Powassan's Drum?

The sun could not answer.
The tense sky burst and went dark
And could not answer.
But the storm answers.
The murdered shadow sinks in the water.
Uprises the storm
And crushes the dark world;
At the core of the rushing fury
Bursting hail, tangled lightning
Wind in a wild vortex
Lives the triumphant throb—throb—throb—throb—
Throbbing of Powassan's Drum.

c. January-February 1925
The Poems of Duncan Campbell Scott, 1926

THOUGHTS

These thoughts of mine
Oh! would they were away.
Thoughts that have progress
Give me stay
And eagerness for life;
But these dead thoughts
Hang like burned forests
By a northern lake,
Whose waters take
The bone-grey skeletons

And mirror the grey bones,
Both dead, the trees and the reflections.

Compare these thoughts
To anything that nothing tells,—
To toads alive for centuries in stone cells,
To a styleless dial on a fiery lawn,
To the trapped bride within the oaken chest,
Or to the dull, intolerable bells
That beat the dawn
And will not let us rest!

1926
The Poems of Duncan Campbell Scott, 1926

PRAIRIE WIND

Indolent wind on the prairie
   Wind that loiters and passes
What are you striving to whisper
   To the dead pale prairie grasses;

Where the alkali lake-shore is blistered,
   Hopeless of dew or shower
Where the buttes are an ashen purple
   Like the wraith of a giant flower;

Are you telling the prairie grasses
   With the sound of whispering fountains,
How you found a tarn that was lonely
   Since the making of the mountains;

You paused on the fern-green margin
   And saw on the surface stilly
The face of a star in the water
   That looked like a water-lily;

Then you rushed on the frail enchantment
   As if 'twere a passionate duty
To carry to far away deserts
   The charm of the virginal beauty;

But the closer you pressed and regarded,
  Ripples rippled over in fretwork
And the vision was twisted and vanished,
  Confused and astray in the network;

You hovered above the surface,
  For the waters to cease their tremble,
For the star to be liquid lily,
  For the colour to reassemble;

But the vision you found in the twilight
  You could never again recapture,
It was lost in one careless impulse
  In the first wild rush of the rapture;

O wind are you thinking ever
  Of the tarn on the eve you caught her,
In her tangle of emerald azure,
  With her lily-star in the water;

Do you think, had you only been quiet,
  The colour and star were conspiring
To tell you their secret of beauty
  And now—only dreams and desiring.

O wind on the desolate prairie,
  Wind that loiters and passes,
Is this your disconsolate whisper
  To the dead pale prairie grasses?

c. 1926
The Poems of Duncan Campbell Scott, 1926

EN ROUTE

The train has stopped for no apparent reason
In the wilds;
A frozen lake is level and fretted over
With rippled wind lines;
The sun is burning in the South; the season
Is winter trembling at a touch of spring.
A little hill with birches and a ring
Of cedars—all so still, so pure with snow—

It seems a tiny landscape in the moon.
Long wisps of shadow from the naked birches
Lie on the white in lines of cobweb-grey;
From the cedar roots the snow has shrunk away,
One almost hears it tinkle as it thaws.
Traces there are of wild things in the snow—
Partridge at play, tracks of the foxes' paws
That broke a path to sun them in the trees.
They're going fast where all impressions go
On a frail substance—images like these,
Vagaries the unconscious mind receives
From nowhere, and lets go to nothingness
With the lost flush of last year's autumn leaves.

c. 1930-31
The Green Cloister: Later Poems, 1935

AT GULL LAKE: AUGUST, 1810

Gull lake set in the rolling prairie—
Still there are reeds on the shore,
As of old the poplars shimmer
As summer passes;
Winter freezes the shallow lake to the core;
Storm passes,
Heat parches the sedges and grasses,
Night comes with moon-glimmer,
Dawn with the morning-star;
All proceeds in the flow of Time
As a hundred years ago.

Then two camps were pitched on the shore,
The clustered teepees
Of Tabashaw Chief of the Saulteaux.
And on a knoll tufted with poplars
Two grey tents of a trader—
Nairne of the Orkneys.
Before his tents under the shade of the poplars
Sat Keejigo, third of the wives
Of Tabashaw Chief of the Saulteaux;

Clad in the skins of antelopes
Broidered with porcupine quills
Coloured with vivid dyes,
Vermilion here and there
In the roots of her hair,
A half-moon of powder-blue
On her brow, her cheeks
Scored with light ochre streaks.
Keejigo daughter of Launay
The Normandy hunter
And Oshawan of the Saulteaux,
Troubled by fugitive visions
In the smoke of the camp-fires,
In the close dark of the teepee,
Flutterings of colour
Along the flow of the prairies,
Spangles of flower tints
Caught in the wonder of dawn,
Dreams of sounds unheard—
The echoes of echo,
Star she was named for
Keejigo, star of the morning,
Voices of storm—
Wind-rush and lightning,—
The beauty of terror;
The twilight moon
Coloured like a prairie lily,
The round moon of pure snow,
The beauty of peace;
Premonitions of love and of beauty
Vague as shadows cast by a shadow.
Now she had found her hero,
And offered her body and spirit
With abject unreasoning passion,
As Earth abandons herself
To the sun and the thrust of the lightning.
Quiet were all the leaves of the poplars,
Breathless the air under their shadow,
As Keejigo spoke of these things to her heart
In the beautiful speech of the Saulteaux.

The flower lives on the prairie,
The wind in the sky,
I am here my beloved;
The wind and the flower.

The crane hides in the sand-hills,
Where does the wolverine hide?
I am here my beloved,
Heart's-blood on the feathers
The foot caught in the trap.

Take the flower in your hand,
The wind in your nostrils;
I am here my beloved;
Release the captive
Heal the wound under the feathers.

A storm-cloud was marching
Vast on the prairie,
Scored with livid ropes of hail,
Quick with nervous vines of lightning—
Twice had Nairne turned her away
Afraid of the venom of Tabashaw,
Twice had the Chief fired at his tents
And now when two bullets
Whistled above the encampment
He yelled "Drive this bitch to her master."

Keejigo went down a path by the lake;
Thick at the tangled edges,
The reeds and the sedges
Were grey as ashes
Against the death-black water;
The lightning scored with double flashes
The dark lake-mirror and loud
Came the instant thunder.
Her lips still moved to the words of her music,
"Release the captive,
Heal the wound under the feathers."

At the top of the bank
The old wives caught her and cast her down
Where Tabashaw crouched by his camp-fire.
He snatched a live brand from the embers,
Seared her cheeks,
Blinded her eyes,
Destroyed her beauty with fire,
Screaming, "Take that face to your lover."
Keejigo held her face to the fury
And made no sound.
The old wives dragged her away

And threw her over the bank
Like a dead dog.

Then burst the storm—
The Indians' screams and the howls of the dogs
Lost in the crash of hail
That smashed the sedges and reeds,
Stripped the poplars of leaves,
Tore and blazed onwards,
Wasting itself with riot and tumult—
Supreme in the beauty of terror.

The setting sun struck the retreating cloud
With a rainbow, not an arc but a column
Built with the glory of seven metals;
Beyond in the purple deeps of the vortex
Fell the quivering vines of the lightning.
The wind withdrew the veil from the shrine of the moon,
She rose changing her dusky shade for the glow
Of the prairie lily, till free of all blemish of colour
She came to her zenith without a cloud or a star,
A lovely perfection, snow-pure in the heaven of midnight.
After the beauty of terror the beauty of peace.

But Keejigo came no more to the camps of her people;
Only the midnight moon knew where she felt her way,
Only the leaves of autumn, the snows of winter
Knew where she lay.

c. 1934
The Green Cloister: Later Poems, 1935

A SCENE AT LAKE MANITOU

In front of the fur-trader's house at Lake Manitou
Indian girls were gathering the hay,
Half labour and half play;
So small the stony field
And light the yield
They gathered it up in their aprons,
Racing and chasing,
And laughing loud with the fun

Of building the tiny cocks.
The sun was hot on the rocks.
The lake was all shimmer and tremble
To the bronze-green islands of cedars and pines;
In the channel between the water shone
Like an inset of polished stone;
Beyond them a shadowy trace
Of the shore of the lake
Was lost in the veil of haze.

Above the field on the rocky point
Was a cluster of canvas tents,
Nearly deserted, for the women had gone
Berry-picking at dawn
With most of the children.
Under the shade of a cedar screen
Between the heat of the rock and the heat of the sun,
The Widow Frederick
Whose Indian name means Stormy Sky,
Was watching her son Matanack
In the sunlight die,
As she had watched his father die in the sunlight.
Worn out with watching,
She gazed at the far-off islands
That seemed in a mirage to float
Moored in the sultry air.
She had ceased to hear the breath in Matanack's throat
Or the joy of the children gathering the hay.
Death, so near, had taken all sound from the day,
And she sat like one that grieves
Unconscious of grief.

With a branch of poplar leaves
She kept the flies from his face,
And her mind wandered in space
With the difficult past
When her husband had faded away;
How she had struggled to live
For Matanack four years old;
Triumphant at last!

She had taught him how and where
To lay the rabbit snare,
And how to set
Under the ice, the net,
The habits of shy wild things
Of the forest and marsh;

To his inherited store
She had added all her lore;
He was just sixteen years old
A hunter crafty and bold;
But there he lay,
And his life with its useless cunning
Was ebbing out with the day.

Fitfully visions rose in her tired brain,
Faded away, and came again and again.
She remembered the first day
He had gone the round of the traps alone,
She saw him stand in the frosty light
Two silver-foxes over his shoulder.
She heard the wolves howl,
Or the hoot of a hunting owl,
Or saw in a sunlit gap
In the woods, a mink in the trap;
Mingled with thoughts of Nanabojou
And the powerful Manitou
That lived in the lake;
Mingled with thoughts of Jesus
Who raised a man from the dead,
So Father Pacifique said.

Suddenly something broke in her heart.
To save him, to keep him forever!
She had prayed to their Jesus,
She had called on Mary His mother
To save him, to keep him forever!
The Holy Water and the Scapular!
She had used all the Holy Water
Father Pacifique had given her;
He had worn his Scapular
Always, and for months had worn hers too;
There was nothing more to be done
That Christians could do.

Now she would call on the Powers of the Earth and the
Air,
The Powers of the Water;
She would give to the Manitou
That lived in the lake
All her treasured possessions,
And He would give her the lad.
The children heard her scream,
The trader and the loafing Indians

Saw her rush into her tent and bring out her blankets
And throw them into the lake,
Screaming demented screams,
Dragging her treasures into the light,
Scattering them far on the water.
First of them all, her gramophone,
She hurled like a stone;
And they caught her and held her
Just as she swung aloft the next of her treasures
Her little hand-sewing-machine.
They threw her down on the rock
And five men held her until,
Not conquered by them,
But subdued by her will
She lay still.

The trader looked at the boy,
"He's done for," he said.
He covered the head
And went down to the Post;
The Indians, never glancing,
Afraid of the ghost,
Slouched away to their loafing.
After a curious quiet
The girls began the play
Of gathering the last of the hay.

She knew it was all in vain;
He was slain by the foe
That had slain his father.
She put up her hair that had fallen over her eyes,
And with movements, weary and listless,
Tidied her dress.
He had gone to his father
To hunt in the Spirit Land
And to be with Jesus and Mary.

She was alone now and knew
What she would do:
The Trader would debit her winter goods,
She would go into the woods
And gather the fur,
Live alone with the stir
Alone with the silence;
Revisit the Post,
Return to hunt in September;
So had she done as long as she could remember.

She sat on the rock beside Matanack
Resolute as of old,
Her strength and her spirit came back.
Someone began to hammer down at the Trader's house.
The late August air was cold
With a presage of frost.
The islands had lost
Their mirage-mooring in air
And lay dark on the burnished water
Against the sunset flare—
Standing ruins of blackened spires
Charred by the fury of fires
That had passed that way,
That were smouldering and dying out in the West
At the end of the day.

c. 1935
The Green Cloister: Later Poems, 1935

AT DELOS

An iris-flower with topaz leaves,
With a dark heart of deeper gold,
Died over Delos when light failed
And the night grew cold.

No wave fell mourning in the sea
Where age on age beauty had died;
For that frail colour withering away
No sea-bird cried.

There is no grieving in the world
As beauty fades throughout the years:
The pilgrim with the weary heart
Brings to the grave his tears.

c. 1939
Queen's Quarterly, 1939
The Circle of Affection and Other Pieces in Prose and Verse, 1947

Marjorie Pickthall

1883–1922

Pickthall was born in Gunnersby, Middlesex, England in 1883 and moved to Toronto with her family in 1889. She showed an early talent for literature as well as music, studying violin into her late teens. At the age of fifteen, she sold a short story to the *Toronto Globe*, a remarkable accomplishment for one so young. She wrote other periodical pieces and brought out three novels between 1905 and 1908. She was evidently never strong physically. She was very close to her parents and the death of her mother in 1910 had a profound effect on her life, causing her to give up writing entirely for a time. After a short period of work in the Victoria College library (University of Toronto), she left for England in 1912 to stay with relatives. Evidently, her spirits rebounded to a degree, for 1913 saw the publication of her first volume of poetry, *The Drift of Pinions*. In 1915 she published another volume of prose, and in 1916, *The Lamp of Poor Souls, and Other Poems*, which includes the contents of *The Drift of Pinions*, as well as new poems, such as "Improvisation on the Flute" and "Two Lyrics". During World War I, she learned to drive an ambulance and also undertook both farm and library work. But death was always close at hand and, amongst others she knew, the War claimed her cousin Roy Pickthall. In 1920 she returned to Canada, moving to British Columbia after a short stay in Toronto, and spending time both in Vancouver and on Vancouver Island. She continued to write, producing a serial novel started in England—*The Bridge: A Story of the Great Lakes*—in 1921. *The Wood Carver's Wife and Later Poems* was published in 1922, the year of her death as the result of an embolism after surgery in Vancouver. Two posthumous works are notable—*Angels' Shoes and Other Stories* (1923) and *Complete Poems* (1925).

Pickthall had long been interested in legend, myth, and Biblical story. Her early years, in particular, were marked by a fascination with the more sublime beauties of the natural world, as can be seen in "The Pool" (1907) and "Bridegroom of Cana" (1907). Her poetic inspiration was predominantly romantic, and it is this voice, with its kinship to Keatsian lyric, that she tends to maintain throughout most of her canon, despite her spiritual preoccupations, which may have as much to do with her apprehension of the brevity of life as with her devout Anglo-Catholicism. Indeed, the romantic strain probably caused her work to fade from fashion. But while some of her prose displays a kind of splendid naïveté, her poems—such as "Quiet" (1917) and "Mary Tired" (1919)—are remarkable personal evocations of a searching, sweet-tempered spirit, showing her to be an innocent visionary for whom faith was sufficient test and guarantee of divine benevolence. She was not a mystic—certainly she did not tread the road delineated by Evelyn Underhill; but the absence of the dark torment of Donnian angst should not be taken as evidence of a lack of suffering. The death of her mother, the proximity of wartime misery, and her own prolonged fragility of health constituted torment enough. There is solace in affirmation and calmness in faith; and her poetic verbalisation, based on her own sense of reality, has to be taken seriously.

While her structures are conventional, Pickthall offers a craftsmanship that is striking and beautiful both in terms of image and sound. In the latter respect, she is profoundly musical, and her sense of assonance—consider her variations of single vowels within a line or in adjacent lines—and alliterative power used for emphasis and unity is unfailing. She was a writer of superb, short lyrics of undeniable romanticism in an increasingly realistic age that would demand a more modernist voice before it would bestow any accolades. Yet, had she lived, one might doubt whether she would have altered her voice to suit the newer trends. Like Carman, she knew how to sing in her own way. What she set out to do in poems such as "Resurgam" she accomplished with a grace and soft-spoken strength that demands attention. In her era, she was not alone in finding older forms sufficient and beautiful, and an awareness of her capacities will serve to remind readers that stylistic trends do not cause *all* writers, or *all* audiences, to march in lock-step.

The largest collection of Pickthall's poetry is *The Complete Poems of Marjorie Pickthall* (1925), with a foreword by Arthur C. Pickthall. Another source is Lorne Pierce's *The Selected Poems of Marjorie Pickthall* (1957).

Works on Pickthall's poetry include: J.D. Logan, *Marjorie Pickthall: Her Poetic Genius and Art* (1922); Lorne Pierce, *Marjorie Pickthall, A Book of Remembrance* (1925); "Dream-Gardens" in W.E. Collin's *The White Savannahs* (1936); Sister St. Cecilia, *Marjorie Pickthall, The Ethereal Minstrel of Canada* (M.A. Thesis, Ottawa University, 1941); Lorne Pierce, "Marjorie Pickthall", *Leading Canadian Poets*, ed. W.P. Percival (1948), 168-76; Janice Williamson, "Framed by History: Marjorie Pickthall's Devices and Desire" in *A Mazing Space: Writing Canadian Women Writing*, ed. Shirley Neuman and Smaro Kamboureli (1986), 167-78; Diana M.A. Relke, "Demeter's Daughter: Marjorie Pickthall and the Quest for Poetic Identity", *Canadian Literature* 115 (Winter 1986), 28-43; and Alex Kizuk, "The Case of the Forgotten Electra: Marjorie Pickthall's Apostrophes and Feminine Poetics", *Studies in Canadian Literature* 12 (1987), 1, 15-34.

A MOTHER IN EGYPT

"About midnight will I go out into the midst of Egypt; and all the firstborn in the land of Egypt shall die, from the firstborn of Pharaoh that sitteth upon the throne, even unto the firstborn of the maid-servant that is behind the mill." —Exodus xi: 4, 5.

Is the noise of grief in the palace over the river
For this silent one at my side?
There came a hush in the night, and he rose with his hands
  a-quiver
Like lotus petals adrift on the swing of the tide.
O small soft hands, the day groweth old for sleeping!
O small still feet, rise up, for the hour is late!
Rise up, my son, for I hear them mourning and weeping
In the temple down by the gate.

Hushed is the face that was wont to brighten with laughter
When I sang at the mill,
And silence unbroken shall greet the sorrowful dawns
  hereafter,
The house shall be still.
Voice after voice takes up the burden of wailing,—
Do you heed, do you hear?—in the high-priest's house by the
  wall;
But mine is the grief, and their sorrow is all unavailing.
Will he wake at their call?

Something I saw of the broad, dim wings half folding
The passionless brow.
Something I saw of the sword the shadowy hands were
  holding,—
What matters it now?
I held you close, dear face, as I knelt and harkened
To the wind that cried last night like a soul in sin,
When the broad, bright stars dropped down and the soft sky
  darkened,
And the Presence moved therein.

I have heard men speak in the market-place of the city,
Low voiced, in a breath,
Of a god who is stronger than ours, and who knows not
  changing nor pity,
Whose anger is death.

Nothing I know of the lords of the outland races,
But Amun is gentle and Hathor the Mother is mild,
And who would descend from the light of the peaceful places
To war on a child?

Yet here he lies, with a scarlet pomegranate petal
Blown down on his cheek.
The slow sun sinks to the sand like a shield of some burnished
metal,
But he does not speak.
I have called, I have sung, but he neither will hear nor waken;
So lightly, so whitely he lies in the curve of my arm,
Like a feather let fall from the bird that the arrow hath taken.
Who could see him, and harm?

"The swallow flies home to her sleep in the eaves of the altar,
And the crane to her nest,"—
So do we sing o'er the mill, and why, ah, why should I falter,
Since he goes to his rest?
Does he play in their flowers as he played among these with
his mother?
Do the gods smile downward and love him and give him their
care?
Guard him well, O ye gods, till I come; lest the wrath of that
Other
Should reach to him there!

1905
Century, April 1905
The Drift of Pinions, 1913

THE BRIDEGROOM OF CANA

"There was a marriage in Cana of Galilee . . . And both Jesus was called, and His disciples, to the marriage."

Veil thine eyes, O belovèd, my spouse,
Turn them away,
Lest in their light my life withdrawn
Dies as a star, as a star in the day,
As a dream in the dawn.

Slenderly hang the olive leaves
Sighing apart;
The rose and silver doves in the eaves
With a murmur of music bind our house.
Honey and wine in thy words are stored,
Thy lips are bright as the edge of a sword
That hath found my heart,
That hath found my heart.

Sweet, I have waked from a dream of thee,—
And of Him.
He who came when the songs were done.
From the net of thy smiles my heart went free
And the golden lure of thy love grew dim.
I turned to them asking, "Who is He,
Royal and sad, who comes to the feast
And sits Him down in the place of the least?"
And they said, "He is Jesus, the carpenter's son."

Hear how my harp on a single string
Murmurs of love.
Down in the fields the thrushes sing
And the lark is lost in the light above,
Lost in the infinite, glowing whole,
As I in thy soul,
As I in thy soul.

Love, I am fain for thy glowing grace
As the pool for the star, as the rain for the rill.
Turn to me, trust to me, mirror me
As the star in the pool, as the cloud in the sea.
Love, I looked awhile in His face
And was still.

The shaft of the dawn strikes clear and sharp;
Hush, my harp.
Hush, my harp, for the day is begun,
And the lifting, shimmering flight of the swallow
Breaks in a curve on the brink of morn,
Over the sycamores, over the corn,
Cling to me, cleave to me, prison me
As the mote in the flame, as the shell in the sea,
For the winds of the dawn say, "Follow, follow
Jesus Bar-Joseph, the carpenter's son."

1907
University Magazine, October 1907
The Drift of Pinions, 1913

THE POOL

Come with me, follow me, swift as a moth,
Ere the wood-doves waken.
Lift the long leaves and look down, look down
Where the light is shaken,
Amber and brown,
On the woven ivory roots of the reed,
On a floating flower and a weft of weed
And a feather of froth.

Here in the night all wonders are,
Lapped in the lift of the ripple's swing,—
A silver shell and a shaken star,
And a white moth's wing.
Here the young moon when the mists unclose
Swims like the bud of a golden rose.

I would live like an elf where the wild grapes cling,
I would chase the thrush
From the red rose-berries.
All the day long I would laugh and swing
With the black choke-cherries.

I would shake the bees from the milkweed blooms,
And cool, O cool,
Night after night I would leap in the pool,
And sleep with the fish in the roots of the rush.
Clear, O clear my dreams should be made
Of emerald light and amber shade,
Of silver shallows and golden glooms.
Sweet, O sweet my dreams should be
As the dark, sweet water enfolding me
Safe as a blind shell under the sea.

1907
Metropolitan, October 1907
The Drift of Pinions, 1913

THE SHEPHERD BOY

When the red moon hangs over the fold,
And the cypress shadow is rimmed with gold,
O, little sheep, I have laid me low,
My face against the old earth's face,
Where one by one the white moths go,
And the brown bee has his sleeping place.
And then I have whispered, Mother hear,
For the owls are awake and the night is near,
And whether I lay me near or far
No lips shall kiss me,
No eye shall miss me,
Saving the eye of a cold white star.

And the old brown woman answers mild,
Rest you safe on my heart, O child.
Many a shepherd, many a king,
I fold them safe from their sorrowing.
Gwenever's heart is bound with dust,
Tristram dreams of the dappled doe,
But the bugle moulders, the blade is rust;
Stilled are the trumpets of Jericho,
And the tired men sleep by the walls of Troy.
Little and lonely,
Knowing me only,
Shall I not comfort you, shepherd-boy?

When the wind wakes in the apple-trees,
And the shy hare feeds on the wild fern stem,
I say my prayers to the Trinity,—
The prayers that are three and the charms that are seven
To the angels guarding the towers of heaven,—
And I lay my head on her raiment's hem,
Where the young grass darkens the strawberry star,
Where the iris buds and the bellworts are.

All night I hear her breath go by
Under the arch of the empty sky.
All night her heart beats under my head,
And I lie as still as the ancient dead,
Warm as the young lambs there with the sheep.
I and no other,

Close to my Mother,
Fold my hands in her hands, and sleep.

1909
Youth's Companion, June 1909
The Drift of Pinions, 1913

THREE ISLAND SONGS

After the wind in the wood,
Peace, and the night.
After the bond and the brood,
Flight.
After the height and the hush
Where the wild hawk swings,
Heart of the earth-loving thrush
Shaken with wings.

After the bloom and the leaf
Rain on the nest.
After the splendour and grief
Rest.
After the hills and the far
Glories and gleams,
Cloud, and the dawn of a star,
And dreams.

O, the grey rocks of the islands and the hemlock green above
them,
The foam beneath the wild rose bloom, the star above the
shoal.
When I am old and weary I'll wake my heart to love them,
For the blue ways of the islands are wound about my soul.

Here in the early even when the young grey dew is falling,
And the king-heron seeks his mate beyond the loneliest wild,
Still your heart in the twilight, and you'll hear the river calling
Through all her outmost islands to seek her last-born child.

I sat among the green leaves, and heard the nuts falling,
The broad red butterflies were gold against the sun,
But in between the silence and the sweet birds calling
The nuts fell one by one.
Why should they fall and the year but half over?
Why should sorrow seek me and I so young and kind?
The leaf is on the bough and the dew is on the clover,
But the green nuts are falling in the wind.

O, I gave my lips away and all my soul behind them.
Why should trouble follow and the quick tears start?
The little birds may love and fly with only God to mind them,
But the green nuts are falling on my heart.

c. 1913
The Drift of Pinions, 1913

PÈRE LALEMANT

I lift the Lord on high,
Under the murmuring hemlock boughs, and see
The small birds of the forest lingering by
And making melody.
These are mine acolytes and these my choir,
And this mine altar in the cool green shade,
Where the wild soft-eyed does draw nigh
Wondering, as in the byre
Of Bethlehem the oxen heard Thy cry
And saw Thee, unafraid.

My boatmen sit apart,
Wolf-eyed, wolf-sinewed, stiller than the trees.
Help me, O Lord, for very slow of heart
And hard of faith are these.
Cruel are they, yet Thy children. Foul are they,
Yet wert Thou born to save them utterly.
Then make me as I pray,
Just to their hates, kind to their sorrows, wise

After their speech, and strong before their free
Indomitable eyes.

Do the French lilies reign
Over Mount Royal and Stadacona still?
Up the St. Lawrence comes the spring again,
Crowning each southward hill
And blossoming pool with beauty, while I roam
Far from the perilous folds that are my home,
There where we built St. Ignace for our needs,
Shaped the rough roof tree, turned the first sweet sod,
St. Ignace and St. Louis, little beads
On the rosary of God.

Pines shall Thy pillars be,
Fairer than those Sidonian cedars brought
By Hiram out of Tyre, and each birch-tree
Shines like a holy thought.
But come no worshippers; shall I confess,
St. Francis-like, the birds of the wilderness?
O, with Thy love my lonely head uphold.
A wandering shepherd I, who hath no sheep:
A wandering soul, who hath no scrip, nor gold,
Nor anywhere to sleep.

My hour of rest is done;
On the smooth ripple lifts the long canoe;
The hemlocks murmur sadly as the sun
Slants his dim arrows through.
Whither I go I know not, nor the way,
Dark with strange passions, vexed with heathen charms,
Holding I know not what of life or death;
Only be Thou beside me day by day,
Thy rod my guide and comfort, underneath
Thy everlasting arms.

c. 1913
The Drift of Pinions, 1913

IMPROVISATION ON THE FLUTE

My lost delight, my guest,
Fled from me when I stirred,
Silently as the bird
That has no nest.

She has gathered darkness to build her a nest
And the little leaves of cloud.
She crouches with her breast against darkness,
And hides as a hare in the meadows of night.
It covers her like long grass
Whose blossom is all of stars;
Crocus-stars, stars of anemone,
Where cling the moths that are the longings of men.
She is born of the evening,
When the moon breathes the scent of young thyme,
And the dead shepherds hear the sheep cropping in the
dew.

She is slain of the morning,
When the thin willow-leaves tremble like fire
Burning the branches,
As if each were a sorrow that burned and shone
Forever.
My shadow, my desire,
Come to me, listen, and stay,
Ah, never?
With the day
She is gone, she is gone
Away
Forever—
My guest, my lost delight,
Come nearer, star by star.
Sweet as the lips of night
Your kisses are.

1915
University Magazine, April 1915
The Lamp of Poor Souls and Other Poems, 1916

TWO LYRICS

I

All in a rainy hazel wood
I watched the hyacinth break
Her lucent sheath, as if she could
Make summer for your sake.

And year by year the hyacinth-tide
Breaks in a foam of flowers
For other loves than we denied
And other griefs than ours.

Long wed, long dead, so I've been told,
But still when Spring's set free,
All in a drift of rainy gold
You walk the wood with me.

II

How looked she when she breathed good-bye?
Most like a bird, whose breast
Across a thousand wastes of sky
Is constant to her nest.

How looked she when she turned away?
Most as a spirit might,
Who shared our sorrow for a day
Yet kept her home in sight.

O, looked she sad or seemed she glad?
Most like a star, that knows
Only the loveliness it had,
The light to which it goes.

c. 1916
The Lamp of Poor Souls and Other Poems, 1916

INHERITANCE

Desolate strange sleep and wild
Came on me while yet a child;
I, before I tasted tears,
Knew the grief of all the years.

I, before I fronted pain,
Felt creation writhe and strain,
Sending ancient terrors through,
My small pulses, sweet and new.

I, before I learned how time
Robs all summers at their prime,
I, few seasons gone from birth,
Felt my body change to earth.

September 1917
The Wood Carver's Wife and Later Poems, 1922

QUIET

Come not the earliest petal here, but only
Wind, cloud, and star,
Lovely and far,
Make it less lonely.

Few are the feet that seek her here, but sleeping
Thoughts sweet as flowers
Linger for hours,
Things winged, yet weeping.

Here in the immortal empire of the grasses,
Time, like one wrong
Note in a song,
With their bloom, passes.

c. 1917
The Dial, 25 October 1917
The Wood Carver's Wife and Later Poems, 1922

THE GARDENER'S BOY

"All day I have fed on lilied thoughts of her,"
The gardener's boy sang in Gethsemane.
"She is quick, her garments make a lovely stir,
Like the wind going in an almond tree.
She is young, she hath doves' eyes, and like the vine
Her hands enclose me,—hers as she is mine.

"She shall feed among the lilies where I am,
Learning their silver names. When evening grows,
One bower shall hold me and my love, my lamb.
Which shall I clasp," he sang, "her or the rose?"
When the palm shadow barred the juniper
He lay at last to sleep and dream of her.

He saw not those who came when night was deep
Up from the city, walking hastily.
One seemed a strong man wan for fear and sleep.
One bore a lantern. One moved stumblingly.
The gardener's boy dreamed on the sunburned sod,
Smiling beside the agony of God.

1917
University Magazine, December 1919
The Wood Carver's Wife and Later Poems, 1922

MARY TIRED

Through the starred Judean night
She went, in travail of the Light.
With the earliest hush she saw
God beside her in the straw.

One poor taper glimmered clear,
Drowsing Joseph nodded near.
All the glooms were rosed with wings.
She that knew the Spirit's kiss
Wearied of the bright abyss.

She was tired of heavenly things.
There between the day and night
These she counted for delight:

Baby kids that butted hard
In the shadowy stable yard;
Silken doves that dipped and preened
Where the crumbling well-curb greened;
Sparrows in the vine, and small
Sapphired flies upon the wall,
So lovely they seemed musical.

In the roof a swift had built.
All the new-born airs were spilt
Out of cups the morning made
Of a glory and a shade.
These her solemn eyelids felt
While unseen the seraphs knelt.
Then a young mouse, sleek and bold,
Rustling in the winnowed gold,
To her shadow crept, and curled
Near the Ransom of the world.

1919
University Magazine, December 1919
The Wood Carver's Wife and Later Poems, 1922

RIDING

If I should live again,
Quick of sinew and vein
O God, let me be young,
With the honeycomb on my tongue,
All in a moment flung
With the dawn on a flowing plain,
Riding, riding, riding, riding
Between the sun and the rain.

If I, having been, must be,
O God, let it be so,
Swift and supple and free
With a long journey to go,

And the clink of the curb and the blow
Of hooves, and the wind at my knee,
Riding, riding, riding, riding
Between the hills and the sea.

c. July 1920
The Wood Carver's Wife and Later Poems, 1922

THE INDIAN DANCER

Over his feet the fringes fell,
The fox-fur fringes, white as noon;
It seemed his feet were musical.
They never stayed in the slow tune
That ran and rippled and changed its bars
And chimed for ever in falling notes,
As when the summer sings in stars
Of music born in bobolink throats.

All his wild strength was given in grace.
Scarce-plumed, the year's young grasses bent,
The warm airs touched his brooding face
Along the pathway that he went;
Giving no light, the full moon stood
Behind the birches on the hill,
The summer silence of the wood
Was a gold cup for love to fill.

Red lily-buds and blackening grapes,
And mandrakes gemmed with ivory bloom,—
The forest held a thousand shapes
Like music in the scented gloom.
She saw, as flower or song made fair,
The last light glow on crest and limb.
One barred owl-plume was in his hair,
Like a white moth it danced with him.

Into her willow flute she breathed
Her soul with delicate outs and ins,
Her soul was with the dew that sheathed
Love's bead work on his moccasins.

Her soul was in the fern that laid
Love's sweetness for his moving feet.
Between the moon-dawn and the shade
Her soul danced with the Malicete.

c. 1920
Canadian Home Journal, September 1920
The Complete Poems of Marjorie Pickthall, 1927

PALOME'S BOOK

Preface to this very private edition.

My dearest Daddy,
I am sending for you, and you only, to see, some of the little poems left by Palome, and found long after by Adam Laurent and Jenny Hurst, in the room painted with doves that had been hers at Paracuando.
Their place in the story I cannot yet show, but they will stand alone. And as in these times one does not quite know when or how any story will be told or any work finished, I am sending them to you, a little foretaste of "The Mountain."
I hope you will be pleased with them.

Your very loving
Daughter.

All days were night before this day's dear prime,
Dust in Time's hand or strewn about his feet,
Ashes of morning, suns and moons outworn.
Now we have back our heritage of Time.
Heaven rounds us like a shell, and very sweet
Sea-voices breathe, Beloved, it is morn.

The little doves go up and down in showers,
Over the spice-bud, underneath the bough,
Till I grow weary, counting little doves
Swift as our thoughts and feathered like our flowers.
Dearest of all, lean nearer, kiss me now.
God has no need of pity on their loves.

The loveliest ladies ever felt the wind
Blow on them from the doorsills of delight
Should stoop to me and give me sisterhood,—
She that was Star of Egypt out of mind,
And one world's rose, and one who led her knight
Weeping about the hollows of the wood.

There was an altar builded in the sun
By shipmen out of Argos, long ago,
Bound in bleak bronze and every stone engraven
With wings and faces, and each face was one,
Helen's. And there they fed a flame, to show
Poor mariners the sea-ways of the haven.

O Love, be very silent. Death will hear.
Helen was proud, she laughed her love and glory
When Paris leaned and kissed her on the lips.
She had another lover that was near.
He kissed her, and she changed into a story,
A half-heard song blown out to wandering ships.

I am Love's weakest, worthless, lost, unwise,
Cities were taken, kings uncrowned for her,
A thousand blades had blossom on her mouth,
A thousand spears were hid in her great eyes.
Over me too the little grasshopper
Shall chirr against the honey-breathing south.

Love, that has raised you higher, casts me down
From my proud places and remembered praise,
Though still a half-hushed worshipper you sit,
Though still you kneel as if I wore a crown,
O Love I love you most for these great ways
Of worship, while I am unworthy it.

Yea, could I grieve you, could I make you weep,
I have crowned you, wronged you, cast aside
Most cruelly for your sake my griefs and fears?
If you leaned closer on the kiss of sleep
And saw that in some silence I had died
Dreaming of you, O would you give me tears?

"Rise up, my love, my fair one, come away,
My love, my dove, my sister, undefiled."
I rose, I followed, but my friend was fled,
Though once I saw him through the morning's grey
And the last starshine, where he turned and smiled,
With amaranth newly bound upon his head.

"Woman, behold thy child, for it is Grief,
Sword-slender grief, the world within her hold.
Give her thy heart, be true to one another."
The voice endured the dropping of a leaf.

Then for so long I heard as when a gold
Ripe apple falls, "O Grief, behold your mother."

O Love, forgive. They know not what they do,
Dealing their little coin of scorn or shame.
I have seen into heaven, and all the floor
White with our thoughts, as fields are white with dew.
Light as young linnets, in a laughing flame,
They beat forever round God's open door.

My Love, my Love, hast Thou forsaken me?
Hyssop I gave you not, nor scourge, nor scars,
While any rose was left of summer's loss,
While any sail flowered white along the sea.
Now the sea darkens, and the angry stars
Born of that bitter water, are a cross.

I thirst, I thirst, though many waters hide me
Drowning in depths where Love will never seek.
There were three waves that broke on me. The first
Was salt as tears, the second rose beside me
In foam of fire, the third against my cheek
Touched like a kiss. My heart aches, and I thirst.

Today we were with Love in Paradise
A little while, and for that while the shade
Stood waiting, and a-wing the swallow slept.
But angels came with anger of bright eyes
And thrust us from the garden where Love laid
His homeless head. He followed us, and wept.

Yea, it is finished, yea, it is enough.
Time hastens, and the tide is gone so far
The faint horizon scarcely gleams in foam.
The gate is narrow and the path is rough,
But through the cloud one silver shepherd-star
Lingers to lead us. Love, we will go home.

Into thy hands, immortal Love. Not ours
The noonday's triumph, the diviner close,
Or the full flood across Time's whispering sands.
We bring you withered sheaves and broken flowers,—
Rue and wild poppy, thorns, one fading rose.
Love, we are sorry. All is in thy hands.

c. 1920
In shortened form, as "Adagio" in *University Magazine*, February 1920
The Complete Poems of Marjorie Pickthall, 1927

THE WOODSMAN IN THE FOUNDRY

Where the trolley's rumble
Jars the bones,
He hears waves that tumble
Green-linked weed along the golden stones.

Where the crane goes clanging
Chains and bars,
He sees branches hanging
Little leaves against the laughing stars.

Where the molten metals
Curdle bright,
He sees cherry petals
Fallen on blue violets in the night.

When the glow is leaping
Redly hurled,
He sees roses sleeping,
Forest-roses in a windy world.

c. 1922
The Wood Carver's Wife and Later Poems, 1922

MARCHING MEN

Under the level winter sky
I saw a thousand Christs go by.
They sang an idle song and free
As they went up to Calvary.

Careless of eye and coarse of lip,
They marched in holiest fellowship.
That heaven might heal the world, they gave
Their earth-born dreams to deck the grave.

With souls unpurged and steadfast breath
They supped the sacrament of death.
And for each one, far off, apart,
Seven swords have rent a woman's heart.

c. 1922
The Wood Carver's Wife and Later Poems, 1922

WHEN WINTER COMES

Rain at Muchalat, rain at Sooke,
And rain, they say, from Yale to Skeena,
And the skid-roads blind, and never a look
Of the Coast Range blue over Malaspina,
And west winds keener
Than jack-knife blades,
And rocks grown greener
With the long drip-drip from the cedar shades
On the drenched deep soil where the footsteps suck,
And the camp half-closed and the pay-roll leaner,—
Say, little horse, shall we hunt our luck?

Yet . . . I don't know . . . there's an hour at night
When the clouds break and the stars are turning
A thousand points of diamond light
Through the old snags of the cedar-burning,
And the west wind's spurning
A hundred highlands,
And the frost-moon's learning
The white fog-ways of the outer islands,
And the shallows are dark with the sleeping duck,
And life's a wonder for our discerning,—
Say, little horse, shall we wait our luck?

c. 1922
The Wood Carver's Wife and Later Poems, 1922

EBB TIDE

(The Sailor's Grave at Clo-oose, V[ancouver]. I[sland].)

Out of the winds' and the waves' riot,
Out of the loud foam,
He has put in to a great quiet
And a still home.

Here he may lie at ease and wonder
Why the old ship waits,
And hark for the surge and the strong thunder
Of the full Straits,

And look for the fishing fleet at morning,
Shadows like lost souls,
Slide through the fog where the seal's warning
Betrays the shoals,

And watch for the deep-sea liner climbing
Out of the bright West,
With a salmon-sky and her wake shining
Like a tern's breast,—

And never know he is done for ever
With the old sea's pride,
Borne from the fight and the full endeavour
On an ebb tide.

c. 1922
Two Poems, privately printed by Lorne Pierce, 1923

RESURGAM

I shall say, Lord, "Is it music, is it morning,
Song that is fresh as sunrise, light that sings?"
When on some hill there breaks the immortal warning
Of half-forgotten springs.

I shall say, Lord, "I have loved you, not another,
Heard in all quiet your footsteps on my road,
Felt your strong shoulder near me, O my brother,
Lightening the load."

I shall say, Lord, "I remembered, working, sleeping,
One face I looked for, one denied and dear.
Now that you come my eyes are blind with weeping,
But you will kiss them clear."

I shall say, Lord, "Touch my lips, and so unseal them;
I have learned silence since I lived and died."
I shall say, Lord, "Lift my hands, and so reveal them,
Full, satisfied."

I shall say, Lord, "We will laugh again to-morrow,
Now we'll be still a little, friend with friend.
Death was the gate and the long way was sorrow.
Love is the end."

c. 1922
Little Songs: A Book of Poems, 1925

WILD ASTERS

Grey lies the field and grey the windless hill,
Topped by the green-black shadow of the pine.
The lower woods are bird-bereft and still,
Save where a lingering robin whistles shrill,
And wakes an echo soft and fairy-fine.

In tangled growth of trees the birches show
All silvery fair and softly colourless.
By drifted leaves the last wild sun-flowers grow
Rain-washed and tall, and pale seed feathers blow
On every breeze that shakes the wilderness.

But far and far upon the sombre wold
Broad mists of tenderest purple lie outspread.
O sturdy blossoms with your eyes of gold,
You hold our hearts when frailer things are dead,
And flame by road and river, mead and mere,
A last, dear, radiant greeting from the year.

c. 1922
Little Songs: A Book of Poems, 1925

TWO SOULS

A Letter from Père Jogues

Most reverend Father, I have borne all wrong,
Agonies, griefs, revengements. Yet not I,
But rather He Who knew and loved us long,
And came at last to die.
In my maimed hands ye see Him, in my face
His poor abiding place,

"Lo, they will hear My voice and understand;
Go, seek My wandering sheep," the Shepherd saith,

So, o'er the world I sought them, hand in hand
With that dark brother of our Order, Death.
Under the shadow of his bitterest rod,
Behold, two souls for God!

Like the reed-feeding swans that cannot choose
But hear the voice of summer, in swift flight
Up from Three Rivers came the long canoes
Through calm of day and night,
I in the foremost, Coupil and Couture,
Whose fiery crowns are sure.

Sweet shines the summer over Normandy,
And bright on Arles among her blossoming vines,
But O, more sweet than any land or sea
The northern summer shines.
Each night a silvered dream to cast away,
Each golden dream a day—

So we went on, and our dark Hurons smiled,
Singing the child-songs of the woodpecker,
Through clear green glooms and amber bars enisled
Of tamarack and fir.
Till one cried, "Lo, a shadow and a dread
Steals from the isles ahead!"

Death laid a sudden silence on his lips.
In tumult of torn waters at the side,
Crashing, he fell, and all our little ships
Shook on that reddening tide.
Then the blue noon was torn with steel and flame,
And the Five Nations came.

c. 1922
Little Songs: A Book of Poems, 1925

MODERN ENDYMION

In the Asylum Garden

You!—
You stealing violets where the snail-tracks glisten
In the dew.
And little secret roses when the doctor's back is turned,—
Listen!
Listen, and I'll tell you how my window burned!

Burning silver ran about the pane in fires,
Piercing silver fires, and their points went creeping
All along the sidewalks and the branches and the wires
And the chimneys of the houses where the smoke was sleeping
O, white, white, white,
Was my window of the night,
And the glass was dripping in the old cold flame,
And soon, soon, soon,
Underneath the little bars that barricade it black,
With the whiteness and the brightness dripping from her
back,
The bare moon came,
Came the moon!

They cannot keep her out, O my secret, O my white
Silver-throated goddess of the night, of the night.
They may stifle me all day, but by night I am free,
Waiting for the goddess to climb the walnut tree
In the grey asylum grounds
Where the watchman goes his rounds.
He never sees her mounting, limb by silver limb.
He never sees her counting the stairway of the stars
With her bright hair twining,—
She's just the moon to him,
Shining,—
Shining through my window with the black strong bars.
And close, close, close,
Closer than the dew-shine to the rose,
And near, near, near
I am holding her all night, my terrible, my dear.
And the four grey walls
Run a drowning sluice of silver, and it falls

Where it will,—
Falls
Fierce and still,
Fierce and still—

Hush!
The little doctor's coming to take away your flowers!
If you run, run, run
Round the candleberry bush
In the pathway of the sun,
Maybe he won't find you, he won't follow you for hours.
But he can't touch me.
He can't find her, he can't feel her, he can't see, see, see
Her climbing to my window by the silver fruited tree.

c. 1922
The Complete Poems of Marjorie Pickthall, 1927

CANADA'S CENTURY

"*Behold, a people shall come from the north, and a great nation.*"

I

Out of the north, O Lord,
Out of the north we have come at Thy word;
The forests have heard,
Yea, the tall cedars have heard, and they bow;
The plains have rejoiced at the wound of the plow,
They have laughed, they have laughed at the kiss of the rain
In the bountiful beauty of grain;
The waters have sung of the ships to be.
We are come, a people new-risen, and free
As our wide deep rivers that run from the snows to the sea.

II

Into our hands they are given, the unknown opening years,
That, like a seed close-furled,
Hide all their growth and sovereignty and fears
And glories from the world.
Ours is the coming time, and ours the stress
To hold from Thee Thy gifts in worthiness,—
Honour and labour, law to right the wrong,
Courage and peace divine,
Life, clean as prairie of the north, and strong
As the rock-rooted pine,—
These shall be ours, and ours, of all, in all, is Thine.

III

Speak yet again,
Thou Who of old to wandering Israel came
In cloud and flame;
But not in wrath
Of human words, nor show an unveiled sword.
Lead us in mercy, Lord.
Behold, the long sweet year Thy word fulfills.
We see Thy prophets' visions on the plain,
Thy signs and wonders writ upon the hills,—
The free hills of the North.

c. 1922
The Complete Poems of Marjorie Pickthall, 1927

E.J. Pratt

1882–1964

Like Duncan Campbell Scott, Edwin John Pratt was the son of a Methodist minister. Born in 1882 in Western Bay, Newfoundland, he grew up by the sea and attended St. John's Methodist College. After working as a teacher and probationary preacher, he went on to study philosophy, theology, and psychology at Victoria College, University of Toronto. He graduated with a Ph.D. in 1917, and in moving towards a literary focus, published *Rachel: A Sea Story of Newfoundland in Verse* in the same year. In 1920, he joined the University of Toronto's Department of English (then headed by Pelham Edgar) and taught there for the rest of his career. He died in 1964, the recipient of numerous literary awards and honours.

Pratt's first volume of poems, *Newfoundland Verse*, appeared in 1923, and was considerably influenced by his youthful experiences, especially in the outports. The book contains thematic and structural characteristics which were to mark much of his later poetry. One thematic element is the struggle of human beings with their mechanical ingenuity and with nature. Another element is his delight in drawing imagery from one area to illustrate another: "The Shark" (1923) is an intriguing example of a creature portrayed in chilling mechanical terms. Yet another noticeable feature is his command of structure (which is ever his servant), even in his long poems.

Again like D.C. Scott, Pratt was prepared to alter stanza and line-lengths to suit the subject, thereby making his rhythms flexible. Pratt's voice was undoubtedly modern: he not only attempted to come to terms with the technology of his age but also to utilize the considerable range of imagery it offered. But Pratt's imagery was not drawn merely from that source—he pulled simile and metaphor from an astonishingly wide variety of sources, and his range of allusion provides many of his works with particular freshness.

As his poetic career progressed Pratt continued—both in short poems such as "The Lee Shore" (1927), "From Stone to Steel" (1932), and "The Man and the Machine" (1932), and in much longer ones such as *The Titanic* (1935) or *Towards the Last Spike* (1952)—to comment on human beings' insatiable desire to dominate the environment. The issue often is not simply the contest and its outcome, but the question of what humans do with their new-found powers, as well as their arrogance and over-confidence in their inventive capacities. Frequently, Pratt's tone is heavily ironic, as in "The Truant" (1942). Nevertheless, there can be a genuine celebration of achievement, "The 6000" being a case in point.

Pratt's considerable interest in history is evident in many pieces, whether *The Titanic*, *Brébeuf and His Brethren*, or *Towards the Last Spike*, for example. All three of these works also demonstrate another of his poetic capacities—the ability to write on a very large scale, to command an extended narrative which is based on extensive research. Pratt was often a historian in verse, with an ability to use his craftsmanship to give dramatic immediacy to an account of national and/or international importance. *The Titanic* is essentially poetic drama; both *Brébeuf and His Brethren* and *Towards the Last Spike* have as an essential element the struggle of the pioneer, involving contention with human as well as natural foes.

If Pratt delved into history, it was frequently in order to come to terms with the place of humankind in the modern world. If he was critical and ironic, it was not to belittle human achievements or negate the wonder of the human spirit, but to offer a clear-eyed view and to warn of the dangers he perceived. Always a teacher, Pratt never forgot his role, but he could still indulge in glimpses of natural loveliness in a way that readers, even from an earlier age, would have enjoyed. In this respect, the brief "Sea Gulls", even viewed alongside the vaster narratives, is more than adequate testimony to his eye and ear, and his very real mastery of his literary realm. The contrasts within the images and the metric control are testimony enough to his poetic prowess; and behind it all is his sense of beauty, which rests as a kind of underlying bass against which even his darker melodies must be set.

The definitive editions of Pratt's poetry include: *Collected Poems, Second Edition*, edited with an introduction by Northrop Frye (1958, rpt. 1962), and Sandra Djwa and R.G. Moyles, eds., *E.J. Pratt: Complete Poems*, Parts I and II (1989). Pratt's manuscript collections are found in the following: E.J. Pratt Library, Victoria University Library, University of Toronto, Toronto; Macmillan Archive, Mills Memorial Library, McMaster University, Hamilton; Lorne Pierce Collection, Queen's University Archives, Kingston.

Secondary sources on Pratt include: H.W. Wells and C.F. Klinck, *Edwin J. Pratt: The Man and His Poetry* (1947); Sister St. Dorothy Marie, "The Epic Note in the Poetry of Edwin John Pratt" (M.A. Thesis, Ottawa University, 1946); Desmond Pacey, "E.J. Pratt" in *Ten Canadian Poets* (1958), 165-93; Earle Birney, "E.J. Pratt and His Critics" in *Our Living Tradition*, ed. R.L. McDougall (1959), 123-47; A.J.M. Smith, *Some Poems of E.J. Pratt: Aspects of Imagery and Theme* (1969); Sandra Djwa, *E.J. Pratt: The Evolutionary Vision* (1974); Glenn Clever, ed., *The E.J. Pratt Symposium* (1977); Glenn Clever, *On E.J. Pratt* (1977); David Pitt, *E.J. Pratt: The Truant Years, 1882-1927*, Vol. I, and *E.J. Pratt, The Master Years, 1927-1964*, Vol. II (1984-87); Robert G. Collins, *E.J. Pratt* (1988); Heinz Tschachler, "The Cost of the Story: Ideology and the Ambivalence in the Verse Narratives of E.J. Pratt", *Canadian Literature* 122-123 (Autumn-Winter 1989), 93-106.

THE DEAR ILLUSION

Dusk—with a grey and silent sea,
The fading outlines of a shore,
A bittern's cry, and evermore
The lonelier cry of memory.

Night—and the lifted clouds afar,
And yonder near a little hill
A cross, above a form so still,
Holds vigil with one raying star.

Sleep falls, and lo! the gift of dreams—
He comes again, I clasp his hands,
Death's bars are broken, and he stands
As once he stood;—or so it seems.

c. 1918
Acta Victoriana, March 1918
E.J. Pratt: Complete Poems, Part I, 1989

SIGNALS

(A man speaks)
Was that a cry you say you heard?
Where? No. The winds would drown it quite.
No sound would reach the shore tonight,
Except the scream of some wild bird.

A flash, you say, that cut the rain
Like a red knife? It could not be;
There's nothing living in this sea.
Don't look so frightened. What—again?

The lifeboat! They are hailing me.
They need a man for the stern oar;
The wind drives dead upon this shore,
A rudder's helpless in this sea.

(A woman speaks)
No. That was not a scream I heard;
One could not hear so far away.
That flash was but the breakers' spray,
That cry, the note of some wild bird.

1920
As "On the Shore" in *Rebel*, March 1920
As "Later" in *New foundland Verse*, 1923

THE SHARK

He seemed to know the harbour,
So leisurely he swam;
His fin,
Like a piece of sheet-iron,
Three-cornered,
And with knife-edge,
Stirred not a bubble
As it moved
With its base-line on the water.

His body was tubular
And tapered
And smoke-blue,
And as he passed the wharf
He turned,
And snapped at a flat-fish
That was dead and floating.
And I saw the flash of a white throat,
And a double row of white teeth,
And eyes of metallic grey,
Hard and narrow and slit.

Then out of the harbour,
With that three-cornered fin
Shearing without a bubble the water
Lithely,
Leisurely,
He swam—

That strange fish,
Tubular, tapered, smoke-blue,
Part vulture, part wolf,
Part neither—for his blood was cold.

c. 1922
Canadian Forum, January 1923
Newfoundland Verse, 1923

NEWFOUNDLAND

Here the tides flow,
And here they ebb;
Not with that dull, unsinewed tread of waters
Held under bonds to move
Around unpeopled shores—
Moon-driven through a timeless circuit
Of invasion and retreat;
But with a lusty stroke of life
Pounding at stubborn gates,
That they might run
Within the sluices of men's hearts,
Leap under throb of pulse and nerve,
And teach the sea's strong voice
To learn the harmonies of new floods,
The peal of cataract,
And the soft wash of currents
Against resilient banks,
Or the broken rhythms from old chords
Along dark passages
That once were pathways of authentic fires.

Red is the sea-kelp on the beach,
Red as the heart's blood,
Nor is there power in tide or sun
To bleach its stain.
It lies there piled thick
Above the gulch-line.
It is rooted in the joints of rocks,

It is tangled around a spar,
It covers a broken rudder,
It is red as the heart's blood,
And salt as tears.

Here the winds blow,
And here they die,
Not with that wild, exotic rage
That vainly sweeps untrodden shores,
But with familiar breath
Holding a partnership with life,
Resonant with the hopes of spring,
Pungent with the airs of harvest.
They call with the silver fifes of the sea,
They breathe with the lungs of men,
They are one with the tides of the sea,
They are one with the tides of the heart,
They blow with the rising octaves of dawn,
They die with the largo of dusk,
Their hands are full to the overflow,
In their right is the bread of life,
In their left are the waters of death.

Scattered on boom
And rudder and weed
Are tangles of shells;
Some with backs of crusted bronze,
And faces of porcelain blue,
Some crushed by the beach stones
To chips of jade;
And some are spiral-cleft
Spreading their tracery on the sand
In the rich veining of an agate's heart;
And others remain unscarred,
To babble of the passing of the winds.

Here the crags
Meet with winds and tides—
Not with that blind interchange
Of blow for blow
That spills the thunder of insentient seas;
But with the mind that reads assault
In crouch and leap and the quick stealth,
Stiffening the muscles of the waves.
Here they flank the harbours,
Keeping watch

On thresholds, altars and the fires of home,
Or, like mastiffs,
Over-zealous,
Guard too well.

Tide and wind and crag,
Sea-weed and sea-shell
And broken rudder—
And the story is told
Of human veins and pulses,
Of eternal pathways of fire,
Of dreams that survive the night,
Of doors held ajar in storms.

c. 1923
Newfoundland Verse, 1923

From THE WITCHES' BREW

THE SUPREME TEST

Now it was clear to every Shade
That some great wonder was before them,
As Tom upon the palisade
Emptied, as fast as Lulu bore them,
The flasks upon the ocean wagon.
And clear it was when Tom had cleaned
The liquor from the hundredth flagon,
The Shades then saw Hell's darkest fiend—
A sea-cat with an awful jag-on.

Up to this time, he did not see
Upon the wide expanse of grey
A single thing approach his way
Which he might call his enemy.
He spent the hours upon the rim,
Leaping, dancing, rarely sitting,

Always grinning, always spitting,
Waiting for a foe to swim
Within his range, but through the night
Not a walrus offered fight,—
A most unusual night for him.
But with the hundredth flagon drink,
He spat at his inactive fate,
And moving closer to the brink,
Began more madly to gyrate.
Upon his face, ironic, grim,
A resolution was ingrained,
If fish would not come unto him
To offer battle, what remained
But that his fighting blood would freeze
Unless he were allowed to go,
Ranging at will upon the seas,
To fight and conquer every foe?
With that, into the cavernous deep
He took a ghastly flying leap.

Gaping, breathless, every Shade
Watched the course of the wild-cat's raid;
And never was an errand run
With means and end so much at one.
For from his birth he was imbued
With hatred of his racial kind;
A more inveterate, blasting feud
Within the world one could not find.
His stock were traitors to the sea,
Had somehow learned the ways of earth,
The need of air, the mystery
Of things warm-blooded, and of birth.
To avenge this shameful derogation,
He had, upon his final flask,
Resolved to carry out his task—
To wit:—the full extermination,
First, of his nearest order, male
And female, then the breed cetacean;
Grampus, porpoise, dolphin, whale—
Humpback, Rorqual, Black and White;
Then the walrus, lion, hood,
Seals of all orders; these he would
Just as they came, in single fight,
Or in the fortunes of mêlée,
Challenge as his lawful prey.

The Blacksmith:
I never knew an ocean steed
Develop such demonic speed.

Sir Isaac Newton:
How he maintains that lightning rate,
Now in air and now in water,
And carries on such heavy slaughter,
Is more than I can formulate.

Blake:
The tiger, though in stretch of limb
And heft of bone is larger; still,
For straight uxoricidal will
Is but a lamb compared to him.

Bottom:
What humour is it makes him flail
His tawny quarters with that tail?

Owen Glendower:
Did any electrician mark
The explosive nature of that spark?

Benjamin Franklin:
I did in truth, but cannot quite
See, on the basis of my kite,
How such a flame should always sit
Upon a wild-cat's caudal tip.

Aesop:
Or what blind fury makes him whip
His smoking sides to capture it—
An ignis fatuus that eludes
The cat's most sanguinary moods.

Euclid:
The reasons for the circles lie
Within the nature of the thing;
This cat must run around a ring
If he would catch his tail. But why
So bloodily he chaseth it
Is past the compass of my wit.

Johnny Walker:
Just why this wild-cat should resolve,
Leaving his nether tip uncaught,
And spend his energy for naught,

The denser Shades will never solve;
But (granting that the speed is quicker)
All we discerning spirits know
It's just the way a man would go,
Grant the night and grant the liquor.

Calvin:
If I had known that such mad brutes
Had found, before the world began,
A place within the cosmic plan,
They would have dished my Institutes.

THE RETURN OF THE CAT

Time: morning
A half-point Nor'ard from the West,
A bluish-tinted spot of light,
Now deep below, now on the crest
Of a high wave, hove into sight;
And by the curves and speed it made,
Conviction came to every Shade
That here the monster was returning
With all those inner fires burning
That no destruction could assuage;
Though through the hours of the night
The floating victims of the fight
Showed how the wild-cat could engage
His foes; achieve his victories;
For those he could not kill outright
Had either died from heart-disease
Or passed out through a haemorrhage.
An unexpected wonder met
His rolling, unabated eye—
For when he reached the parapet
He found the witches' cauldron dry.
And there was something which surprised
Him even more; the drunken riot
Was followed by a holy quiet;
The fish lay dead or paralysed;
No witch this time came forth to serve
His inbred hunger for assault
With either rum or wine or malt.
The thing told heavily on his nerve,
That near that massive banquet place
Not one lone member of his race,
Outside the fortress or within,
Survived to give him grin for grin,

Or swish a tail across his face.
And so this wild-cat, now bereft
Of all of life's amenities,
Took one blood-curdling leap and left
Magellan's for the vacant seas.
Sullen and dangerous he ripped
A gleaming furrow through the water,
Magnificently still equipped
For combat with rapine and slaughter.
Now with his tail electro-tipped,
Swiftly but leisurely he made
Around the steaming palisade
A blazing spiral which outshone
The fiercest glow of Acheron.
Then suddenly, as if aware,
By a deep ferment in his soul
Or something psychic in his hair,
Of some ulterior, mystic goal,
He sharply turned, began a lonely
Voyage pregnant of immortal raids
And epic plunder. But the Shades
Saw him no more in the flesh. Only
To Satan and the witches three
(In touch with his galvanic tail,
By more occulted masonry)
Appeared a phosphorescent trail
That headed for the Irish Sea.

c. 1925
The Witches' Brew, 1925

THE LEE-SHORE

Her heart cried out—"Come home, come home,"
When the storm beat in at the door,
When the window showed a spatter of foam,
And her ear rang with the roar
Of the reef; and she called again, "Come home,"
To the ship in reach of the shore.

"But not tonight," flashed the signal light
From the Cape that guarded the bay,

"No, not tonight," rang the foam where the white
Hard edge of the breakers lay;
"Keep away from the crash of the storm at its height,
Keep away from the land, keep away."

"Come home," her heart cried out again,
"For the edge of the reef is white."
But she pressed her face to the window-pane,
And read the flash of the signal light;
Then her voice called out when her heart was slain,
"Keep away, my love, tonight."

c. 1927
Canadian Forum, October 1927
Verses of the Sea, 1930

SEA-GULLS

For one carved instant as they flew
The language had no simile—
Silver, crystal, ivory
Were tarnished. Etched upon the horizon blue,
The frieze must go unchallenged, for the lift
And carriage of the wings would stain the drift
Of stars against a tropic indigo
Or dull the parable of snow.

Now settling one by one
Within green hollows or where curled
Crests caught the spectrum from the sun,
A thousand wings are furled.
No clay-born lilies of the world
Could blow as free
As those wild orchids of the sea.

c. 1930
Acta Victoriana, December 1930
Many Moods, 1932

EROSION

It took the sea a thousand years,
A thousand years to trace
The granite features of this cliff,
In crag and scarp and base.

It took the sea an hour one night,
An hour of storm to place
The sculpture of these granite seams
Upon a woman's face.

c. 1931
Canadian Forum, June 1931
Many Moods, 1932

THE 6000

For creatures of this modern breed,
Reared from the element of flame,
Designed to match a storm for speed,
Ionia would have found a name,
Like Mercury or Bucephalus—
Some picturesque immortal label
That lifts a story into fable,
Out of the myths of Uranus;
Then changed its root to demonize
The nature of its strength and size
With fictions out of Tartarus.

Those giants of Vulcan, leather-skinned,
Whose frightful stare monocular
Made mad the coursers of the wind,
And chased the light of the morning star
Away from the Sicilian shore,
Would have been terror-blind before
This forehead which, had it been known
In Greek or Scandinavian lore,

Had turned the hierarchs to stone,
Had battered down the Martian walls,
Reduced to dust Jove's arsenals,
Or rammed the battlements of Thor.
His body black as Erebus
Accorded with the hue of night;
His central eye self-luminous
Threw out a cone of noon-day light,
Which split the gloom and then flashed back
The diamond levels of the track.
No ancient poet ever saw
Just such a monster as could draw
The Olympian tonnage of a load
Like this along an iron road;
Or ever thought that such a birth—
The issue of an inventor's dream—
With breath of fire and blood of steam,
Could find delivery on this earth.
In his vast belly was a pit,
Which even Homer would admit,
Or Dante, searching earth and hell,
Possessed no perfect parallel.
Evolved from no Plutonian forge,
The tender, like a slave, that followed,
Conveyed bitumen to his gorge,
Which on the instant it was swallowed
Ran black through crimson on to white.
Above the mass floated a swirl
Of crystal shapes, agate and pearl
And rose, like imps a-chase, and light
As thistledown, while the blast roared
With angry temperatures that soared
To seven hundred Fahrenheit.
Outside, the engine's dorsal plate,
Above the furnace door ajar,
Revealed the boiler's throbbing rate,
By dial fingers animate,
Like pulses at the jugular.

For every vital inch of steel,
A vibrant indicator read
Two hundred pounds plus twenty-five,
Waiting for the hour to drive
Their energy upon the wheel
In punches from the piston head.

And there another one supplied
The measure of the irrigation,
Whereby the lubricating tide,
Through linear runs and axle curves,
Made perfect his articulation.
And ramifying copper wire
Made up the system of his nerves,
In keeping with his lungs of fire.

Now with his armoured carapace
On head and belly, back and breast,
The Taurian prepared to face
The blurring stretches of the west.
To him it was of no concern
The evening gale was soon to turn
To the full stature of a storm
That would within an hour transform
The ranges for a thousand miles,
Close up all human thoroughfares,
Sweep down through canyons and defiles,
And drive the cougars to their lairs.

A lantern flashed out a command,
A bell was ringing as a hand
Clutched at a throttle, and the bull,
At once obedient to the pull,
Began with bellowing throat to lead
By slow accelerating speed
Six thousand tons of caravan
Out to the spaces—there to toss
The blizzard from his path across
The prairies of Saskatchewan.

c. 1931
As "No. 6000" in *CNR Magazine*, December 1931
Many Moods, 1932

FROM STONE TO STEEL

From stone to bronze, from bronze to steel
Along the road-dust of the sun,
Two revolutions of the wheel
From Java to Geneva run.

The snarl Neanderthal is worn
Close to the smiling Aryan lips,
The civil polish of the horn
Gleams from our praying finger tips.

The evolution of desire
Has but matured a toxic wine,
Drunk long before its heady fire
Reddened Euphrates or the Rhine.

Between the temple and the cave
The boundary lies tissue thin:
The yearlings still the altars crave
As satisfaction for a sin.

The road goes up, the road goes down—
Let Java or Geneva be—
But whether to the cross or crown,
The path lies through Gethsemane.

1932
As "From Java to Geneva" in *Canadian Journal of Religious Thought*, September/October 1932
Many Moods, 1932

THE MAN AND THE MACHINE

By right of fires that smelted ore
Which he had tended years before,
The man whose hands were on the wheel
Could trace his kinship through her steel,
Between his body warped and bent

In every bone and ligament,
And this "eight-cylinder" stream-lined,
The finest model yet designed.
He felt his lesioned pulses strum
Against the rhythm of her hum,
And found his nerves and sinews knot
With sharper spasm as she climbed
The steeper grades, so neatly timed
From storage tank to piston shot—
This creature with the cougar grace,
This man with slag upon his face.

1932
New Outlook, November 1932
Many Moods, 1932

THE EMPTY ROOM

I know that were my soul tonight
Strung to the silence of this room,
I'd hear remembered footfalls light
As wayward drift of lotus bloom.

Nor would it just be make-believe,
Were I to find her in this chair,
Or catch the rustle of her sleeve,
Or note the glint upon her hair.

Say, would you blame me if I knelt
To put faith to its enterprise?
So surely must her touch be felt
In liquid coolness on my eyes.

Now listen! If the veil should part
Within this holy ritual,
You'll hear a voice call to my heart
More lovely than a madrigal.

1933
Canadian Magazine, June 1933
The Fable of the Goats and Other Poems, 1937

From THE TITANIC

HARLAND & WOLFF WORKS, BELFAST, MAY 31, 1911

The hammers silent and the derricks still,
And high-tide in the harbour! Mind and will
In open test with time and steel had run
The first lap of a schedule and had won.
Although a shell of what was yet to be
Before another year was over, she,
Poised for the launching signal, had surpassed
The dreams of builder or of navigator.
The Primate of the Lines, she had out-classed
That rival effort to eliminate her
Beyond the North Sea where the air shots played
The laggard rhythms of their fusillade
Upon the rivets of the *Imperator*.
The wedges in, the shores removed, a girl's
Hand at a sign released a ribbon braid;
Glass crashed against the plates; a wine cascade,
Netting the sunlight in a shower of pearls,
Baptized the bow and gave the ship her name;
A slight push of the rams as a switch set free
The triggers in the slots, and her proud claim
On size—to be the first to reach the sea—
Was vindicated, for whatever fears
Stalked with her down the tallow of the slip
Were smothered under by the harbour cheers,
By flags strung to halyards of the ships.

MARCH 31, 1912

Completed! Waiting for her trial spin—
Levers and telegraphs and valves within
Her intercostal spaces ready to start
The power pulsing through her lungs and heart.
An ocean lifeboat in herself—so ran
The architectural comment on her plan.
No wave could sweep those upper decks—unthinkable!
No storm could hurt that hull—the papers said so.
The perfect ship at last—the first unsinkable,
Proved in advance—had not the folders read so?

. . .

Voices From the Deck:

"There goes the Special with the toffs. You'll make
New York tonight rowing like that. You'll take
Your death o'cold out there with all the fish
And ice around."
        "Make sure your butlers dish
You up your toddies now, and bring hot rolls
For breakfast."
        "Don't forget the finger bowls."

The engineering staff of thirty-five
Are at their stations: those off-duty go
Of their free will to join their mates below
In the grim fight for steam, more steam, to drive
The pressure through the pumps and dynamo.
Knee-deep, waist-deep in water they remain,
Not one of them seen on the decks again.
The under braces of the rudder showing,
The wing propeller blades begin to rise,
And with them, through the hawse-holes, water flowing—
The angle could not but assault the eyes.
At fifteen minutes, and the fo'c'sle head
Was under. And five more, the sea had shut
The lower entrance to the stairs that led
From C deck to the boat deck—the short cut
For the crew. Another five, the upward flow
Had covered the wall brackets where the glow
Diffusing from the frosted bulbs turned green
Uncannily through their translucent screen.

ON THE *CARPATHIA*

White Star—Cunarder, forty miles apart,
Still eighteen knots! From coal to flame to steam—
Decision of a captain to redeem
Errors of brain by hazards of the heart!
Showers of sparks danced through the funnel smoke,
The firemen's shovels, rakes and slice-bars broke
The clinkers, fed the fires, and ceaselessly
The hoppers dumped the ashes on the sea.

As yet no panic, but none might foretell
The moment when the sight of that oblique
Breath-taking lift of the taffrail and the sleek
And foamless undulation of the swell
Might break in meaning on those diverse races,
And give them common language. As the throng

Came to the upper decks and moved along
The incline, the contagion struck the faces
With every lowering of a boat and backed
Them towards the stern. And twice between the hush
Of fear and utterance the gamut cracked,
When with the call for women and the flare
Of an exploding rocket, a short rush
Was made for the boats—fifteen and two.
'Twas nearly done—the sudden clutch and tear
Of canvas, a flurry of fists and curses met
By swift decisive action from the crew,
Supported by a quartermaster's threat
Of three revolver shots fired on the air.

But still the fifteenth went with five inside,
Who, seeking out the shadows, climbed aboard
And, lying prone and still, managed to hide
Under the thwarts long after she was lowered.

Jingle bells, jingle bells,
Jingle all the way,
O what fun....

"Some men in number two, sir!"
The boat swung
Back.
"Chuck the fellows out."
Grabbed by the feet,
The lot were pulled over the gunwale and flung
Upon the deck.
"Hard at that forward cleat!
A hand there for that after fall. Lower
Away—port side, the second hatch, and wait."

With six hands of his watch, the bosun's mate,
Sent down to open up the gangway door,
Was trapped and lost in a flooded alley way,
And like the seventh, impatient of delay,
The second left with room for twenty more.

The fiddley leading from a boiler room
Lay like a tortuous exit from a tomb.
A stoker climbed it, feeling by the twist
From vertical how steep must be the list.
He reached the main deck where the cold night airs
Enswathed his flesh with steam. Taking the stairs,
He heard the babel by the davits, faced
The forward, noticed how the waters raced

To the break of the fo'c'sle and lapped
The foremast root. He climbed again and saw
The resolute manner in which Murdoch's rapped
Command put a herd instinct under law;
No life-preserver on, he stealthily
Watched Phillips in his room, bent at the key,
And thinking him alone, he sprang to tear
The jacket off. He leaped too soon. "Take that!"
The second stove him with a wrench. "Lie there,
Till hell begins to singe your lids—you rat!"

But set against those scenes where order failed,
Was the fine muster at the fourteenth where,
Like a zone of calm along a thoroughfare,
The discipline of sea-worn laws prevailed.
No women answering the repeated calls,
The men filled up the vacant seats: the falls
Were slipping through the sailors' hands,
When a steerage group of women, having fought
Their way over five flights of stairs, were brought
Bewildered to the rails. Without commands
Barked from the lips of officers; without
A protest registered in voice or face,
The boat was drawn up and the men stepped out
Back to the crowded stations with that free
Barter of life for life done with the grace
And air of a Castilian courtesy.

I've just got here through Paris,
From the sunny Southern shore,
I to Monte Carlo went. . . .

ISIDOR AND IDA STRAUS

At the sixteenth—a woman wrapped her coat
Around her maid and placed her in the boat;
Was ordered in but seen to hesitate
At the gunwale, and more conscious of her pride
Than of her danger swiftly took her fate
With open hands, and without show of tears
Returned unmurmuring to her husband's side;
"We've been together now for forty years,
Whither you go, I go."

A boy of ten,
Ranking himself within the class of men,
Though given a seat, made up his mind to waive

The privilege of his youth and size, and piled
The inches on his stature as he gave
Place to a Magyar woman and her child.

And men who had in the world's run of trade,
Or in pursuit of the professions, made
Their reputation, looked upon the scene
Merely as drama in a life's routine:
Millet was studying eyes as he would draw them
Upon a canvas; Butt, as though he saw them
In the ranks; Astor, social, debonair,
Waved "Good-bye" to his bride—"See you tomorrow,"
And tapped a cigarette on a silver case;
Men came to Guggenheim as he stood there
In evening suit, coming this time to borrow
Nothing but courage from his calm, cool face.

And others unobserved, of unknown name
And race, just stood behind, pressing no claim
Upon priority but rendering proof
Of their oblation, quiet and aloof
Within the maelstrom towards the rails. And some
Wavered a moment with the panic urge,
But rallied to attention on the verge
Of flight as if the rattle of a drum
From quarters faint but unmistakable
Had put the stiffening in the blood to check
The impulse of the feet, leaving the will
No choice between the lifeboats and the deck.

The four collapsibles, their lashings ripped,
Half-dragged, half-lifted by the hooks, were slipped
Over the side. The first two luckily
Had but the forward distance to the sea.
Its canvas edges crumpled up, the third
Began to fill with water and transferred
Its cargo to the twelfth, while number four,
Abaft and higher, nose-dived and swamped its score.

The wireless cabin—Phillips in his place,
Guessing the knots of the Cunarder's race.
Water was swirling up the slanted floor
Around the chair and sucking at his feet.
Carpathia's call—the last one heard complete—
Expect to reach position half-past four.
The operators turned—Smith at the door
With drawn incredulous face. "Men, you have done
Your duty. I release you. Everyone

Now for himself." They stayed ten minutes yet,
The power growing fainter with each blue
Crackle of flame. Another stammering jet—
Virginian heard "a tattering C.Q."
Again a try for contact but the code's
Last jest had died between the electrodes.

Even yet the spell was on the ship: although
The last lifeboat had vanished, there was no
Besieging of the heavens with a crescendo
Of fears passing through terror into riot—
But on all lips the strange narcotic quiet
Of an unruffled ocean's innuendo.
In spite of her deformity of line,
Emergent like a crag out of the sea,
She had the semblance of stability,
Moment by moment furnishing no sign,
So far as visible, of that decline
Made up of inches crawling into feet.
Then, with the electric circuit still complete,
The miracle of day displacing night
Had worked its fascination to beguile
Direction of the hours and cheat the sight.
Inside the recreation rooms the gold
From Arab lamps shone on the burnished tile.
What hindered the return to shelter while
The ship clothed in that irony of light
Offered her berths and cabins as a fold?

And, was there not the *Californian*?
Many had seen her smoke just over there,
But two hours past—it seemed a harbour span—
So big, so close, she could be hailed, they said;
She must have heard the signals, seen the flare
Of those white stars and changed at once her course.
There under the *Titanic*'s foremast head,
A lamp from the look-out cage was flashing Morse.
No ship afloat, unless deaf, blind and dumb
To those three sets of signals but would come.
And when the whiz of a rocket bade men turn
Their faces to each other in concern
At shattering facts upon the deck, they found
Their hearts take reassurance with the sound
Of the violins from the gymnasium, where
The bandsmen in their blithe insouciance
Discharged the sudden tension of the air
With the fox-trot's sublime irrelevance.

The fo'c'sle had gone under the creep
Of the water. Though without a wind, a lop
Was forming on the wells now fathoms deep.
The seventy feet—the boat deck's normal drop—
Was down to ten. Rising, falling, and waiting,
Rising again, the swell that edged and curled
Around the second bridge, over the top
Of the air-shafts, backed, resurged and whirled
Into the stokehold through the fiddley grating.
Under the final strain the two wire guys
Of the forward funnel tugged and broke at the eyes:
With buckled plates the stack leaned, fell and smashed
The starboard wing of the flying bridge, went through
The lower, then tilting at the davits crashed
Over, driving a wave aboard that drew
Back to the sea some fifty sailors and
The captain with the last of the bridge command.

Out on the water was the same display
Of fear and self-control as on the deck—
Challenge and hesitation and delay,
The quick return, the will to save, the race
Of snapping oars to put the realm of space
Between the half-filled lifeboats and the wreck.
The swimmers whom the waters did not take
With their instant death-chill struck out for the wake
Of the nearer boats, gained on them, hailed
The steersmen and were saved: the weaker failed
And fagged and sank. A man clutched at the rim
Of a gunwale, and a woman's jewelled fist
Struck at his face: two others seized his wrist,
As he released his hold, and gathering him
Over the side, they staunched the cut from the ring.
And there were many deeds envisaging
Volitions where self-preservation fought
Its red primordial struggle with the "ought",
In those high moments when the gambler tossed
Upon the chance and uncomplaining lost.

Aboard the ship, whatever hope of dawn
Gleamed from the *Carpathia*'s riding lights was gone,
For every knot was matched by each degree
Of list. The stern was lifted bodily
When the bow had sunk three hundred feet, and set
Against the horizon stars in silhouette
Were the blade curves of the screws, hump of the rudder.
The downward pull and after buoyancy

Held her a minute poised but for a shudder
That caught her frame as with the upward stroke
Of the sea a boiler or a bulkhead broke.

Climbing the ladders, gripping shroud and stay,
Storm-rail, ringbolt or fairlead, every place
That might befriend the clutch of hand or brace
Of foot, the fourteen hundred made their way
To the heights of the aft decks, crowding the inches
Around the docking bridge and cargo winches.
And now that last salt tonic which had kept
The valour of the heart alive—the bows
Of the immortal seven that had swept
The strings to outplay, outdie their orders, ceased.
Five minutes more, the angle had increased
From eighty on to ninety when the rows
Of deck and port-hole lights went out, flashed back
A brilliant second and again went black.
Another bulkhead crashed, then following
The passage of the engines as they tore
From their foundations, taking everything
Clean through the bows from 'midships with a roar
Which drowned all cries upon the deck and shook
The watchers in the boats, the liner took
Her thousand fathoms journey to her grave.

And out there in the starlight, with no trace
Upon it of its deed but the last wave
From the *Titanic* fretting at its base,
Silent, composed, ringed by its icy broods,
The grey shape with the palaeolithic face
Was still the master of the longitudes.

1935
The Titanic, 1935

SILENCES

There is no silence upon the earth or under the earth like the silence under the sea;
No cries announcing birth,
No sounds declaring death.
There is silence when the milt is laid on the spawn in the weeds and fungus of the rock-clefts;
And silence in the growth and struggle for life.
The bonitos pounce upon the mackerel,
And are themselves caught by the barracudas,
The sharks kill the barracudas
And the great molluscs rend the sharks,
And all noiselessly—
Though swift be the action and final the conflict,
The drama is silent.

There is no fury upon the earth like the fury under the sea.
For growl and cough and snarl are the tokens of spendthrifts who know not the ultimate economy of rage.
Moreover, the pace of the blood is too fast.
But under the waves the blood is sluggard and has the same temperature as that of the sea.

There is something pre-reptilian about a silent kill.

Two men may end their hostilities just with their battle-cries,
"The devil take you," says one.
"I'll see you in hell first," says the other.
And these introductory salutes followed by a hail of gutturals and sibilants are often the beginning of friendship, for who would not prefer to be lustily damned than to be half-heartedly blessed?
No one need fear oaths that are properly enunciated, for they belong to the inheritance of just men made perfect, and, for all we know, of such may be the Kingdom of Heaven.
But let silent hate be put away for it feeds upon the heart of the hater.
Today I watched two pairs of eyes. One pair was black and the other grey. And while the owners thereof, for the space of five seconds, walked past each other, the grey snapped at the black and the black riddled the grey.
One looked to say—"The cat,"

And the other—"The cur."
But no words were spoken;
Not so much as a hiss or a murmur came through the perfect enamel of the teeth; not so much as a gesture of enmity.
If the right upper lip curled over the canine, it went unnoticed.
The lashes veiled the eyes not for an instant in the passing.
And as between the two in respect to candour of intention or eternity of wish, there was no choice, for the stare was mutual and absolute.
A word would have dulled the exquisite edge of the feeling.
An oath would have flawed the crystallization of the hate.
For only such culture could grow in a climate of silence—
Away back before emergence of fur or feather, back to the unvocal sea and down deep where the darkness spills its wash on the threshold of light, where the lids never close upon the eyes, where the inhabitants slay in silence and are as silently slain.

1936
Canadian Forum, March 1936
The Fable of the Goats and Other Poems, 1937

THE SUBMARINE

The young lieutenant in command
Of the famous submarine, the K-
148, had scanned
The sea circumference all day:
A thousand times or so his hand
Revolved the prism in the hope
That the image of the ship expected,
But overdue, might be reflected
Through the lenses of his periscope.
'Twas getting late, and not a mark
Had troubled the monotony
Of every slow expanding arc
Of the horizon. Suddenly
His grip froze to the handle! What
Was that amorphous yellow spot
To the north-east? Was it the lift
Of a wave, a curl of foam, a drift
Of cloud? Too slow for foam, too fast
For cloud. A minute more. At last
The drift was taking shape; his stroke
Of luck had fallen —it was SMOKE!

An hour of light in the western sky,
And thirty seconds for descent;
The quarry ten miles off. Stand by!
The valves were opened—flood and vent—
And the water like a rumble of thunder
Entered the tanks. Two generators
Sparked her fins and drove her under
Down the ocean escalators.

No forebear of the whale or shark,
No saurian of the Pleiocene,
Piercing the sub-aquatic dark
Could rival this new submarine.
The evolution of the sea
Had brought forth many specimens
Conceived in horror—denizens
Whose vast inside economy
Not only reproduced their broods,
But having shot them from their wombs,
Devoured them in their family feuds

And passed them through their catacombs.
But was there one in all their race
Combined such terror with such grace,
As this disturber of the glooms,
This rapid sinuous oval form
Which knew unerringly the way
To sound and circumvent a storm
Or steal a march upon her prey?
No product she of Nature's dower,
No casual selection wrought her
Or gave her such mechanic power
To breathe above or under water.

In her thoracic cavities
One hundred tons of batteries
Were ready, on the dive, to start
The musculation of the heart.
And where outside a Ming museum
Could any antiquarian find
An assemblage such as here was shrined
Within the vault of her peritoneum?
Electric switches, indicators,
Diving alarm-horns, oscillators,
Rudder controls, and tubes and dials,
Yellow, white, magenta vials,
Pipes to force out battery gases,
Pressure gauges, polished brasses,
Surrounded human figures caught
At their positions, silent, taut,
Like statues in the tungsten light,
While just outside the cell was night
And a distant engine's monotone
Tapping at a telephone.
And now two hundred feet below
She held her bearings towards her foe,
While silence and the darkness flowed
Along an unnavigated road.

In half an hour she stopped and blew
The water ballast with her air,
Rose stealthily to surface where
Upon the mirror in full view,
Cutting an Atlantic swarth
The trail of smoke turned out to be
A fat mammalian of the sea,
Set on a course north-east by north,
And heavy with maternity.

Within her framework iron-walled
A thousand bodies were installed,
A snug and pre-lacteal brood
Drawing from her warmth and food,
Awaiting in two days or three
A European delivery.
Blood of tiger, blood of shark,
What a prey to stalk and strike
From an ambush in the dark
Thicket of the sea!

Now like
The tiger-shark viviparous
Who with her young grown mutinous
Before the birth-hour with the smell
Of blood inside the mother, will expel
Them from her body to begin
At once the steerage of the fin,
The seizure of the jaw, the click
Of serried teeth fashioned so well
Pre-natally to turn the trick
Upon a shoal of mackerel—
So like the shark, the submarine
Ejected from her magazine
The first one of her foetal young.
It ran along the trolley, swung
Into a flooded tube and there
Under a jet of compressed air
It found the sea. A trip-latch in
The tube a second later sprung
A trigger, and the turbine power
Acting on the driving fin
Paced it a fifty miles per hour.
So huge and luscious was this feast,
The 148 released
Three others to offset the chance
Of some erratic circumstance
Of aim or speed or tide or weather.
And during this time nothing was seen
Except to an eye in the submarine
Of that bevy of sharks on the sea together,
So accurately spaced one after the other,
And driven by thirst derived from the mother.
Each seemed on the glass a tenuous feather
Of gold such as a curlew in flight

Would make with its nether wing skimming the swell;
Not a hint of a swerve to the left or right,
The gyros were holding the balance so well.

The rich-ripe mammal was swimming straight
On the course of her chart with unconcerned leisure,
Her steady keel and uniform rate
Combining so perfectly with the deep black
Of the hull—silhouette against the back-
Drop of the sunset to etch and measure
The target—when three of those shafts of foam
At the end of their amber stretch struck home.
The first one barely missed—to plough
A harmless path across her bow:
The next tore like a scimitar
Through flesh to rip the jugular;
Boilers and bulkheads broke apart
When the third torpedo struck the heart;
And with what logic did the fourth
Cancel the course north-east by north,
Hitting abaft the beam to rut
The exploding nitrates through her gut.
The young commander's time was short
To log the items for report.
Upon the mirror he descried
Three cavernous wounds in the mammal's side—
Three crumbled dykes through which the tide
Of a gluttonous Atlantic poured;
A heavy starboard list with banks
Of smoke fluted with steam which soared
From a scramble of pipes within her flanks;
Twin funnel-nostrils belching red,
A tilting stern, a plunging head,
The foundering angle in position,
And the sea's reach for a thousand souls
In the last throe of the parturition.

Now with her hyper-sensitive feel
Of her master's hands on the controls—
A pull of a switch, a turn of a wheel,
The submarine, like the deep-sea shark,
Went under cover, away from the light
And limn of the sunset, from the sight
Of the stars, to a native lair as dark
As a kraken's grave. She took her course
South-west by south—for what was the source

Of that hum to the port picked up by the oscillator?
A rhythm too rapid, too hectic for freighter
Or liner! This was her foe, not her prey:
Faster and louder, and heading her way!
Beyond the depth where the tanks could flood 'er,
She drove her nose down with the diving rudder,
Far from the storm of shells or thrust
Of the ram, away from the gear-wrenching zone
Of the depth-bomb, away from the scent and lust
Of a killer whose might was as great as her own.

c. 1938
Canadian Forum, December 1938
Still Life and Other Verse, 1943

From BRÉBEUF AND HIS BRETHREN

II

1629

Four years at home could not abate his zeal.
Brébeuf, absorbed within his meditations,
Made ready to complete his early vows.
Each year in France but served to clarify
His vision. At Rouen he gauged the height
Of the Cathedral's central tower in terms
Of pines and oaks around the Indian lodges.
He went to Paris. There as worshipper,
His eyes were scaling transepts, but his mind,
Straying from window patterns where the sun
Shed rose ellipses on the marble floor,
Rested on glassless walls of cedar bark.
To Rennes—the Jesuits' intellectual home,
Where, in the *Summa* of Aquinas, faith
Laid hold on God's existence when the last
Link of the Reason slipped, and where Loyola
Enforced the high authoritarian scheme
Of God's vicegerent on the priestly fold.
Between the two nostalgic fires Brébeuf
Was swung—between two homes; in one was peace

Within the holy court, the ecstasy
Of unmolested prayer before the Virgin,
The daily and vicarious offering
On which no hand might dare lay sacrilege:
But in the other would be broken altars
And broken bodies of both Host and priest.
Then of which home, the son? From which the exile?
With his own blood Brébeuf wrote his last vow—
"Lord Jesus! You redeemed me with your blood;
By your most precious death; and this is why
I make this pledge to serve you all my life
In the Society of Jesus—never
To serve another than Thyself. Hereby
I sign this promise in my blood, ready
To sacrifice it all as willingly
As now I give this drop."—Jean de Brébeuf.

Nor did the clamour of the *Thirty Years*,
The battle-cries at La Rochelle and Fribourg,
Blow out the flame. Less strident than the names
Of Richelieu and Mazarin, Condé,
Turenne, but just as mighty, were the calls
Of the new apostolate. A century
Before had Xavier from the Indies summoned
The world to other colours. Now appeals
Were ringing through the history of New France.
Le Jeune, following the example of Biard
And Charles Lalemant, was capturing souls
By thousands with the fire of the *Relations*:
Noble and peasant, layman, priest and nun
Gave of their wealth and power and personal life.

Among his new recruits were Chastellain,
Pijart, Le Mercier, and Isaac Jogues,
The Lalemants—Jerome and Gabriel—
Jerome who was to supervise and write,
With Ragueneau, the drama of the Mission;
Who told of the survivors reaching France
When the great act was closed that "all of them
Still hold their resolution to return
To the combat at the first sound of the trumpets."
The other, Gabriel, who would share the crown
With Jean Brébeuf, pitting the frailest body
Against the hungers of the wilderness,
The fevers of the lodges and the fires
That slowly wreathed themselves around a stake.

Then Garnier, comrade of Jogues. The winds
Had fanned to a white heat the hearth and placed
Three brothers under vows—the Carmelite,
The Capuchin, and his, the Jesuit.
The gentlest of his stock, he had resolved
To seek and to accept a post that would
Transmit his nurture through a discipline
That multiplied the living martyrdoms
Before the casual incident of death.

To many a vow did Chabanel subject
His timid nature as the evidence
Of trial came through the Huronian records.
He needed every safeguard of the soul
To fortify the will, for every day
Would find him fighting, mastering his revolt
Against the native life and practices.
Of all the priests he could the least endure
The sudden transformation from the Chair
Of College Rhetoric to the heat and drag
Of portages, from the monastic calm
To the noise and smoke and vermin of the lodges,
And the insufferable sights and stinks
When, at the High Feast of the Dead, the bodies
Lying for months or years upon the scaffolds
Were taken down, stripped of their flesh, caressed,
Strung up along the cabin poles and then
Cast in a pit for common burial.
The day would come when in the wilderness,
The weary hand protesting, he would write
This final pledge—"I, Noel Chabanel,
Do vow, in presence of the Sacrament
Of Thy most precious blood and body, here
To stay forever with the Huron Mission,
According to commands of my Superiors.
Therefore I do beseech Thee to receive me
As Thy perpetual servant and to make
Me worthy of so sublime a ministry."

And the same spirit breathed on Chaumonot,
Making his restless and undisciplined soul
At first seek channels of renunciation
In abstinence, ill health and beggary.
His months of pilgrimages to the shrines
At Rome and to the Lady of Loretto,
The static hours upon his knees had sapped
His strength, turning an introspective mind

Upon the weary circuit of its thoughts,
Until one day a letter from Brébeuf
Would come to burn the torpors of his heart
And galvanize a raw novitiate.

. . .

1634

He had not come to stack the arquebuses
Against the mountains of the beaver pelts.
He had not come to kill. Between the two
—Barter and battle—what was left to explain
A stranger in their midst? The name *Echon*
Had solved the riddle.

So with native help
The Fathers built their mission house—the frame
Of young elm-poles set solidly in earth;
Their supple tops bent, lashed and braced to form
The arched roof overlaid with cedar-bark.
"No Louvre or palace is this cabin," wrote
Brébeuf, "no stories, cellar, garret, windows,
No chimney—only at the top a hole
To let the smoke escape. Inside, three rooms
With doors of wood alone set it apart
From the single long-house of the Indians.
The first is used for storage; in the second
Our kitchen, bedroom and refectory;
Our bedstead is the earth; rushes and boughs
For mattresses and pillows; in the third,
Which is our chapel, we have placed the altar,
The images and vessels of the Mass."
It was the middle room that drew the natives,
Day after day, to share the sagamite
And raisins, and to see the marvels brought
From France—marvels on which the Fathers built
A basis of persuasion, recognizing
The potency of awe for natures nurtured
On charms and spells, invoking kindly spirits
And exorcising demons.

. . .

AUGUST 27, 1635

A moon eclipse was due— Brébeuf had known it—
Had told the Indians of the moment when
The shadow would be thrown across the face.

Nor was there wastage in the prayers as night,
Uncurtained by a single cloud, produced
An orb most perfect. No one knew the lair
Or nest from which the shadow came; no one
The home to which it travelled when it passed.
Only the vague uncertainties were left—
Was it the dread invasion from the south?
Such portent was the signal for the braves
To mass themselves outside the towns and shoot
Their multitudes of arrows at the sky
And fling their curses at the Iroquois.
Like a crow's wing it hovered, broodily
Brushing the face—five hours from rim to rim
While midnight darkness stood upon the land.
This was prediction baffling all their magic.
Again, when weeks of drought had parched the land
And burned the corn, when dancing sorcerers
Brought out their tortoise shells, climbed on the roofs,
Clanging their invocation to the Bird
Of Thunder to return, day after day,
Without avail, the priests formed their processions,
Put on their surplices above their robes,
And the Bird of Thunder came with heavy rain,
Released by the nine masses at Saint Joseph.

Nor were the village warriors slow to see
The value of the Frenchmen's strategy
In war. Returning from the eastern towns,
They told how soldiers had rebuilt the forts,
And strengthened them with corner bastions
Where through the embrasures enfilading fire
Might flank the Iroquois bridging the ditches,
And scaling ramparts. Here was argument
That pierced the thickest prejudice of brain
And heart, allaying panic ever present,
When with the first news of the hated foe
From scouts and hunters, women with their young
Fled to the dubious refuge of the forest
From terror blacker than a pestilence.
On such a soil tilled by those skilful hands
Those passion flowers and lilies of the East,
The *Aves* and the *Paternosters* bloomed.
The *Credos* and the *Thou-shalt-nots* were turned
By Daniel into simple Huron rhymes
And taught to children, and when points of faith
Were driven hard against resistant rock,

The Fathers found the softer crevices
Through deeds which readily the Indian mind
Could grasp—where hands were never put to blows
Nor the swift tongues used for recrimination.

Acceptance of the common lot was part
Of the original vows. But that the priests
Who were to come should not misread the text,
Brébeuf prepared a sermon on the theme
Of Patience:— "Fathers, Brothers, under call
Of God! Take care that you foresee the perils,
Labours and hardships of this Holy Mission.
You must sincerely love the savages
As brothers ransomed by the blood of Christ.
All things must be endured. To win their hearts
You must perform the smallest services.
Provide a tinder-box or burning mirror
To light their fires. Fetch wood and water for them;
And when embarking never let them wait
For you; tuck up your habits, keep them dry
To avoid water and sand in their canoes. Carry
Your load on portages. Always appear
Cheerful—their memories are good for faults.
Constrain yourselves to eat their sagamite
The way that they prepare it, tasteless, dirty."

And by the priests upon the ground all dots
And commas were observed. They suffered smoke
That billowed from the back-draughts at the roof,
Smothered the cabin, seared the eyes; the fire
That broiled the face, while frost congealed the spine;
The food from unwashed platters where refusal
Was an offence; the rasp of speech maintained
All day by men who never learned to talk
In quiet tones; the drums of the Diviners
Blasting the night—all this without complaint!
And more—whatever sleep was possible
To snatch from the occasional lull of cries
Was broken by uncovenanted fleas
That fastened on the priestly flesh like hornets.
Carving the curves of favour on the lips,
Tailoring the man into the Jesuit coat,
Wrapping the smiles round inward maledictions,
And sublimating hoary Gallic oaths
Into the *Benedicite* when dogs
And squaws and reeking children violated
The hours of rest, were penances unnamed

Within the iron code of good Ignatius.
Was there a limit of obedience
Outside the jurisdiction of this Saint?
How often did the hand go up to lower
The flag? How often by some ringing order
Was it arrested at the halliard touch?
How often did Brébeuf seal up his ears
When blows and insults woke ancestral fifes
Within his brain, blood-cells, and viscera,
Is not explicit in the written story.

But never could the Indians infer
Self-gain or anything but simple courage
Inspired by a zeal beyond reproof,
As when the smallpox spreading like a flame
Destroying hundreds, scarifying thousands,
The Fathers took their chances of contagion,
Their broad hats warped by rain, their moccasins
Worn to the kibes, that they might reach the huts,
Share with the sick their dwindled stock of food—
A sup of partridge broth or raisin juice,
Inscribe the sacred sign of the cross, and place
A touch of moisture from the Holy Water
Upon the forehead of a dying child.

Before the year was gone the priests were shown
The way the Hurons could prepare for death
A captive foe. The warriors had surprised
A band of Iroquois and had reserved
The one survivor for a fiery pageant.
No cunning of an ancient Roman triumph,
Nor torment of a Medici confession
Surpassed the subtle savagery of art
Which made the dressing for the sacrifice
A ritual of mockery for the victim.
What visions of the past came to Brébeuf,
And what forebodings of the days to come,
As he beheld this weird compound of life
In jest and intent taking place before
His eyes—the crude unconscious variants
Of reed and sceptre, robe and cross, brier
And crown! Might not one day baptismal drops
Be turned against him in a rain of death?
Whatever the appeals made by the priests,
They could not break the immemorial usage
Or vary one detail. The prisoner
Was made to sing his death-song, was embraced,

Hailed with ironic greetings, forced to state
His willingness to die.
"See how your hands
Are crushed. You cannot thus desire to live.
No.
Then be of good courage—you shall die.

True! What shall be the manner of my death?

By fire.
When shall it be?
Tonight.
What hour?
At sunset.
All is well."
Eleven fires
Were lit along the whole length of the cabin.
His body smeared with pitch and bound with belts
Of bark, the Iroquois was forced to run
The fires, stopped at each end by the young braves,
And swiftly driven back, and when he swooned,
They carried him outside to the night air,
Laid him on fresh damp moss, poured cooling water
Into his mouth, and to his burns applied
The soothing balsams. With resuscitation
They lavished on him all the courtesies
Of speech and gesture, gave him food and drink,
Compassionately spoke of his wounds and pain.
The ordeal every hour was resumed
And halted, but, with each recurrence, blows
Were added to the burns and gibes gave place
To yells until the sacrificial dawn,
Lighting the scaffold, dimming the red glow
Of the hatchet collar, closed the festival.

Brébeuf had seen the worst. He knew that when
A winter pack of wolves brought down a stag
There was no waste of time between the leap
And the business click upon the jugular,
Such was the forthright honesty in death
Among the brutes. They had not learned the sport
Of dallying around the nerves to halt
A quick despatch. A human art was torture,
Where reason crept into the veins, mixed tar
With blood and brewed its own intoxicant.
Brébeuf had pleaded for the captive's life,
But as the night wore on, would not his heart,

Colliding with his mind, have wished for death?
The plea refused, he gave the Iroquois
The only consolation in his power.
He went back to his cabin, heavy in heart.
To stem that viscous melanotic current
Demanded labour, time, and sacrifice.
Those passions were not altered over-night.
Two plans were in his mind—the one concerned
The seminary started in Quebec.
The children could be sent there to be trained
In Christian precepts, weaned from superstition
And from the savage spectacle of death.
He saw the way the women and their broods
Danced round the scaffold in their exaltation.
How much of this was habit and how much
Example? Curiously Brébeuf revolved
The facets of the Indian character.
A fighting courage equal to the French—
It could be lifted to crusading heights
By a battle speech. Endurance was a code
Among the braves, and impassivity.
Their women wailing at the Feast of Death,
The men sat silent, heads bowed to the knees.
"Never in nine years with but one exception,"
Wrote Ragueneau, "did I see an Indian weep
For grief." Only the fires evoked the cries,
And these like scalps were triumphs for the captors.
But then their charity and gentleness
To one another and to strangers gave
A balance to the picture. Fugitives
From villages destroyed found instant welcome
To the last communal share of food and land.
Brébeuf's stay at Toanché gave him proof
Of how the Huron nature could respond
To kindness. But last night upon that scaffold!
Could that be scoured from the heart? Why not
Try out the nurture plan upon the children
And send the boys east, shepherded by Daniel?

The other need was urgent—labourers!
The villages were numerous and were spread
Through such a vast expanse of wilderness
And shore. Only a bell with a bronze throat
Must summon missionaries to these fields.
With the last cry of the captive in his ears,
Brébeuf strode from his cabin to the woods

To be alone. He found his tabernacle
Within a grove, picked up a stone flat-faced,
And going to a cedar-crotch, he jammed
It in, and on this table wrote his letter.
"Herein I show you what you have to suffer.
I shall say nothing of the voyage—that
You know already. If you have the courage
To try it, that is only the beginning,
For when after a month of river travel
You reach our village, we can offer you
The shelter of a cabin lowlier
Than any hovel you have seen in France.
As tired as you may be, only a mat
Laid on the ground will be your bed. Your food
May be for weeks a gruel of crushed corn
That has the look and smell of mortar paste.
This country is the breeding place of vermin.
Sandflies, mosquitoes haunt the summer months.
In France you may have been a theologian,
A scholar, master, preacher, but out here
You must attend a savage school; for months
Will pass before you learn even to lisp
The language. Here barbarians shall be
Your Aristotle and Saint Thomas. Mute
Before those teachers you shall take your lessons.
What of the winter? Half the year is winter.
Inside your cabins will be smoke so thick
You may not read your Breviary for days.
Around your fireplace at mealtime arrive
The uninvited guests with whom you share
Your stint of food. And in the fall and winter,
You tramp unbeaten trails to reach the missions,
Carrying your luggage on your back. Your life
Hangs by a thread. Of all calamities
You are the cause—the scarcity of game,
A fire, famine or an epidemic.
There are no natural reasons for a drought
And for the earth's sterility. You are
The reasons, and at any time a savage
May burn your cabin down or split your head.
I tell you of the enemies that live
Among our Huron friends. I have not told
You of the Iroquois our constant foes.
Only a week ago in open fight
They killed twelve of our men at Contarea,
A day's march from the village where we live.

Treacherous and stealthy in their ambuscades,
They terrorize the country, for the Hurons
Are very slothful in defence, never
On guard and always seeking flight for safety.

. . .

XII

No doubt in the mind of Brébeuf that this was the last
Journey—three miles over the snow. He knew
That the margins as thin as they were by which he escaped
From death through the eighteen years of his mission toil
Did not belong to this chapter: not by his pen
Would this be told. He knew his place in the line,
For the blaze of the trail that was cut on the bark by Jogues
Shone still. He had heard the story as told by writ
And word of survivors—of how a captive slave
Of the hunters, the skin of his thighs cracked with the frost,
He would steal from the tents to the birches, make a rough
  cross
From two branches, set it in snow and on the peel
Inscribe his vows and dedicate to the Name
In "litanies of love" what fragments were left
From the wrack of his flesh; of his escape from the tribes;
Of his journey to France where he knocked at the door of the
  College
Of Rennes, was gathered in as a mendicant friar,
Nameless, unknown, till he gave for proof to the priest
His scarred credentials of faith, the nail-less hands
And withered arms—the signs of the Mohawk fury.
Nor yet was the story finished—he had come again
Back to his mission to get the second death.
And the comrades of Jogues—Goupil, Eustache and Couture,
Had been stripped and made to run the double files
And take the blows—one hundred clubs to each line—
And this as the prelude to torture, leisured, minute,
Where thorns on the quick, scallop shells to the joints of the
  thumbs,
Provided the sport for children and squaws till the end.
And adding salt to the blood of Brébeuf was the thought
Of Daniel—was it months or a week ago?
So far, so near, it seemed in time, so close
In leagues—just over there to the south it was
He faced the arrows and died in front of his church.

But winding into the greater artery
Of thought that bore upon the coming passion

Were little tributaries of wayward wish
And reminiscence. Paris with its vespers
Was folded in the mind of Lalemant,
And the soft Gothic lights and traceries
Were shading down the ridges of his vows.
But two years past at Bourges he had walked the cloisters,
Companioned by St Augustine and Francis,
And wrapped in quiet holy mists. Brébeuf,
His mind a moment throwing back the curtain
Of eighteen years, could see the orchard lands,
The *cidreries*, the peasants at the Fairs,
The undulating miles of wheat and barley,
Gardens and pastures rolling like a sea
From Lisieux to Le Havre. Just now the surf
Was pounding on the limestone Norman beaches
And on the reefs of Calvados. Had dawn
This very day not flung her surplices
Around the headlands and with golden fire
Consumed the silken argosies that made
For Rouen from the estuary of the Seine?
A moment only for that veil to lift—
A moment only for those bells to die
That rang their matins at Condé-sur-Vire.

By noon St Ignace! The arrival there
The signal for the battle-cries of triumph,
The gauntlet of the clubs. The stakes were set
And the ordeal of Jogues was re-enacted
Upon the priests—even with wilder fury,
For here at last was trapped their greatest victim,
Echon. The Iroquois had waited long
For this event. Their hatred for the Hurons
Fused with their hatred for the French and priests
Was to be vented on this sacrifice,
And to that camp had come apostate Hurons,
United with their foes in common hate
To settle up their reckoning with *Echon*.

Now three o'clock, and capping the height of the passion,
Confusing the sacraments under the pines of the forest,
Under the incense of balsam, under the smoke
Of the pitch, was offered the rite of the font. On the head,
The breast, the loins and the legs, the boiling water!
While the mocking paraphrase of the symbols was hurled
At their faces like shards of flint from the arrow heads —

"We baptize thee with water . . .
That thou mayest be led
To Heaven . . .
To that end we do anoint thee.
We treat thee as a friend: we are the cause
Of thy happiness; we are thy priests; the more
Thou sufferest, the more thy God will reward thee,
So give us thanks for our kind offices."

The fury of taunt was followed by fury of blow.
Why did not the flesh of Brébeuf cringe to the scourge,
Respond to the heat, for rarely the Iroquois found
A victim that would not cry out in such pain—yet here
The fire was on the wrong fuel. Whenever he spoke,
It was to rally the soul of his friend whose turn
Was to come through the night while the eyes were uplifted in prayer,
Imploring the Lady of Sorrows, the mother of Christ,
As pain brimmed over the cup and the will was called
To stand the test of the coals. And sometimes the speech
Of Brébeuf struck out, thundering reproof to his foes,
Half-rebuke, half-defiance, giving them roar for roar.
Was it because the chancel became the arena,
Brébeuf a lion at bay, not a lamb on the altar,
As if the might of a Roman were joined to the cause
Of Judaea? Speech they could stop for they girdled his lips,
But never a moan could they get. Where was the source
Of his strength, the home of his courage that topped the best
Of their braves and even out-fabled the lore of their legends?
In the bunch of his shoulders which often had carried a load
Extorting the envy of guides at an Ottawa portage?
The heat of the hatchets was finding a path to that source.
In the thews of his thighs which had mastered the trails of the Neutrals?
They would gash and beribbon those muscles. Was it the blood?
They would draw it fresh from its fountain. Was it the heart?
They dug for it, fought for the scraps in the way of the wolves.
But not in these was the valour or stamina lodged;
Nor in the symbol of Richelieu's robes or the seals
Of Mazarin's charters, nor in the stir of the *lilies*
Upon the Imperial folds; nor yet in the words
Loyola wrote on a table of lava-stone
In the cave of Manresa—not in these the source—
But in the sound of invisible trumpets blowing
Around two slabs of board, right-angled, hammered
By Roman nails and hung on a Jewish hill.

The wheel had come full circle with the visions
In France of Brébeuf poured through the mould of St Ignace.
Lalemant died in the morning at nine, in the flame
Of the pitch belts. Flushed with the sight of the bodies, the
  foes
Gathered their clans and moved back to the north and west
To join in the fight against the tribes of the Petuns.
There was nothing now that could stem the Iroquois blast.
However undaunted the souls of the priests who were left,
However fierce the sporadic counter attacks
Of the Hurons striking in roving bands from the ambush,
Or smashing out at their foes in garrison raids,
The villages fell before a blizzard of axes
And arrows and spears, and then were put to the torch.

The days were dark at the fort and heavier grew
The burdens on Ragueneau's shoulders. Decision was his.
No word from the east could arrive in time to shape
The step he must take. To and fro—from altar to hill,
From hill to altar, he walked and prayed and watched.
As governing priest of the mission he felt the pride
Of his Order whipping his pulse, for was not St Ignace
The highest test of the Faith? And all that torture
And death could do to the body was done. The Will
And the Cause in their triumph survived. Loyola's mountains,
Sublime at their summits, were scaled to the uttermost peak.
Ragueneau, the Shepherd, now looked on a battered fold.
In a whirlwind of fire St Jean, like St Joseph, crashed
Under the Iroquois impact. Firm at his post,
Garnier suffered the fate of Daniel. And now
Chabanel, last in the roll of the martyrs, entrapped
On his knees in the woods met death at apostate hands.

The drama was drawing close to its end. It fell
To Ragueneau's lot to perform a final rite—
To offer the fort in sacrificial fire!
He applied the torch himself. "Inside an hour,"
He wrote, "we saw the fruit of ten years' labour
Ascend in smoke—then looked our last at the fields,
Put altar-vessels and food on a raft of logs,
And made our way to the island of St Joseph."
But even from there was the old tale retold—
Of hunger and the search for roots and acorns;
Of cold and persecution unto death
By the Iroquois; of Jesuit will and courage
As the shepherd-priest with Chaumonot led back
The remnant of a nation to Quebec.

THE MARTYRS' SHRINE

Three hundred years have passed, and the winds of God
Which blew over France are blowing once more through the
pines
That bulwark the shores of the great Fresh Water Sea.
Over the wastes abandoned by human tread,
Where only the bittern's cry was heard at dusk;
Over the lakes where the wild ducks built their nests,
The skies that had banked their fires are shining again
With the stars that guided the feet of Jogues and Brébeuf.

The years as they turned have ripened the martyrs' seed,
And the ashes of St Ignace are glowing afresh.
The trails, having frayed the threads of the cassocks, sank
Under the mould of the centuries, under fern
And brier and fungus—there in due time to blossom
Into the highways that lead to the crest of the hill
Which havened both shepherd and flock in the days of their
trial.
For out of the torch of Ragueneau's ruins the candles
Are burning today in the chancel of Sainte Marie.
The Mission sites have returned to the fold of the Order.
Near to the ground where the cross broke under the hatchet,
And went with it into the soil to come back at the turn
Of the spade with the carbon and calcium char of the bodies,
The shrines and altars are built anew; the *Aves*
And prayers ascend, and the Holy Bread is broken.

1938-40
Brébeuf and His Brethren, 1940

COME AWAY, DEATH

Willy-nilly, he comes or goes, with the clown's logic,
Comic in epitaph, tragic in epithalamium,
And unseduced by any mused rhyme.
However blow the winds over the pollen,
Whatever the course of the garden variables,
He remains the constant,
Ever flowering from the poppy seeds.

There was a time he came in formal dress,
Announced by Silence tapping at the panels
In deep apology.
A touch of chivalry in his approach,
He offered sacramental wine,
And with acanthus leaf
And petals of the hyacinth
He took the fever from the temples
And closed the eyelids,
Then led the way to his cool longitudes
In the dignity of the candles.

His mediaeval grace is gone—
Gone with the flame of the capitals
And the leisured turn of the thumb
Leafing the manuscripts,
Gone with the marbles
And the Venetian mosaics,
With the bend of the knee
Before the rose-strewn feet of the Virgin.
The *paternosters* of his priests,
Committing clay to clay,
Have rattled in their throats
Under the gride of his traction tread.

One night we heard his footfall—one September night—
In the outskirts of a village near the sea.
There was a moment when the storm
Delayed its fist, when the surf fell
Like velvet on the rocks—a moment only;
The strangest lull we ever knew!
A sudden truce among the oaks
Released their fratricidal arms;
The poplars straightened to attention
As the winds stopped to listen
To the sound of the motor drone—
And then the drone was still.
We heard the tick-tock on the shelf,
And the leak of valves in our hearts.
A calm condensed and lidded
As at the core of a cyclone ended breathing.
This was the monologue of Silence
Grave and unequivocal.

What followed was a bolt
Outside the range and target of the thunder,

And human speech curved back upon itself
Through Druid runways and the Piltdown scarps,
Beyond the stammers of the Java caves,
To find its origins in hieroglyphs
On mouths and eyes and cheeks
Etched by a foreign stylus never used
On the outmoded page of the Apocalypse.

1941
Poetry, April 1941
Collected Poems, 1944

THE TRUANT

"What have you there?" the great Panjandrum said
To the Master of the Revels who had led
A bucking truant with a stiff backbone
Close to the foot of the Almighty's throne.

"Right Reverend, most adored,
And forcibly acknowledged Lord
By the keen logic of your two-edged sword!
This creature has presumed to classify
Himself—a biped, rational, six feet high
And two feet wide; weighs fourteen stone;
Is guilty of a multitude of sins.
He has abjured his choric origins,
And like an undomesticated slattern,
Walks with tangential step unknown
Within the weave of the atomic pattern.
He has developed concepts, grins
Obscenely at your Royal bulletins,
Possesses what he calls a will
Which challenges your power to kill."

"What is his pedigree?"

"The base is guaranteed, your Majesty—
Calcium, carbon, phosphorus, vapour
And other fundamentals spun
From the umbilicus of the sun,
And yet he says he will not caper

Around your throne, nor toe the rules
For the ballet of the fiery molecules."

"His concepts and denials—scrap them, burn them—
To the chemists with them promptly."

"Sire,
The stuff is not amenable to fire.
Nothing but their own kind can overturn them.
The chemists have sent back the same old story—
'With our extreme gelatinous apology,
We beg to inform your Imperial Majesty,
Unto whom be dominion and power and glory,
There still remains that strange precipitate
Which has the quality to resist
Our oldest and most trusted catalyst.
It is a substance we cannot cremate
By temperatures known to our Laboratory.' "

And the great Panjandrum's face grew dark—
"I'll put those chemists to their annual purge,
And I myself shall be the thaumaturge
To find the nature of this fellow's spark.
Come, bring him nearer by yon halter rope:
I'll analyse him with the cosmoscope."

Pulled forward with his neck awry,
The little fellow six feet short,
Aware he was about to die,
Committed grave contempt of court
By answering with a flinchless stare
The Awful Presence seated there.

The ALL HIGH swore until his face was black.
He called him a coprophagite,
A genus *homo*, egomaniac,
Third cousin to the family of worms,
A sporozoan from the ooze of night,
Spawn of a spavined troglodyte:
He swore by all the catalogue of terms
Known since the slang of carboniferous Time.
He said that he could trace him back
To pollywogs and earwigs in the slime.
And in his shrillest tenor he began
Reciting his indictment of the man,
Until he closed upon this capital crime—
"You are accused of singing out of key,
(A foul unmitigated dissonance)

Of shuffling in the measures of the dance,
Then walking out with that defiant, free
Toss of your head, banging the doors,
Leaving a stench upon the jacinth floors.
You have fallen like a curse
On the mechanics of my Universe.

"Herewith I measure out your penalty—
Hearken while you hear, look while you see:
I send you now upon your homeward route
Where you shall find
Humiliation for your pride of mind.
I shall make deaf the ear, and dim the eye,
Put palsy in your touch, make mute
Your speech, intoxicate your cells and dry
Your blood and marrow, shoot
Arthritic needles through your cartilage,
And having parched you with old age,
I'll pass you wormwise through the mire;
And when your rebel will
Is mouldered, all desire
Shrivelled, all your concepts broken,
Backward in dust I'll blow you till
You join my spiral festival of fire.
Go, Master of the Revels—I have spoken."

And the little genus *homo*, six feet high,
Standing erect, countered with this reply—
"You dumb insouciant invertebrate,
You rule a lower than a feudal state—
A realm of flunkey decimals that run,
Return; return and run; again return,
Each group around its little sun,
And every sun a satellite.
There they go by day and night,
Nothing to do but run and burn,
Taking turn and turn about,
Light-year in and light-year out,
Dancing, dancing in quadrillions,
Never leaving their pavilions.

"Your astronomical conceit
Of bulk and power is anserine.
Your ignorance so thick,
You did not know your own arithmetic.
We flung the graphs about your flying feet;
We measured your diameter—

Merely a line
Of zeros prefaced by an integer.
Before we came
You had no name.
You did not know direction or your pace;
We taught you all you ever knew
Of motion, time and space.
We healed you of your vertigo
And put you in our kindergarten show,
Perambulated you through prisms, drew
Your mileage through the Milky Way,
Lassoed your comets when they ran astray,
Yoked Leo, Taurus, and your team of Bears
To pull our kiddy cars of inverse squares.

"Boast not about your harmony,
Your perfect curves, your rings
Of *pure and endless light*—'Twas we
Who pinned upon your seraphim their wings,
And when your brassy heavens rang
With joy that morning while the planets sang
Their choruses of archangelic lore,
'Twas we who ordered the notes upon their score
Out of our winds and strings.
Yes! all your shapely forms
Are ours—parabolas of silver light,
Those blueprints of your spiral stairs
From nadir depth to zenith height,
Coronas, rainbows after storms,
Auroras on your eastern tapestries
And constellations over western seas.

"And when, one day, grown conscious of your age,
While pondering an eolith,
We turned a human page
And blotted out a cosmic myth
With all its baby symbols to explain
The sunlight in Apollo's eyes,
Our rising pulses and the birth of pain,
Fear, and that fern-and-fungus breath
Stalking our nostrils to our caves of death—
That day we learned how to anatomize
Your body, calibrate your size
And set a mirror up before your face
To show you what you really were—a rain
Of dull Lucretian atoms crowding space,
A series of concentric waves which any fool

Might make by dropping stones within a pool,
Or an exploding bomb forever in flight
Bursting like hell through Chaos and Old Night.

"You oldest of the hierarchs
Composed of electronic sparks,
We grant you speed,
We grant you power, and fire
That ends in ash, but we concede
To you no pain nor joy nor love nor hate,
No final tableau of desire,
No causes won or lost, no free
Adventure at the outposts—only
The degradation of your energy
When at some late
Slow number of your dance your sergeant-major Fate
Will catch you blind and groping and will send
You reeling on that long and lonely
Lockstep of your wave-lengths towards your end.

"We who have met
With stubborn calm the dawn's hot fusillades;
Who have seen the forehead sweat
Under the tug of pulleys on the joints,
Under the liquidating tally
Of the cat-and-truncheon bastinades;
Who have taught our souls to rally
To mountain horns and the sea's rockets
When the needle ran demented through the points;
We who have learned to clench
Our fists and raise our lightless sockets
To morning skies after the midnight raids,
Yet cocked our ears to bugles on the barricades,
And in cathedral rubble found a way to quench
A dying thirst within a Galilean valley—
No! by the Rood, we will not join your ballet."

1942
Canadian Forum, December 1942
Still Life and Other Verse, 1943

STILL LIFE

To the poets who have fled
To pools where little breezes dusk and shiver,
Who need still life to deliver
Their souls of their songs,
We offer roses blanched of red
In the Orient gardens,
With April lilies to limn
On the Japanese urns—
And time, be it said,
For a casual hymn
To be sung for the hundred thousand dead
In the mud of the Yellow River.

And if your metric paragraphs
Incline to Western epitaphs,
Be pleased to return to a plain
Where a million lie
Under a proletarian sky,
Waiting to trouble
Your lines on the scorched Ukrainian stubble.
On the veined marble of their snows
Indite a score to tether
The flight of your strain;
Or should you need a rougher grain
That will never corrode with weather,
Let us propose
A stone west of the bend where the Volga flows
To lick her cubs on the Stalingrad rubble.

Hasten, for time may pass you by,
Mildew the reed and rust the lyre;
Look—that Tunisian glow will die
As died the Carthaginian fire!
Today the autumn tints are on
The trampled grass at Marathon.
Here are the tales to be retold,
Here are the songs to be resung.
Go, find a cadence for that field-grey mould
Outcropping on the Parthenon.
Invoke, in other than the Latin tongue,
A Mediterranean Muse

To leave her pastoral loves—
The murmurs of her soft Theocritean fold,
Mimosa, oleander,
Dovecotes and olive groves,
And court the shadows where the night bedews
A Roman mausoleum hung
Upon the tides from Candia to Syracuse.

1943
Saturday Night, October 1939 [variant]
Still Life and Other Verse, 1943

BLIND FROM SINGAPORE

("Our orders are to burn the city")

Only in memory is petroleum burning:
Why do you keep your lids turning
Upward as though you feared light from the sun?

There was economy
In what was said, in what was done:—
A second just to read
The signal, just an hour for the deed.
As for your memory,
Was not six years enough to have consumed the city?
The physical fear has gone
A substitute has come:
You find it hard to take our pity,
This the hardest of all—better the dumb
Gestures you cannot see.

Your enemy
Is light,
Although withdrawn
In ambush through the stars.

Your friend is Night.
Wise to the clock in candid ambiguity,
She sidles to your bed at dawn,
Carries no mirror for your scars
And stays with you till dewfall. We

Alone can read those figures on the page
That multiplied your age.

1949
Northern Review, December/January 1949/50
E.J. Pratt: Complete Poems, Part II, 1989

THE GOOD EARTH

Let the mind rest awhile, lower the eyes,
Relieve the spirit of its Faustian clamour:
An atom holds more secrets than the skies;
Be patient with the earth and do not cram her

With seed beyond the wisdom of her soil.
She knows the foot and hoof of man and ox,
She learned the variations of their toil—
The ploughshare's sensitivity to rocks.

Gather the stones for field and garden walls,
Build cellars for your vegetable stores,
Forgo the architecture of your halls,
Until your hands have fashioned stable doors.

She likes the smell of nitrates from the stalls,
She hates a disciplined tread, the scorching roar
At the grain's roots: she is nervous at the calls
Of men in panic at a strike of ore.

Patient she is in her flesh servitude,
Tolerant to curry ticklings of the harrow,
But do not scratch past her agrarian mood
To cut the calcium in her bone and marrow.

Hold that synthetic seed, for underneath
Deep down she'll answer to your horticulture:
She has a way of germinating teeth
And yielding crops of carrion for the vulture.

c. 1950
Canadian Poetry Magazine, September 1950
Collected Poems, 1958

From TOWARDS THE LAST SPIKE

It was the same world then as now—the same,
Except for little differences of speed
And power, and means to treat myopia
To show an axe-blade infinitely sharp
Splitting things infinitely small, or else
Provide the telescopic sight to roam
Through curved dominions never found in fables.
The same, but for new particles of speech—
Those algebraic substitutes for nouns
That sky cartographers would hang like signboards
Along the trespass of our thoughts to stop
The stutters of our tongues with their equations.

As now, so then, blood kept its ancient colour,
And smoothly, roughly, paced its banks;
Preserving them, in riot rupturing them.
Wounds needed bandages and stomachs
The hands outstretched had joined the lips in prayer—
"Give us our daily bread, give us our pay."
The past flushed in the present and tomorrow
Would dawn upon today: only the rate
To sensitize or numb a nerve would change;
Only the quickening of a measuring skill
To gauge the onset of a birth or death
With the precision of micrometers.
Men spoke of acres then and miles and masses,
Velocity and steam, cables that moored
Not ships but continents, world granaries,
The east-west cousinship, a nation's rise,
Hail of identity, a world expanding,
If not the universe: the feel of it
Was in the air—"Union required the Line."
The theme was current at the banquet tables,
And arguments profane and sacred rent
God-fearing families into partisans.
Pulpit, platform and floor were sounding-boards;
Cushions beneath the pounding fists assumed
The hues of western sunsets; nostrils sniffed
The prairie tang; the tongue rolled over texts:
Even St Paul was being invoked to wring
The neck of Thomas in this war of faith

With unbelief. Was ever an adventure
Without its cost? Analogies were found
On every page of history or science.
A nation, like the world, could not stand still.
What was the use of records but to break them?
The tougher armour followed the new shell;
The newer shell the armour; lighthouse rockets
Sprinkled their stars over the wake of wrecks.
Were not the engineers at work to close
The lag between the pressures and the valves?
The same world then as now thirsting for power
To crack those records open, extra pounds
Upon the inches, extra miles per hour.
The mildewed static schedules which before
Had like asbestos been immune to wood
Now curled and blackened in the furnace coal.
This power lay in the custody of men
From down-and-outers needing roofs, whose hands
Were moulded by their fists, whose skins could feel
At home incorporate with dolomite,
To men who with the marshal instincts in them,
Deriving their authority from wallets,
Directed their battalions from the trestles.

THE GATHERING

("Oats—a grain which in England is generally given to horses, but in Scotland supports the people."—Dr Samuel Johnson. "True, but where will you find such horses, where such men?"—Lord Elibank's reply as recorded by Sir Walter Scott.)

Oatmeal was in their blood and in their names.
Thrift was the title of their catechism.
It governed all things but their mess of porridge
Which, when it struck the hydrochloric acid
With treacle and skim-milk, became a mash.
Entering the duodenum, it broke up
Into amino acids: then the liver
Took on its natural job as carpenter:
Foreheads grew into cliffs, jaws into juts.
The meal, so changed, engaged the follicles:
Eyebrows came out as gorse, the beards as thistles,
And the chest-hair the fell of Grampian rams.
It stretched and vulcanized the human span:
Nonagenarians worked and thrived upon it.
Out of such chemistry run through by genes,
The food released its fearsome racial products:—

The power to strike a bargain like a foe,
To win an argument upon a burr,
Invest the language with a Bannockburn,
Culloden or the warnings of Lochiel,
Weave loyalties and rivalries in tartans,
Present for the amazement of the world
Kilts and the civilized barbaric Fling,
And pipes which, when they acted on the mash,
Fermented lullabies to *Scots wha hae*.

Their names were like a battle muster—Angus
(He of the Shops) and Fleming (of the Transit),
Hector (of the *Kicking Horse*), Dawson,
"Cromarty" Ross, and Beatty (Ulster Scot),
Bruce, Allan, Galt and Douglas, and the "twa"—
Stephen (Craigellachie) and Smith (Strathcona)—
Who would one day climb from their Gaelic hide-outs,
Take off their plaids and wrap them round the mountains.
And then the everlasting tread of the Macs,
Vanguard, centre and rear, their roving eyes
On summits, rivers, contracts, beaver, ledgers;
Their ears cocked to the skirl of Sir John A.,
The general of the patronymic march.

(Sir John revolving round the Terms of Union with British Columbia. Time, late at night.)

Insomnia had ripped the bed-sheets from him
Night after night. How long was this to last?
Confederation had not played this kind
Of trickery on him. That was rough indeed,
So gravelled, that a man might call for rest
And take it for a life accomplishment.
It was his laurel though some of the leaves
Had dried. But this would be a longer tug
Of war which needed for his team thick wrists
And calloused fingers, heavy heels to dig
Into the earth and hold—men with bull's beef
Upon their ribs. Had he himself the wind,
The anchor-waist to peg at the rope's end?
'Twas bad enough to have these questions hit
The waking mind: 'twas much worse when he dozed;
For goblins had a way of pinching him,
Slapping a nightmare on to dwindling snoozes.
They put him and his team into a tug
More real than life. He heard a judge call out—
"Teams settle on the ropes and take the strain!"

And with the coaches' *heave*, the running welts
Reddened his palms, and then the gruelling *backlock*
Inscribed its indentations on his shoulders.
This kind of burn he knew he had to stand;
It was the game's routine; the other fire
Was what he feared the most for it could bake him—
That white dividing rag tied to the rope
Above the centre pole had with each heave
Wavered with chances equal. With the backlock,
Despite the legs of Tupper and Cartier,
The western anchor dragged; the other side
Remorselessly was gaining, holding, gaining.
No sleep could stand this strain and, with the nightmare
Delivered of its colt, Macdonald woke.

Tired with the midnight toss, lock-jawed with yawns,
He left the bed and, shuffling to the window,
He opened it. The air would cool him off
And soothe his shoulder burns. He felt his ribs:
Strange, nothing broken—how those crazy drowses
Had made the fictions tangle with the facts!
He must unscramble them with steady hands.
Those Ranges pirouetting in his dreams
Had their own knack of standing still in light,
Revealing peaks whose known triangulation
Had to be read in prose severity.
Seizing a telescope, he swept the skies,
The north-south drift, a self-illumined chart.
Under Polaris was the Arctic Sea
And the sub-Arctic gates well stocked with names:
Hudson, Davis, Baffin, Frobisher;
And in his own day Franklin, Ross and Parry
Of the Canadian Archipelago;
Kellett, McClure, McClintock, of *The Search*.
Those straits and bays had long been kicked by keels,
And flags had fluttered on the Capes that fired
His youth, making familiar the unknown.
What though the odds were nine to one against,
And the Dead March was undertoning trumpets,
There was enough of strychnine in the names
To make him flip a penny for the risk,
Though he had palmed the coin reflectively
Before he threw and watched it come down *heads*.
That stellar path looked too much like a road map
Upon his wall—the roads all led to market—
The north-south route. He lit a candle, held

It to a second map full of blank spaces
And arrows pointing west. Disturbed, he turned
The lens up to the zenith, followed the course
Tracked by a cloud of stars that would not keep
Their posts—Capella, Perseus, were reeling;
Low in the north-west, Cassiopeia
Was qualmish, leaning on her starboard arm-rest,
And Aries was chasing, butting Cygnus,
Just diving. Doubts and hopes struck at each other.
Why did those constellations look so much
Like blizzards? And what lay beyond the blizzards?

'Twas chilly at the window. He returned
To bed and savoured soporific terms:
Superior, the *Red River, Selkirk, Prairie,*
Port Moody and *Pacific*. Chewing them,
He spat out *Rocky* grit before he swallowed.
Selkirk! This had the sweetest taste. Ten years
Before, the Highland crofters had subscribed
Their names in a memorial for the Rails.
Sir John reviewed the story of the struggle,
That four months' journey from their native land—
The Atlantic through the Straits to Hudson Bay,
Then the Hayes River to Lake Winnipeg
Up to the Forks of the Assiniboine.
He could make use of that—just what he needed,
A Western version of the Arctic daring,
Romance and realism, double dose.
How long ago? Why, this is '71.
Those fellows came the time Napoleon
Was on the steppes. For sixty years they fought
The seasons, 'hoppers, drought, hail, wind and snow;
Survived the massacre at Seven Oaks,
The "Pemmican War" and the Red River floods.
They wanted now the Road—those pioneers
Who lived by spades instead of beaver traps.
Most excellent word that, pioneers! Sir John
Snuggled himself into his sheets, rolling
The word around his tongue, a theme for song,
Or for a peroration to a speech.

THE HANGOVER AT DAWN

He knew the points that had their own appeal.
These did not bother him: the patriot touch,
The Flag, the magnetism of explorers,
The national unity. These could burn up

The phlegm in most of the provincial throats.
But there was one tale central to his plan
(The focus of his headache at this moment),
Which would demand the limit of his art—
The ballad of his courtship in the West:
Better reveal it soon without reserve.

. . .

NUMBER TWO

On the North Shore a reptile lay asleep—
A hybrid that the myths might have conceived,
But not delivered, as progenitor
Of crawling, gliding things upon the earth.
She lay snug in the folds of a huge boa
Whose tail had covered Labrador and swished
Atlantic tides, whose body coiled itself
Around the Hudson Bay, then curled up north
Through Manitoba and Saskatchewan
To Great Slave Lake. In continental reach
The neck went past the Great Bear Lake until
Its head was hidden in the Arctic Seas.
This folded reptile was asleep or dead:
So motionless, she seemed stone dead—just seemed:
She was too old for death, too old for life,
For as if jealous of all living forms
She had lain there before bivalves began
To catacomb their shells on western mountains.
Somewhere within this life-death zone she sprawled,
Torpid upon a rock-and-mineral mattress.
Ice-ages had passed by and over her,
But these, for all their motion, had but sheared
Her spotty carboniferous hair or made
Her ridges stand out like the spikes of molochs.
Her back grown stronger every million years,
She had shed water by the longer rivers
To Hudson Bay and by the shorter streams
To the great basins to the south, had filled
Them up, would keep them filled until the end
Of Time.

Was this the thing Van Horne set out
To conquer? When Superior lay there
With its inviting levels? Blake, Mackenzie,
Offered this water like a postulate.
"Why those twelve thousand men sent to the North?

Nonsense and waste with utter bankruptcy."
And the Laurentian monster at the first
Was undisturbed, presenting but her bulk
To the invasion. All she had to do
Was lie there neither yielding nor resisting.
Top-heavy with accumulated power
And overgrown survival without function,
She changed her spots as though brute rudiments
Of feeling foreign to her native hour
Surprised her with a sense of violation
From an existence other than her own—
Or why take notice of this unknown breed,
This horde of bipeds that could toil like ants,
Could wake her up and keep her irritated?
They tickled her with shovels, dug pickaxes
Into her scales and got under her skin,
And potted holes in her with drills and filled
Them up with what looked like fine grains of sand,
Black sand. It wasn't noise that bothered her,
For thunder she was used to from her cradle—
The head-push and nose-blowing of the ice,
The height and pressure of its body: these
Like winds native to clime and habitat
Had served only to lull her drowsing coils.
It was not size or numbers that concerned her.
It was their foreign build, their gait of movement.
They did not crawl—nor were they born with wings.
They stood upright and walked, shouted and sang;
They needed air—that much was true—their mouths
Were open but the tongue was alien.
The sounds were not the voice of winds and waters,
Nor that of any beasts upon the earth.
She took them first with lethargy, suffered
The rubbing of her back—those little jabs
Of steel were like the burrowing of ticks
In an elk's hide needing an antler point,
Or else left in a numb monotony.
These she could stand but when the breed
Advanced west on her higher vertebrae,
Kicking most insolently at her ribs,
Pouring black powder in her cavities,
And making not the clouds but her insides
The home of fire and thunder, then she gave
Them trial of her strength: the trestles tottered;
Abutments, bridges broke; her rivers flooded:
She summoned snow and ice, and then fell back

On the last weapon in her armoury—
The first and last—her passive corporal bulk,
To stay or wreck the schedule of Van Horne.

NUMBER THREE

The big one was the mountains—seas indeed!
With crests whiter than foam: they poured like seas,
Fluting the green banks of the pines and spruces.
An eagle-flight above they hid themselves
In clouds. They carried space upon their ledges.
Could these be overridden frontally,
Or like typhoons outsmarted on the flanks?
And what were on the flanks? The troughs and canyons,
Passes more dangerous to the navigator
Than to Magellan when he tried to read
The barbarous language of his Strait by calling
For echoes from the rocky hieroglyphs
Playing their pranks of hide-and-seek in fog:
As stubborn too as the old North-West Passage,
More difficult, for ice-packs could break up;
And as for bergs, what polar architect
Could stretch his compass points to draught such peaks
As kept on rising there beyond the foothills?
And should the bastions of the Rockies yield
To this new human and unnatural foe,
Would not the Selkirks stand? This was a range
That looked like some strange dread outside a door
Which gave its name but would not show its features,
Leaving them to the mind to guess at. This
Meant tunnels—would there be no end to boring?
There must be some day. Fleming and his men
Had nosed their paths like hounds; but paths and trails,
Measured in every inch by chain and transit,
Looked easy and seductive on a chart.
The rivers out there did not flow: they tumbled.
The cataracts were fed by glaciers;
Eddies were thought as whirlpools in the Gorges,
And gradients had paws that tore up tracks.

Terror and beauty like twin signal flags
Flew on the peaks for men to keep their distance.
The two combined as in a storm at sea—
"Stay on the shore and take your fill of breathing,
But come not to the decks and climb the rigging."
The Ranges could put cramps in hands and feet
Merely by the suggestion of the venture.

They needed miles to render up their beauty,
As if the gods in high aesthetic moments,
Resenting the profanity of touch,
Chiselled this sculpture for the eye alone.

(Van Horne in momentary meditation at the Foothills.)

His name was now a legend. The North Shore,
Though not yet conquered, yet had proved that he
Could straighten crooked roads by pulling at them,
Shear down a hill and drain a bog or fill
A valley overnight. Fast as a bobcat,
He'd climb and run across the shakiest trestle
Or, with a locomotive short of coal,
He could supply the head of steam himself.
He breakfasted on bridges, lunched on ties;
Drinking from gallon pails, he dined on moose.
He could tire out the lumberjacks; beat hell
From workers but no more than from himself.
Only the devil or Paul Bunyan shared
With him the secret of perpetual motion,
And when he moved among his men they looked
For shoulder sprouts upon the Flying Dutchman.

But would his legend crack upon the mountains?
There must be no retreat: his bugles knew
Only one call—the summons to advance
Against two fortresses: the mind, the rock.
To prove the first defence was vulnerable,
To tap the treasury at home and then
Untie the purse-strings of the Londoners,
As hard to loosen as salt-water knots—
That job was Stephen's, Smith's, Tupper's, Macdonald's.
He knew its weight: had heard, as well as they,
Blake pumping at his pulmonary bellows,
And if the speeches made the House shock-proof
Before they ended, they could still peal forth
From print more durable than spoken tones.
Blake had returned to the attack and given
Sir John the ague with another phrase
As round and as melodious as the first:
"The Country's wealth, its millions after millions
Squandered—LOST IN THE GORGES OF THE FRASER":
A beautiful but ruinous piece of music
That could only be drowned with drums and fifes.
Tupper, fighting with fists and nails and toes,
Had taken the word *scandal* which had cut

His master's ballots, and had turned the edge
With his word *slander*, but Blake's *sea*, how turn
That edge? Now this last devastating phrase!
But let Sir John and Stephen answer this
Their way. Van Horne must answer it in his.

INTERNECINE STRIFE

The men were fighting foes which had themselves
Waged elemental civil wars and still
Were hammering one another at this moment.
The peaks and ranges flung from ocean beds
Had wakened up one geologic morning
To find their scalps raked off, their lips punched in,
The colour of their skins charged with new dyes.
Some of them did not wake or but half-woke;
Prone or recumbent with the eerie shapes
Of creatures that would follow them. Weather
Had acted on their spines and frozen them
To stegosaurs or, taking longer cycles,
Divining human features, had blown back
Their hair and, pressing on their cheeks and temples,
Bestowed on them the gravity of mummies.
But there was life and power which belied
The tombs. Guerrilla evergreens were climbing
In military order: at the base
The *ponderosa* pine; the fir backed up
The spruce; and it the Stoney Indian lodge-poles;
And these the white-barks; then, deciduous,
The outpost suicidal Lyell larches
Aiming at summits, digging scraggy roots
Around the boulders in the thinning soil,
Till they were stopped dead at the timber limit—
Rock *versus* forest with the rock prevailing.
Or with the summer warmth it was the ice,
In treaty with the rock to hold a line
As stubborn as a Balkan boundary,
That left its caves to score the Douglases,
And smother them with half a mile of dirt,
And making snow-sheds, covering the camps,
Futile as parasols in polar storms.
One enemy alone had battled rock
And triumphed: searching levels like lost broods,
Keen on their ocean scent, the rivers cut
The quartzite, licked the slate and softened it,
Till mud solidified was mud again,
And then, digesting it like earthworms, squirmed

Along the furrows with one steering urge—
To navigate the mountains in due time
Back to their home in worm-casts on the tides.

Into this scrimmage came the fighting men,
And all but rivers were their enemies.
Whether alive or dead the bush resisted:
Alive, it must be slain with axe and saw,
If dead, it was in tangle at their feet.
The ice could hit men as it hit the spruces.
Even the rivers had betraying tricks,
Watched like professed allies across a border.
They smiled from fertile plains and easy runs
Of valley gradients: their eyes got narrow,
Full of suspicion at the gorges where
They leaped and put the rickets in the trestles.
Though natively in conflict with the rock,
Both leagued against invasion. At Hell's Gate
A mountain laboured and brought forth a bull
Which, stranded in mid-stream, was fighting back
The river, and the fight turned on the men,
Demanding from this route their bread and steel.
And there below the Gate was the Black Canyon
With twenty-miles-an-hour burst of speed.

(Onderdonk builds the "Skuzzy" to force the passage.)

'Twas more than navigation: only eagles
Might follow up this run; the spawning salmon
Gulled by the mill-race had returned to rot
Their upturned bellies in the canyon eddies.
Two engines at the stern, a forrard winch,
Steam-powered, failed to stem the cataract.
The last resource was shoulders, arms and hands.
Fifteen men at the capstan, creaking hawsers,
Two hundred Chinese tugging at shore ropes
To keep her bow-on from the broadside drift,
The *Skuzzy* under steam and muscle took
The shoals and rapids, and warped through the Gate,
Until she reached the navigable water—
The adventure was not sailing; it was climbing.

As hard a challenge were the precipices
Worn water-smooth and sheer a thousand feet.
Surveyors from the edges looked for footholds,
But, finding none, they tried marine manoeuvres.
Out of a hundred men they drafted sailors
Whose toes as supple as their fingers knew

The wash of reeling decks, whose knees were hardened
Through tying gaskets at the royal yards:
They lowered them with knotted ropes and drew them
Along the face until the lines were strung
Between the juts. Barefooted, dynamite
Strapped to their waists, the sappers followed, treading
The spider films and chipping holes for blasts,
Until the cliffs delivered up their features
Under the civil discipline of roads.

. . .

(The Government grants the Directors the right to issue $35,000,000, guarantees $20,000,000, the rest to be issued by the Railway Directors. Stephen goes to London, and Lord Revelstoke, speaking for the House of Baring, takes over the issue.)

SUSPENSE IN THE MONTREAL BOARD ROOM

Evening had settled hours before its time
Within the Room and on the face of Angus.
Dejection overlaid his social fur,
Rumpled his side-burns, left moustache untrimmed.
The vision of his Bank, his future Shops,
Was like his outlook for the London visit.
Van Horne was fronting him with a like visage
Except for two spots glowing on his cheeks—
Dismay and anger at those empty pay-cars.
His mutterings were indistinct but final
As though he were reciting to himself
The Athanasian damnatory clauses.
He felt the Receiver's breath upon his neck:
To come so near the end, and then this hurdle!

Only one thing could penetrate that murk—
A cable pledge from London, would it come?
Till now refusal or indifference
Had met the overtures. Would Stephen turn
The trick?
                A door-knock and a telegram
With Stephens' signature! Van Horne ripped it
Apart. Articulation failed his tongue,
But Angus got the meaning from his face
And from a noisy sequence of deductions:—
An inkstand coasted through the office window,
Followed by shredded maps and blotting-pads,
Fluttering like shad-flies in a summer gale;

A bookshelf smitten by a fist collapsed;
Two chairs flew to the ceiling—one retired,
The other roosted on the chandelier.
Some thirty years erased like blackboard chalk,
Van Horne was in a school at Illinois.
Triumphant over his two-hundred weight,
He leaped and turned a cartwheel on the table,
Driving heel sparables into the oak,
Came down to teach his partner a Dutch dance:
And in the presence of the messenger,
Who stared immobilized at what he thought
New colours in the managerial picture,
Van Horne took hold of Angus bodily,
Tore off his tie and collar, mauled his shirt,
And stuffed a Grand Trunk folder down his breeches.

(The last gap in the mountains — between the Selkirks and Savona's Ferry — is closed.)

The Road itself was like a stream that men
Had coaxed and teased or bullied out of Nature.
As if watching for weak spots in her codes,
It sought for levels like the watercourses.
It sinuously took the bends, rejoiced
In plains and easy grades, found gaps, poured through them,
But hating steep descents avoided them.
Unlike the rivers which in full rebellion
Against the canyons' hydrophobic slaver
Went to the limit of their argument:
Unlike again, the stream of steel had found
A way to climb, became a mountaineer.
From the Alberta plains it reached the Summit,
And where it could not climb, it cut and curved,
Till from the Rockies to the Coastal Range
It had accomplished what the Rivers had,
Making a hundred clean Caesarian cuts,
And bringing to delivery in their time
Their smoky, lusty-screaming locomotives.

THE SPIKE

Silver or gold? Van Horne had rumbled "Iron."
No flag or bands announced this ceremony,
No Morse in circulation through the world,
And though the vital words like Eagle Pass,
Craigellachie, were trembling in their belfries,
No hands were at the ropes. The air was taut
With silences as rigid as the spruces

Forming the background in November mist.
More casual than camera-wise, the men
Could have been properties upon a stage,
Except for road maps furrowing their faces.

Rogers, his both feet planted on a tie,
Stood motionless as ballast. In the rear,
Covering the scene with spirit-level eyes,
Predestination on his chin, was Fleming.
The only one groomed for the ritual
From smooth silk hat and well-cut square-rig beard
Down through his Caledonian longitude,
He was outstaturing others by a foot,
And upright as the mainmast of a brig.
Beside him, barely reaching to his waist,
A water-boy had wormed his way in front
To touch this last rail with his foot, his face
Upturned to see the cheek-bone crags of Rogers.
The other side of Fleming, hands in pockets,
Eyes leaden-lidded under square-crowned hat,
And puncheon-bellied under overcoat,
Unsmiling at the focused lens—Van Horne.
Whatever ecstasy played round that rail
Did not leap to his face. Five years had passed,
Less than five years—so well within the pledge.
The job was done. Was this the slouch of rest?
Not to the men he drove through walls of granite.
The embers from the past were in his soul,
Banked for the moment at the rail and smoking,
Just waiting for the future to be blown.

At last the spike and Donald with the hammer!
His hair like frozen moss from Labrador
Poked out under his hat, ran down his face
To merge with streaks of rust in a white cloud.
What made him fumble the first stroke? Not age:
The snow belied his middle sixties. Was
It lapse of caution or his sense of thrift,
That elemental stuff which through his life
Never pockmarked his daring but had made
The man the canniest trader of his time,
Who never missed a rat-count, never failed
To gauge the size and texture of a pelt?
Now here he was caught by the camera,
Back bent, head bowed, and staring at a sledge,
Outwitted by an idiotic nail.
Though from the crowd no laughter, yet the spike

With its slewed neck was grinning up at Smith.
Wrenched out, it was replaced. This time the hammer
Gave a first tap as with apology,
Another one, another, till the spike
Was safely stationed in the tie and then
The Scot, invoking his ancestral clan,
Using the hammer like a battle-axe,
His eyes bloodshot with memories of Flodden,
Descended on it, rammed it to its home.

The stroke released a trigger for a burst
Of sound that stretched the gamut of the air.
The shouts of engineers and dynamiters,
Of locomotive-workers and explorers,
Flanking the rails, were but a tuning-up
For a massed continental chorus. Led
By Moberly (of the Eagles and *this* Pass)
And Rogers (of *his own*), followed by Wilson,
And Ross (charged with the Rocky Mountain Section),
By Egan (general of the Western Lines),
Cambie and Marcus Smith, Harris of Boston,
The roar was deepened by the bass of Fleming,
And heightened by the laryngeal fifes
Of Dug McKenzie and John H. McTavish.
It ended when Van Horne spat out some phlegm
To ratify the tumult with "Well Done"
Tied in a knot of monosyllables.

Merely the tuning up! For on the morrow
The last blow on the spike would stir the mould
Under the drumming of the prairie wheels,
And make the whistles from the steam out-crow
The Fraser. Like a gavel it would close
Debate, making Macdonald's "sea to sea"
Pour through two oceanic megaphones—
Three thousand miles of *Hail* from port to port;
And somewhere in the middle of the line
Of steel, even the lizard heard the stroke.
The breed had triumphed after all. To drown
The traffic chorus, she must blend the sound
With those inaugural, narcotic notes
Of storm and thunder which would send her back
Deeper than ever in Laurentian sleep.

1950-52
Towards the Last Spike, 1952

INDEX